THE
GOLF
TOUR

Written by Jackie Staddon and Hilary Weston

© Automobile Association Developments Limited 2007
Maps © Automobile Association Developments Limited
2007

First published 2007

ISBN: 978-0-7495-5676-1

Published by AA Publishing, a trading name of
Automobile Association Developments Limited,
whose registered office is Fanum House, Basing View,
Basingstoke, Hampshire RG21 4EA. Registered number
1878835.

Automobile Association Developments Limited retains
the copyright in the original edition © 2007 and in all
subsequent editions, reprints and amendments

A CIP catalogue record for this book is available from the
British Library

Project management by
Bookwork Creative Associates Ltd
Design and artwork by Andrew Milne Design Ltd
Picture research by Sarah Hopper
Editorial management by Apostrophe S Ltd
Colour Separation by Keenes, Andover
Printed and bound in China by Leo Paper Products
Mountain High Maps ® Copyright © 1993 Digital Wisdom Inc.

A03311

THE GOLF TOUR
GREAT BRITAIN & IRELAND

The essential guide to 43 major courses

AA

Contents

Introduction: The Story of Golf   6

Golf Etiquette and advice   9

ENGLAND

① **The Belfry**   12
Warwickshire

② **East Sussex National**   16
East Sussex

③ **Manor House**   20
Wiltshire

④ **Marriott Forest of Arden**   24
West Midlands

⑤ **Marriott Hanbury Manor**   28
Hertfordshire

⑥ **National Golf Centre**   32
Lincolnshire

⑦ **Old Thorns**   36
Hampshire

⑧ **Royal Birkdale**   40
Merseyside

⑨ **Royal Cinque Ports**   44
Kent

⑩ **Royal Liverpool**   48
Merseyside

⑪ **Royal Lytham St. Annes**   52
Lancashire

⑫ **Royal St. George's**   56
Kent

⑬ **St. Mellion**   60
Cornwall

⑭ **Sunningdale**   64
Berkshire

⑮ **Walton Heath**   68
Surrey

⑯ **Wentworth**   72
Surrey

⑰ **Woburn**   76
Buckinghamshire

SCOTLAND

⑱ **Carnoustie**   82
Angus

⑲ **Duke's Course**   86
Fife

⑳ **Fairmont St. Andrews**   90
Fife

㉑ **Gleneagles Hotel**   94
Perth & Kinross

㉒ **Marriott Dalmahoy**   98
Edinburgh

㉓ **Prestwick**   102
South Ayrshire

㉔ **Royal Dornoch**   106
Highland

㉕ **Royal Troon**   110
South Ayrshire

㉖ **St. Andrews Links**   114
Fife

㉗ **Westerwood Hotel**   118
North Lanarkshire

㉘ **Westin Turnberry Resort**   122
South Ayrshire

WALES

㉙ **Aberdovey**   128
Gwynedd

㉚ **Celtic Manor Resort**   132
Newport

㉛ **Marriott St. Pierre**   136
Monmouthshire

㉜ **Royal St. David's**   140
Gwynedd

㉝ **Royal Porthcawl**   144
Mid-Glamorgan

IRELAND

(34) **Ballybunion** 150
Co. Kerry

(35) **Dromoland Castle** 154
Co. Clare

(36) **Druids Glen** 158
Co. Wicklow

(37) **Fota Island Resort** 162
Co. Cork

(38) **The K Club** 166
Co. Kildare

(39) **Mount Juliet** 170
Co. Kilkenny

(40) **Portmarnock** 174
Co. Dublin

(41) **Rathsallagh House** 178
Co. Wicklow

(42) **Royal County Down** 182
Co. Down

(43) **Royal Portrush** 186
Co. Antrim

Glossary of Golf Terms 190

Acknowledgements 192

SCOTLAND

IRELAND

ENGLAND

WALES

The Story of Golf

Above: Playing the game of golf from the *Book of Hours* by Gerhard Hoombach

Right: An early 20th-century golfer

Below: Mr Robertson, the manager of Tom Morris's workshop in St. Andrews, tests a golf club for balance while two men work on new clubs

Several countries lay claim to be the originators of golf in its earliest form. It seems that where man could find a stick and a pebble he would attempt to hit it, be it in Scotland, Holland or China. Golf proper, however, began when that pebble was hit into a hole, at first probably a rabbit hole in the sand dunes. The game of *kolven* from Holland no doubt influenced the game that was introduced into Scotland in the early 15th century—in fact the word golf derives from the Dutch *kolf*, meaning club or stick. But the game we know today undoubtedly has its roots in Scotland. Early golf was played on rough terrain, with the holes randomly cut into the ground wherever the surface was flat. These early clubs were crude, carved by individuals from wood, and balls comprised of thin leather bags stuffed with feathers that did not travel far.

In 1744 the Gentlemen Golfers of Leith, later to become the Honourable Company of Edinburgh Golfers, drafted a set of 13 rules to regulate the first annual tournament. These rules formed the basis for the game that's played today. The next 100 years saw interest in the game wane and its survival owed much to the Freemasons, who continued to play. However, by the height of the era of the British Empire golf had gained momentum and was championed by royalty and the aristocracy. William IV bestowed St. Andrews with the title of Royal & Ancient in 1834 and it became the most respected club in the country. Golf was now popular as far away as India and the United States. The ladies' game began to gain in popularity when the first golf club for women was founded in 1867 at St. Andrews. By the 1890s it was a common sight to see women out on the course. American Patty Berg dominated ladies' golf from 1930 until 1960, winning 15 majors.

During the 19th century new technology changed the face of golf. Better equipment such as lawnmowers to service the greens and golf balls made from rubber—guaranteeing an extra 20 yards—was introduced. By the early 20th century clubs were made with metal shafts and then with metal heads, too. In the 1980s the use of light graphite materials for shafts added a different dimension.

Over the years great legends have emerged from this compelling game. From the very beginning Old Tom Morris (1821–1908), as he was known to differentiate him from his son, had a huge influence on the sport. Apart from being a great player, Morris worked as a greens keeper first at Prestwick and then St. Andrews, and went on to pioneer new approaches to greens keeping. He was responsible for standardizing the golf course length at 18 holes and introduced the concept of each nine holes returning to the clubhouse. He also pioneered the placing of hazards in the way, such as lakes and bunkers, which added much more drama to a round of golf. As one of the first great course designers, he took a role in shaping around 75 courses—including Prestwick, Royal Dornoch, Carnoustie and Royal County Down. Old Tom won four Opens and played in every one until 1895.

MEMORABLE GOLFING ACHIEVEMENTS

Some of the greatest moments in golfing history have taken place at the Open, the world's oldest golf championship. Amazing players from all over the world have stamped their authority on this event and have had the privilege of lifting the famous trophy, the Claret Jug. When it comes to outstanding achievements in golf the list is awesome. From Englishman Harry Vardon in the early 20th century, who won seven majors, to Americans such as Walter Hagan (11 majors), Bobby Jones (13 majors), Ben Hogan (9 majors), Tom Watson (8 majors), Arnold Palmer (7 majors), and South African Gary Player (9 majors). But what stands out is the supreme dominance of Jack Nicklaus, who achieved an incredible 18 majors between 1962 and 1986. The astonishing progress of Tiger Woods, who in just over five years as a professional has already completed one Grand Slam and captured eight majors, could well mean he is the man to steal Nicklaus's crown. By the end of 2006 more than half the top-rated women golfers in the world were from Korea and Japan. Currently, the world number one is Annika Sörenstam from Sweden, who has already won 10 majors and is well on the way to becoming the most successful female golfer ever.

Above: At the 18th during the 1990 Open at St. Andrews.

Left: Nick Faldo kisses the trophy at the 1990 Open at St. Andrews.

Below: Tiger Woods on the final day of the 2006 Ryder Cup at The K Club.

66 I have always believed
there are far too many rules
in golf. For me, if you cannot
write them all on the back of
a matchbox then something
is wrong **99**

HENRY LONGHURST

GOLF ETIQUETTE AND ADVICE

Golf etiquette is an essential part of the game. Consideration should be shown to others and the course at all times. Here are some basic guidelines that will help you, and those around you, to have a safe round and gain maximum enjoyment from your game of golf.

• Get the day off to a good start by not turning up late for your tee time.

• Ensure that no one is standing too close when you swing your club and keep your distance when others are swinging.

• When practising your swing, never swing in the direction of another player. There may be objects in the grass that could fly up and injure them.

• Do not hit the ball until you are sure that players in front are out of range.

• If you play a ball and it appears to be going in the direction of another player, shout out the warning "Fore!"

• Do not disturb another player's concentration by talking or making unnecessary noise when they are taking a shot. Keep mobile phones turned off.

• Observe cart rules and keep to the designated routes. Some courses will post "cart path only" signs; others will ask you to observe the "90-degree rule"—stay on the cart path until you are even (at a 90 degree angle) with your ball. Then you may drive your cart out to your ball and when you've taken your shot, drive straight back to the cart path.

• To save wasting time, when walking from a golf cart to your ball, take a couple of clubs at a time so you don't have to keep returning to the cart.

• Never throw clubs in anger. In addition to being rude and not in the spirit of the game, it could also be dangerous.

• Play at a good pace and keep the round moving. Do not spend too much time looking for a lost ball (five minutes is the allotted time). If there is a group behind waiting to play you should invite them to play through. Equally, it is just as important to keep pace with the group ahead of you. If space opens up, allow a faster group to play through.

• Carefully repair all divots made after you have taken a shot and any damage made on the green caused by the impact of the ball or golf shoes.

• Before leaving a bunker, always rake the sand after hitting to erase your footprints and any disturbance to the area where your ball landed.

• Don't stand in a place that causes your shadow to be cast across a player's putting line and never walk through a player's putting line—footprints can alter the path of a putt. Leave the green as soon as the hole has been completed.

• When a golfer is putting another member of the group should remove the flagstick from the hole first, as the ball must not strike the flagstick in the hole—if hit from off the green it's okay.

• Take care when handling the flagstick and make sure it is properly replaced. Remove the ball carefully from the hole.

• Do not mark your scores on the green. Wait until you are at the next tee, allowing the next group to begin their shots to the green as soon as you are done.

• The majority of golf courses have a dress code. A pair of smart slacks or shorts and a collared golf shirt will normally meet the requirements, but it's a good idea to check with the course beforehand. Correct golf shoes are required, but gloves are up to the golfer.

• Outside of tournament golf, it is accepted practice to play "ready golf". This means the golfer who is ready to hit can do so even though he or she may not be farthest away from the hole. This should be agreed with your group beforehand.

BOOKING YOUR ROUND

It is not possible to just turn up and play on the courses listed within this book. Telephone or check the website for booking details.

ENGLAND

(1) **The Belfry**   12
Warwickshire

(2) **East Sussex National**   16
East Sussex

(3) **Manor House**   20
Wiltshire

(4) **Marriott Forest of Arden**   24
West Midlands

(5) **Marriott Hanbury Manor**   28
Hertfordshire

(6) **National Golf Centre**   32
Lincolnshire

(7) **Old Thorns**   36
Hampshire

(8) **Royal Birkdale**   40
Merseyside

(9) **Royal Cinque Ports**   44
Kent

(10) **Royal Liverpool**   48
Merseyside

(11) **Royal Lytham St. Annes**   52
Lancashire

(12) **Royal St. George's**   56
Kent

(13) **St. Mellion**   60
Cornwall

(14) **Sunningdale**   64
Berkshire

(15) **Walton Heath**   68
Surrey

(16) **Wentworth**   72
Surrey

(17) **Woburn**   76
Buckinghamshire

The Belfry
WARWICKSHIRE

The Belfry is the only venue to have staged the biggest golf event in the world, the Ryder Cup, an unprecedented four times. Regarded throughout the world as a great championship course, the superbly sculpted Brabazon (see plan page 14) has some of the most demanding holes in golf, drawing players from around the globe. The 10th, known as Ballesteros's Hole, and the 18th, with its dangerous lakes and amphitheatre around the final green, are particularly renowned.

Alternatively, you can pit your wits against a new legend in the making, the PGA National Course, which has won plaudits from near and far. Designed by Dave Thomas and Peter Alliss in 1997, this course has been used for professional competition and is already established as one of Britain's leading venues. For those who prefer their golf a little easier or like to get back into the swing gently, the Derby is ideal and can be played by golfers of any standard.

Tour Notes

1977 The Belfry becomes the headquarters of the Professional Golf Association (PGA), officially opened with a challenge match between Seve Ballesteros and Johnny Miller against Tony Jacklin and Brian Barnes.

1993 Raymond Floyd tees up for the Ryder Cup to become the oldest Ryder Cup member in the event's history, at 51 years, 20 days. Nick Faldo makes a hole-in-one on the 14th, only the second hole-in-one during the history of the Ryder Cup.

2002 The Ryder Cup is back in Europe's hands after a magnificent show of strength in the decisive singles matches. Jubilant captain Sam Torrance celebrates with his team after an exciting victory.

Left: The Ryder Cup

Hole 1
Distance **411 yds** / Par **4**
Stroke Index **9**

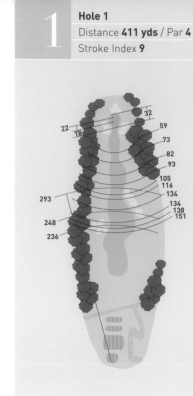

22
18
32
59
73
82
93
105
116
134
134
138
151
293
248
236

Hole 2
Distance **379 yds** / Par **4**
Stroke Index **17**

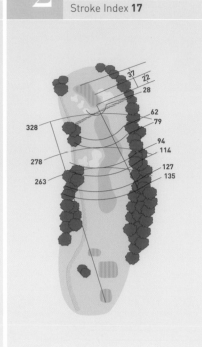

37
22
28
62
79
94
114
127
135
328
278
263

Hole 3
Distance **538 yds** / Par **5**
Stroke Index **13**

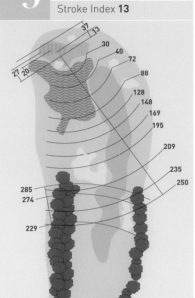

37
13
30
40
72
88
128
148
169
195
209
235
250
27 20
285
274
229

Hole 4
Distance **442 yds** / Par **4**
Stroke Index **3**

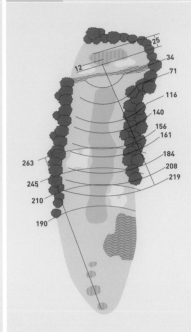

25
12
34
71
116
140
156
161
184
208
219
263
245
210
190

Hole 5
Distance **408 yds** / Par **4**
Stroke Index **11**

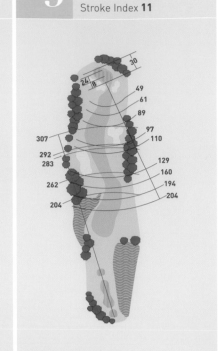

30
24
8
49
61
89
97
110
129
160
194
204
307
292
283
262
204

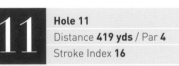
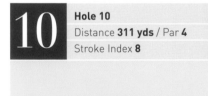

Hole 10
Distance **311 yds** / Par **4**
Stroke Index **8**

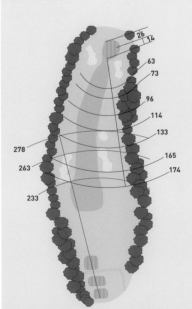

41
23
41
65
87
104
125
261
238
223
190

Hole 11
Distance **419 yds** / Par **4**
Stroke Index **16**

26
14
63
73
96
114
133
165
174
278
263
233

Hole 12
Distance **208 yds** / Par **3**
Stroke Index **6**

37 15
189

Hole 13
Distance **384 yds** / Par **4**
Stroke Index **18**

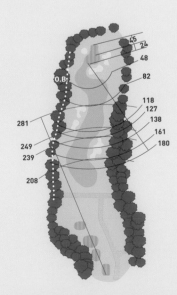

45
24
48
82
118
127
138
161
180
O.B.
281
249
239
208

Hole 14
Distance **190 yds** / Par **3**
Stroke Index **14**

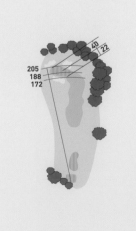

40
22
205
188
172

Hole 6
Distance **430 yds** / Par **4**
Stroke Index **5**

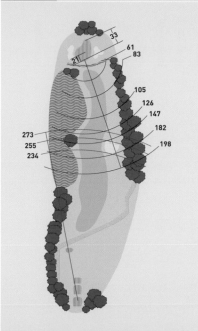

35 20
86
128
304
288 141
175
195
215
218

Hole 7
Distance **177 yds** / Par **3**
Stroke Index **15**

30 10
23
162

Hole 8
Distance **428 yds** / Par **4**
Stroke Index **1**

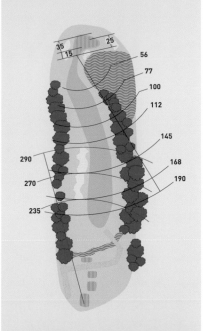

33
61
83
21
105
126
147
182
273
255 198
234

Hole 9
Distance **433 yds** / Par **4**
Stroke Index **7**

35 25
15
56
77
100
112
145
290
270 168
190
235

CONTACT DETAILS

Address
Wishaw B76 9PR

Telephone
01675 470301

Website
www.thebelfry.co.uk

Hole 15
Distance **545 yds** / Par **5**
Stroke Index **2**

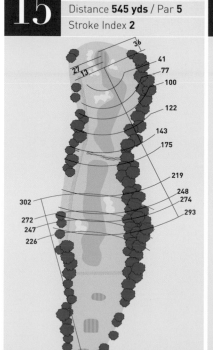

36
41
27 13 77
100
122
143
175
219
302 248
274
272 293
247
226

Hole 16
Distance **413 yds** / Par **4**
Stroke Index **12**

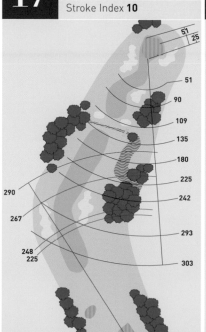

28
13 45
68
88
270 116
255 158
220 175
200 181

Hole 17
Distance **564 yds** / Par **5**
Stroke Index **10**

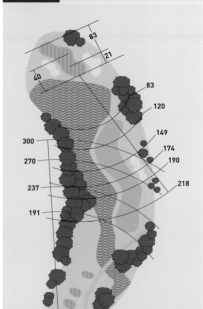

51
25
51
90
109
135
180
225
290 242
267
293
248
225 303

Hole 18
Distance **473 yds** / Par **4**
Stroke Index **4**

83
21
40
83
120
149
300 174
270 190
237 218
191

BRABAZON COURSE

All distance measurements in
yards from the blue tees.

Out	
Distance	**3646 yds**
Par	**36**
In	
Distance	**3507 yds**
Par	**36**

Totals	
Distance	**7153 yds**
Par	**72**

East Sussex National
EAST SUSSEX

East Sussex National offers two huge courses ideal for big-hitting professionals. Many tournaments have been staged here and it is home to the European headquarters of the David Leadbetter Golf Academy, with indoor and outdoor video analysis. The West Course is longer than the East, but both are designed with championship golf in mind. Designer Robert Cupp incorporated 'bent' grass from tee to green, resulting in an American-style layout to test everyone.

The East Course (see plan page 18) was the first of its kind to be galleried. Many consider the 18th tee to be one of the most demanding finishing holes in golf—measuring 454 yards off the tee, it is an uphill par 4 that can catch out the finest golfers. The 17th has the added difficulty of a creek to be negotiated. Unlike the West Course, it has two loops of nine holes. The West Course, also galleried, has been chosen for international events, and is reserved for members and their guests; visitors are welcome on the East Course.

Tour Notes

1990 Both courses are officially opened for play. No expense has been spared—a huge £32.5 million—in getting a top architect from the Jack Nicklaus stable to design them.

1993 and 1994 The East Course hosts the European Open Championships. Gordon Brand Jnr. of Scotland takes the accolade in 1993 and British contender David Gilford wins in 1994.

1994–98 Over a period of 5 years, the East Course is chosen to host five European Challenge Tour events and four PGA European Tour qualifying schools.

Hole 1
Distance **361 yds** / Par **4**
Stroke Index **14**

Hole 2
Distance **517 yds** / Par **5**
Stroke Index **12**

Hole 3
Distance **448 yds** / Par **4**
Stroke Index **8**

Hole 4
Distance **216 yds** / Par **3**
Stroke Index **10**

Hole 5
Distance **460 yds** / Par **4**
Stroke Index **6**

> **" Professional golf is the only sport where, if you win 20 percent of the time, you're the best "**
>
> *JACK NICKLAUS*

Hole 10
Distance **510 yds** / Par **5**
Stroke Index **5**

Hole 11
Distance **394 yds** / Par **4**
Stroke Index **7**

Hole 12
Distance **386 yds** / Par **4**
Stroke Index **15**

Hole 13
Distance **194 yds** / Par **3**
Stroke Index **17**

Hole 14
Distance **575 yds** / Par **5**
Stroke Index **9**

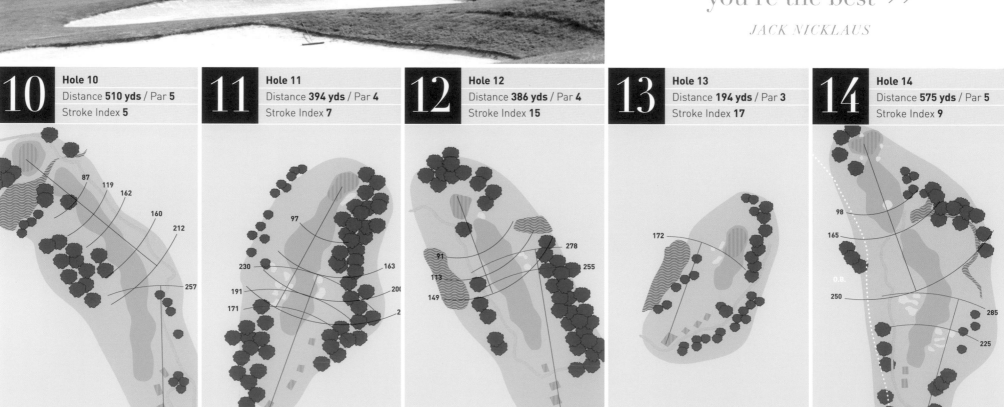

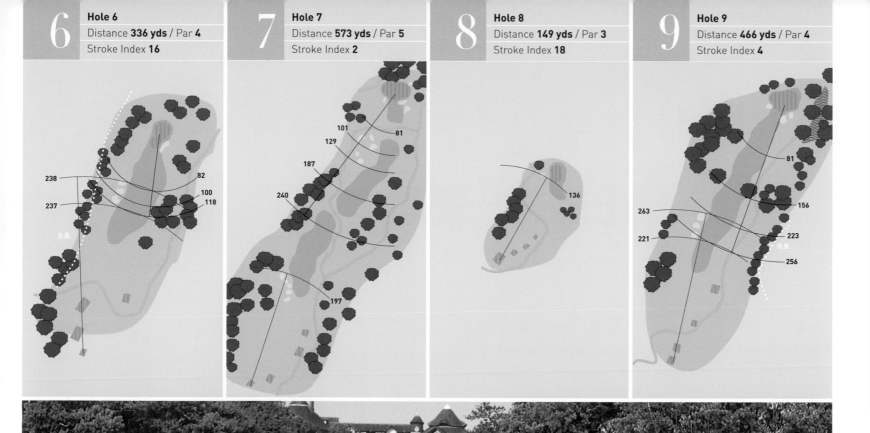

6 | **Hole 6**
Distance **336 yds** / Par **4**
Stroke Index **16**

7 | **Hole 7**
Distance **573 yds** / Par **5**
Stroke Index **2**

8 | **Hole 8**
Distance **149 yds** / Par **3**
Stroke Index **18**

9 | **Hole 9**
Distance **466 yds** / Par **4**
Stroke Index **4**

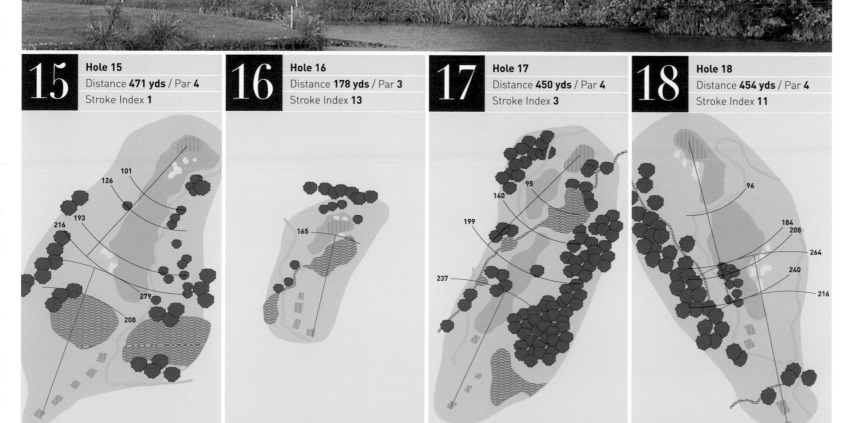

15 | **Hole 15**
Distance **471 yds** / Par **4**
Stroke Index **1**

16 | **Hole 16**
Distance **178 yds** / Par **3**
Stroke Index **13**

17 | **Hole 17**
Distance **450 yds** / Par **4**
Stroke Index **3**

18 | **Hole 18**
Distance **454 yds** / Par **4**
Stroke Index **11**

CONTACT DETAILS

Address
Little Horsted, Uckfield
TN22 5ES

Telephone
01825 880088

Website
www.eastsussexnational.
co.uk

EAST COURSE

All distance measurements in
yards from the back tees.

Out	
Distance	**3526 yds**
Par	**36**
In	
Distance	**3612 yds**
Par	**36**
Totals	
Distance	**7138 yds**
Par	**72**

Manor House
WILTSHIRE

Dramatic, varied, entertaining, exciting and exhausting all sum up the Manor House golf course. There is no doubting this course is set in one of the most picturesque spots you'll ever play, nestled within the 365-acre wooded estate of the 14th-century Manor House.

Stately oak and beech trees line the magnificent fairways, giving the impression that the course is more mature than it is. The course is famed for its spectacular par-3 holes; the 17th, known as Burton Brook, with an incredible double green, is one of the best and most exciting par 3s in England. The River Bybrook meanders through the middle of the course, the perfect complement to the manicured fairways and hand-cut greens. Walking can be a struggle at times and it's wise to take advantage of the buggy service. Wonderful views await you over the 18th tee from the modern clubhouse, which provides an informal area for golfers to relax and have a chilled beer or glass of wine after a game. Other leisure facilities in the grounds include clay pigeon shooting, tennis and archery.

Tour Notes

1992 The golf course opens for play. Designers Peter Alliss and Clive Clark make creative use of the rolling Wiltshire countryside.

2006 Manor House Golf Club is awarded the coveted HSBC Gold Star and is voted within the top 100 courses in the country. The course is attracting top golfers such as Colin Montgomerie.

2007 Manor House unveils its restructured course, bringing many new features into play and creating a longer, challenging course that is ready to host professional championships.

1 Bailey
Distance **363 yds** / Par **4**
Stroke Index **9**

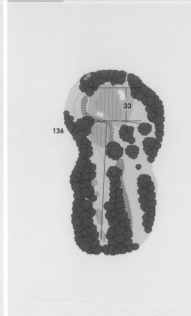

2 Dipper Bridge
Distance **151 yds** / Par **3**
Stroke Index **13**

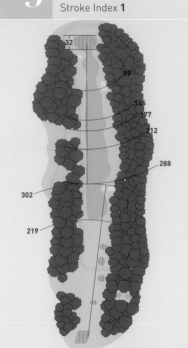

3 Hatch
Distance **600 yds** / Par **5**
Stroke Index **1**

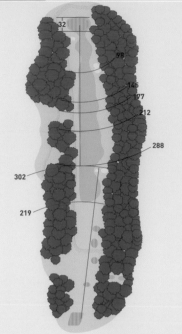

4 Dunstaville
Distance **220 yds** / Par **3**
Stroke Index **7**

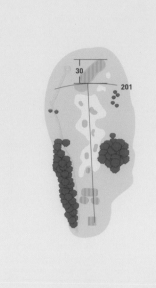

5 Triangle
Distance **467 yds** / Par **4**
Stroke Index **3**

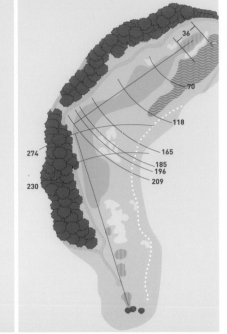

10 Old Plantation
Distance **378 yds** / Par **4**
Stroke Index **14**

11 School
Distance **222 yds** / Par **3**
Stroke Index **6**

12 Doolittle
Distance **498 yds** / Par **5**
Stroke Index **2**

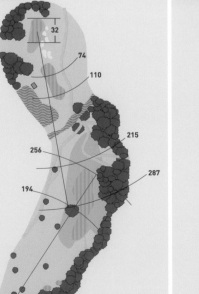

13 Broadmead Brook
Distance **289 yds** / Par **4**
Stroke Index **8**

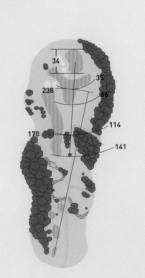

14 Nettleton
Distance **332 yds** / Par **4**
Stroke Index **16**

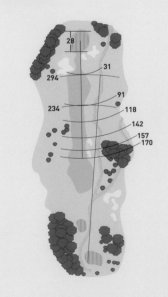

6 Lake
Distance **507 yds** / Par **5**
Stroke Index **15**

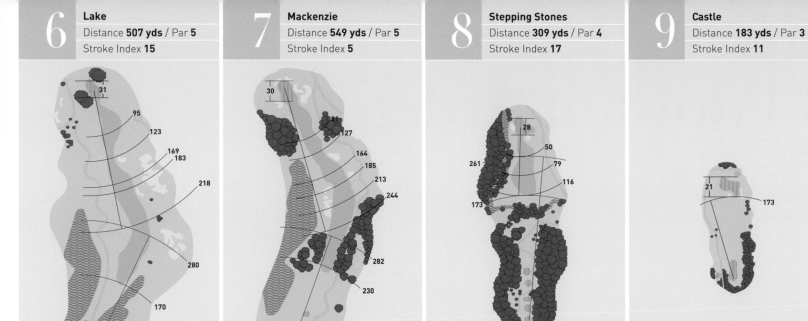

31
95
123
169
183
218
280
170

7 Mackenzie
Distance **549 yds** / Par **5**
Stroke Index **5**

30
81
127
164
185
213
244
282
230

8 Stepping Stones
Distance **309 yds** / Par **4**
Stroke Index **17**

28
50
79
116
261
173

9 Castle
Distance **183 yds** / Par **3**
Stroke Index **11**

21
173

CONTACT DETAILS

Address
Castle Combe SN14 7HR

Telephone
01249 782206

Website
www.exclusivehotels.co.uk

15 Fosseway
Distance **492 yds** / Par **5**
Stroke Index **12**

35
69
150
171
207
233
281

16 Gatcombe
Distance **402 yds** / Par **4**
Stroke Index **4**

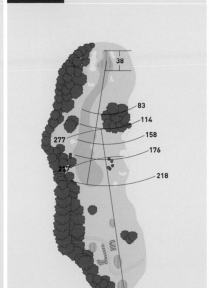

38
83
114
158
176
277
217
218

17 Burton Brook
Distance **154 yds** / Par **3**
Stroke Index **18**

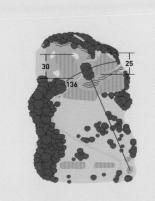

30
25
136

18 Woodbury
Distance **384 yds** / Par **4**
Stroke Index **10**

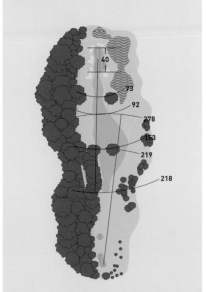

40
73
92
278
153
219
218

MANOR HOUSE COURSE

All distance measurements in yards from the back tees.

Out	
Distance	**3349 yds**
Par	**36**
In	
Distance	**3151 yds**
Par	**36**

Totals	
Distance	**6500 yds**
Par	**72**

Marriott Forest of Arden
WEST MIDLANDS

Forest of Arden ranks among the finest golf destinations in the UK, with a range of facilities to impress every golfer. The jewel in the crown is the Arden (see plan page 26) championship parkland course, set in 10,000 acres of the Packington Estate. Opened in 1979 and subsequently redesigned by one of the most creative golf-course architects, Donald Steel, it presents one of the country's most spectacular challenges.

The first nine holes are set in parkland with lakes placed in strategic locations. The back nine thread their way between ancient oaks inside a deer park. Beware the signature 18th hole overlooking the lakes, which is enough to stretch the nerves of any golfer. The shorter Aylesford course offers a varied and enjoyable challenge, which golfers of all abilities will find rewarding. The club has hosted a succession of international tournaments, including the British Masters and English Open. Golf events are a speciality and there is also a golf academy. Extensive leisure facilities provide the chance for relaxation after the game.

Tour Notes

1992 Donald Steel redesigns the course. The new layout aims to make golfers play a wider range of shots. Its variety of tee boxes, water hazards and trees neatly outline the fairways, offering a tougher and more exhilarating challenge.

2000/2002 Playing on the Arden course, Ulsterman Darren Clarke takes the 2000 and 2002 titles of the English Open, bringing his record to three wins. This is the final time the English Open is played as the championship is discontinued.

2007 The Arden course hosts the Brabazon Trophy, the prestigious men's amateur championships, and Romain Bechu and Jamie Moul come out joint winners.

1 Lakeside
Distance **385 yds** / Par **4**
Stroke Index **16**

2 The Church
Distance **364 yds** / Par **4**
Stroke Index **12**

3 Dingle Dell
Distance **563 yds** / Par **5**
Stroke Index **8**

4 Keys Corner
Distance **381 yds** / Par **4**
Stroke Index **6**

5 The Spinney
Distance **195 yds** / Par **3**
Stroke Index **14**

10 Deers Leap
Distance **435 yds** / Par **4**
Stroke Index **7**

11 Badens Drive
Distance **422 yds** / Par **4**
Stroke Index **13**

12 Coots Island
Distance **547 yds** / Par **5**
Stroke Index **11**

13 Old Hall
Distance **479 yds** / Par **4**
Stroke Index **1**

14 St. James
Distance **451 yds** / Par **4**
Stroke Index **5**

6 Foxes Den
Distance **466 yds** / Par **4**
Stroke Index **4**

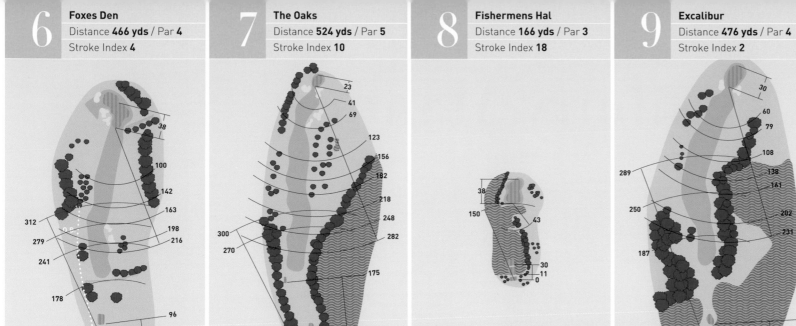

7 The Oaks
Distance **524 yds** / Par **5**
Stroke Index **10**

8 Fishermens Hal
Distance **166 yds** / Par **3**
Stroke Index **18**

9 Excalibur
Distance **476 yds** / Par **4**
Stroke Index **2**

CONTACT DETAILS

Address
Maxstoke Lane, Meriden
CV7 7HR

Telephone
0870 400 7272

Website
www.marriott.com/cvtgs

15 Road hole
Distance **201 yds** / Par **3**
Stroke Index **17**

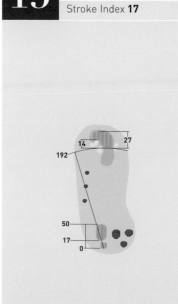

16 Horseshoe
Distance **431 yds** / Par **4**
Stroke Index **3**

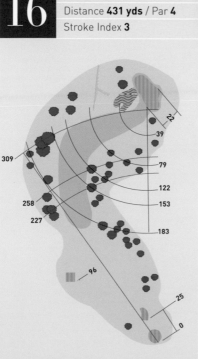

17 Elbow
Distance **516 yds** / Par **5**
Stroke Index **15**

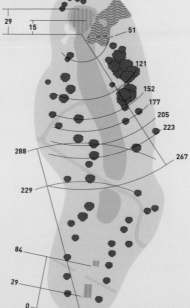

18 Tontine
Distance **211 yds** / Par **3**
Stroke Index **9**

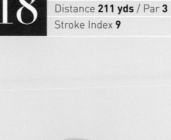
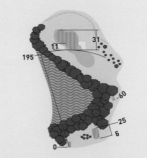

ARDEN COURSE

All distance measurements in yards from the blue tees.

All illustrations are based upon original Strokesaver artwork.

Out	
Distance	**3520 yds**
Par	**36**
In	
Distance	**3693 yds**
Par	**36**

Totals	
Distance	**7213 yds**
Par	**72**

Marriott Hanbury Manor
HERTFORDSHIRE

There can be few golf venues that combine so successfully the old and the new. The old is the site itself, dominated by a Jacobean-style manor built for the Hanbury family in 1890, where the wonderful grounds included a nine-hole parkland course designed by the legendary Harry Vardon. The new is the conversion of the estate into a golf and country club, which now presents itself as a five-star country hotel and conference centre, surrounded by an 18-hole course designed by Jack Nicklaus's eldest son.

Nicklaus's American-style design took the best of Vardon's original and added meadowland to produce a relatively open course with the rolling Hertfordshire countryside opening up in front of you. Its scattering of mature trees, water hazards and good bunkering offer a challenge to all golfers. The 8th hole is the trickiest, with an elevated green—along the left-hand side of the approach fairway is a lake and there is a grassy hollow to the right, and the ground and green slope ominously towards the lake.

Tour Notes

1991 Like father like son, Jack Nicklaus II follows in his father's footsteps by designing his first ever course. His father, Tony Jacklin and Dave Stockton play an exhibition match to celebrate the official opening of the new course.

1996 Hanbury Manor's tournament potential is recognized when the Women's European Open is hosted here; Trish Johnson claims victory by five clear shots.

1997–99 The Men's PGA European Tour arrives at Hanbury in the form of the English Open, which is won respectively by Per Ulrik Johannson, Lee Westwood and Darren Clarke.

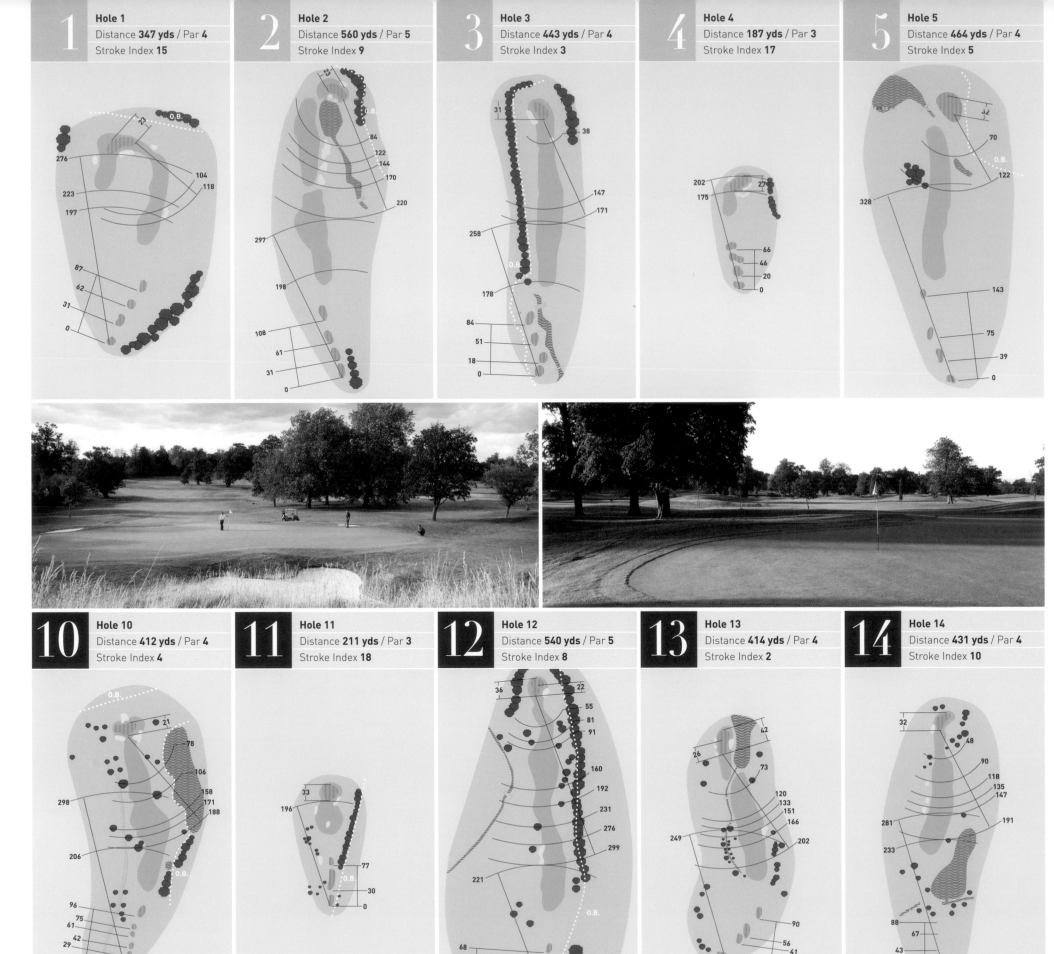

Hole 1
Distance **347 yds** / Par **4**
Stroke Index **15**

Hole 2
Distance **560 yds** / Par **5**
Stroke Index **9**

Hole 3
Distance **443 yds** / Par **4**
Stroke Index **3**

Hole 4
Distance **187 yds** / Par **3**
Stroke Index **17**

Hole 5
Distance **464 yds** / Par **4**
Stroke Index **5**

Hole 10
Distance **412 yds** / Par **4**
Stroke Index **4**

Hole 11
Distance **211 yds** / Par **3**
Stroke Index **18**

Hole 12
Distance **540 yds** / Par **5**
Stroke Index **8**

Hole 13
Distance **414 yds** / Par **4**
Stroke Index **2**

Hole 14
Distance **431 yds** / Par **4**
Stroke Index **10**

6	**Hole 6**
	Distance **189 yds** / Par **3**
	Stroke Index **11**

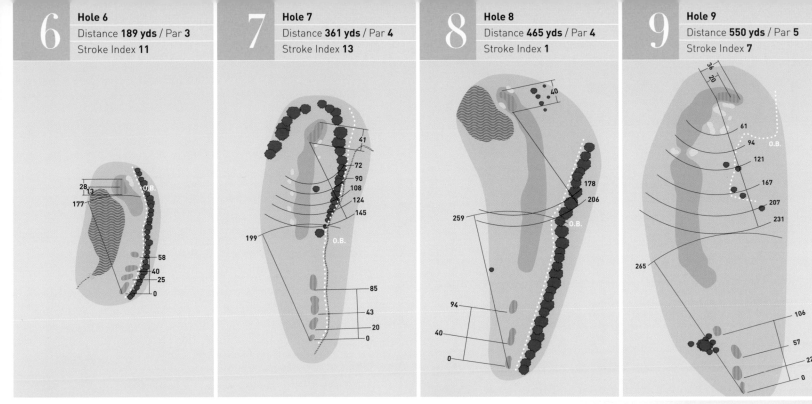

28
13
177
O.B.
58
40
25
0

7	**Hole 7**
	Distance **361 yds** / Par **4**
	Stroke Index **13**

41
72
90
108
124
145
199
O.B.
85
43
20
0

8	**Hole 8**
	Distance **465 yds** / Par **4**
	Stroke Index **1**

40
178
206
259
O.B.
94
40
0

9	**Hole 9**
	Distance **550 yds** / Par **5**
	Stroke Index **7**

36
20
61
94
O.B.
121
167
207
231
265
106
57
22
0

CONTACT DETAILS

Address
Ware SG12 0SD

Telephone
01920 487722

Website
www.marriott.co.uk/stngs

15	**Hole 15**
	Distance **406 yds** / Par **4**
	Stroke Index **14**

O.B.
O.B.
41
93
133
157
224
162
89
33
0

16	**Hole 16**
	Distance **185 yds** / Par **3**
	Stroke Index **16**

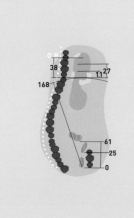

38
27
11
168
61
25
0

17	**Hole 17**
	Distance **496 yds** / Par **5**
	Stroke Index **6**

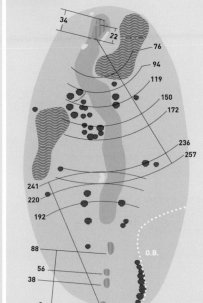

34
22
76
94
119
150
172
236
257
241
220
192
88
56
38
0
O.B.

18	**Hole 18**
	Distance **391 yds** / Par **4**
	Stroke Index **12**

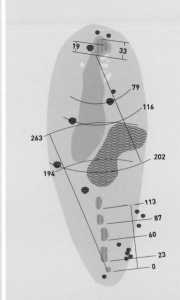

19
33
79
116
263
202
194
113
87
60
23
0

CHAMPIONSHIP COURSE

All distance measurements in yards from the blue tees.

All illustrations are based upon original Strokesaver artwork.

Out	
Distance	**3566 yds**
Par	**36**
In	
Distance	**3486 yds**
Par	**36**

Totals	
Distance	**7052 yds**
Par	**72**

National Golf Centre
LINCOLNSHIRE

Golf has been played here for over 100 years. The championship course at Woodhall Spa, now known as the Hotchkin (see plan page 34), is arguably the best inland course in Britain. Although not a tournament course, it has hosted many distinguished national and international amateur events. The Hotchkin is a heathland course and is notorious for its deep cavernous bunkers and narrow, heather-lined fairways—it is helpful if you can hit the ball long and straight to avoid a difficult second shot. The sandy soil offers good playing conditions year round.

A second course, the Bracken, was opened in 1998 along with extensive practice facilities, including one of Europe's finest short-game practice areas. Laid out on woodland, scrub and arable farmland, Donald Steel's imaginative design is quite different to the Hotchkin. Many of the holes are in a parkland setting and the fairways, greenside bunkers and large undulating greens resemble an American-style course.

Tour Notes

1905 The championship course opens for play. Originally laid out by Harry Vardon, Harry Colt makes some modifications and, in the 1920s, the owner Colonel Hotchkin sets about a major redesign phase.

1995 The English Golf Union (EGU), the governing body of men's amateur golf, acquires Woodhall Spa Golf Club for a reputed £8 million and turn it into their headquarters.

1998 The EGU builds an additional course (the Bracken) and an academy to create a centre of excellence to be enjoyed by players of all levels. The EGU is a non-profit organization looking after the interests of over 1,900 golf clubs and 740,000 club members in England.

Hole 1
Distance **361 yds** / Par **4**
Stroke Index **17**

Hole 2
Distance **442 yds** / Par **4**
Stroke Index **7**

Hole 3
Distance **415 yds** / Par **4**
Stroke Index **3**

Hole 4
Distance **414 yds** / Par **4**
Stroke Index **11**

Hole 5
Distance **148 yds** / Par **3**
Stroke Index **16**

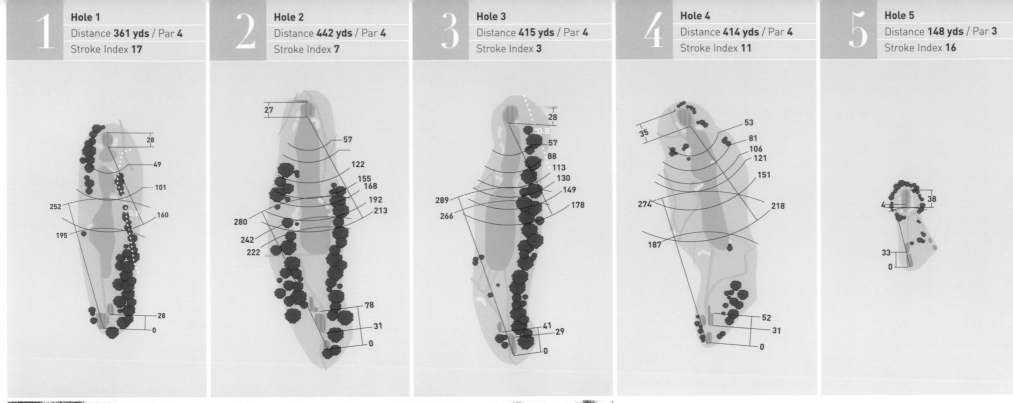

> **If a man comes home with sand in his cuffs and cockleburs in his pants, don't ask him what he shot**
>
> *SAM SNEAD*

Hole 10
Distance **338 yds** / Par **4**
Stroke Index **12**

Hole 11
Distance **437 yds** / Par **4**
Stroke Index **6**

Hole 12
Distance **172 yds** / Par **3**
Stroke Index **18**

Hole 13
Distance **451 yds** / Par **4**
Stroke Index **2**

Hole 14
Distance **521 yds** / Par **5**
Stroke Index **8**

6

Hole 6
Distance **526 yds** / Par **5**
Stroke Index **1**

7

Hole 7
Distance **470 yds** / Par **4**
Stroke Index **9**

8

Hole 8
Distance **209 yds** / Par **3**
Stroke Index **13**

9

Hole 9
Distance **584 yds** / Par **5**
Stroke Index **5**

Hole 6 diagram:
26, 82, 109, 128, 148, 183, 372, 220, 295, 88, 62, 16, 0

Hole 7 diagram:
33, 66, 102, 119, 153, 164, 183, 200, 289, 239, 100, 84, 61, 33, 0

Hole 8 diagram:
31, 197, 37, 31, 17, 0

Hole 9 diagram:
32, 82, 104, 138, 154, 191, 207, 222, 270, 315, 341, 351, 258, 232, O.B., 123, 105, 29, 0

National Golf Centre LINCO_NSHIRE

CONTACT DETAILS

Address
The Broadway, Woodhall
Spa LN10 6PU

Telephone
01526 352511

Website
www.woodhallspagolf.com

6

15

Hole 15
Distance **321 yds** / Par **4**
Stroke Index **14**

16

Hole 16
Distance **395 yds** / Par **4**
Stroke Index **4**

17

Hole 17
Distance **336 yds** / Par **4**
Stroke Index **15**

18

Hole 18
Distance **540 yds** / Par **5**
Stroke Index **10**

Hole 15 diagram:
29, 35, 276, 101, 123, 139, 206, 185, 40, 0

Hole 16 diagram:
29, 47, 335, 110, 123, 274, 160, 70, 28, 0

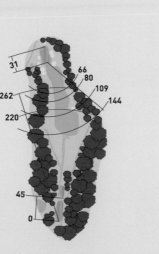

Hole 17 diagram:
31, 66, 80, 109, 144, 262, 220, 45, 0

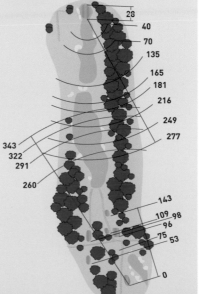

Hole 18 diagram:
28, 40, 70, 135, 165, 181, 216, 249, 277, 343, 322, 291, 260, 143, 109, 98, 96, 75, 53, 0

HOTCHKIN COURSE

All distance measurements in
yards from the championship tees.

All illustrations are based upon
original Strokesaver artwork.

Out	
Distance	**3569 yds**
Par	**36**
In	
Distance	**3511 yds**
Par	**37**

Totals	
Distance	**7080 yds**
Par	**73**

THE GOLF TOUR

35

Old Thorns
HAMPSHIRE

Situated in a 400-acre country estate, Old Thorns boasts a wonderful location and idyllic golf terrain. The demanding 18-hole championship course winds its way through rolling hills peppered with mature trees, natural springs and lakes. Many of the elevated greens have spectacular views across the glorious Hampshire countryside, while clever water features and testing bunkers add character to the course.

Although suitable for the less proficient golfer, Old Thorns holds some surprises for those who enjoy being tested. The tricky 10th is a long par 3 with water in front and to the left; if you try to drive right there are two bunkers waiting to catch your ball. Look out for the sign on the 16th tee that reads "if you miss the green could you please put a pound in the charity box on the bar"—guaranteed to bring out a competitive nature.

Tour Notes

1976 Commander John Harris produces the first blueprint for Old Thorns golf course, but sadly does not live to see the project sanctioned.

1981 Former golfer and broadcaster Peter Alliss—now honorary president of Old Thorns—and Dave Thomas see the construction of the course designed by Commander John Harris through to completion.

1982 The golf course is officially inaugurated on 10 July, endorsed by a high-profile fourball played in front of a large crowd, between four of the greatest golfers in history:

Isao Aoki shoots a score of 69, beating Jack Nicklaus, Seve Ballesteros and the reigning Open champion Bill Rogers.

1984 Kosaido Development Company, which owns many golf courses around the world, becomes owner of Old Thorns. It introduces a number of new features, and Old Thorns evolves into the luxury country club it is today.

2007 A new era at Old Thorns sees new ownership, with many exciting plans for redevelopment.

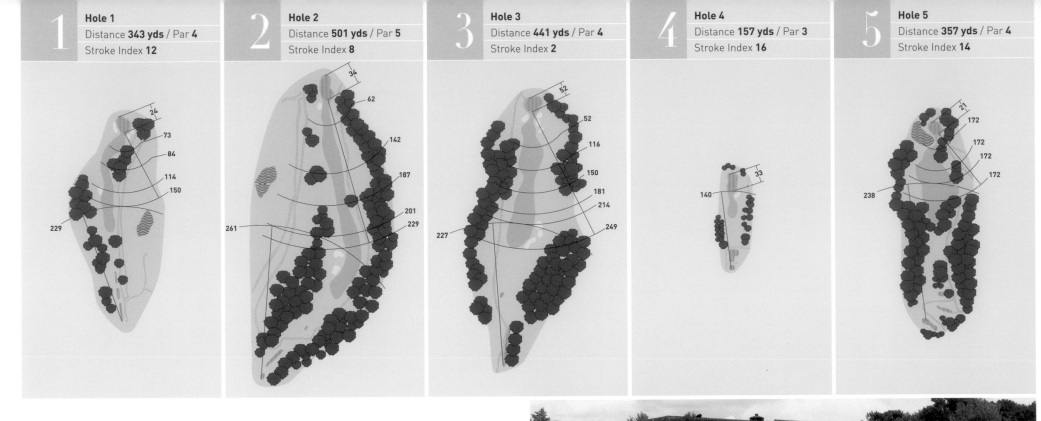

Hole 1
Distance **343 yds** / Par **4**
Stroke Index **12**

24
73
84
114
150
229

Hole 2
Distance **501 yds** / Par **5**
Stroke Index **8**

34
62
142
187
201
229
261

Hole 3
Distance **441 yds** / Par **4**
Stroke Index **2**

52
52
116
150
181
214
249
227

Hole 4
Distance **157 yds** / Par **3**
Stroke Index **16**

33
140

Hole 5
Distance **357 yds** / Par **4**
Stroke Index **14**

21
172
172
172
172
238

> *66 Golf, like the measles,*
> *should be caught young, for,*
> *if postponed to riper years,*
> *the results may be serious* **99**
>
> *P. G. WODEHOUSE*

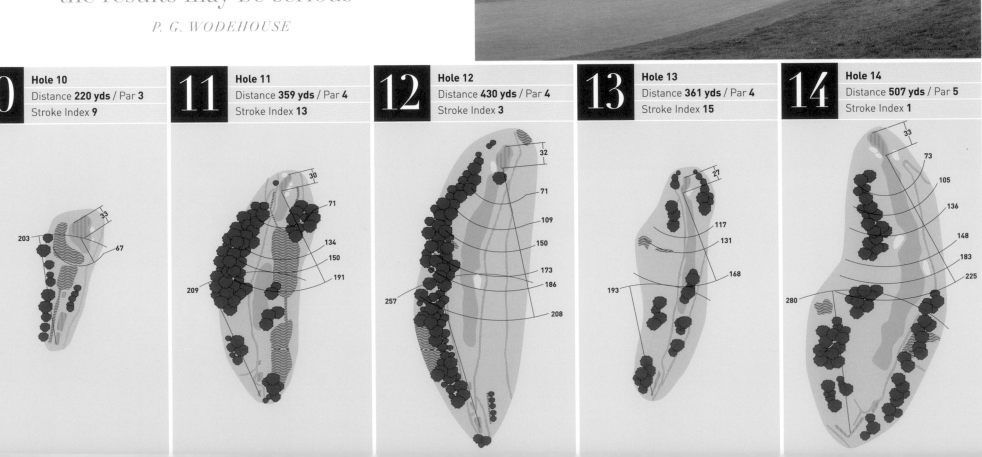

Hole 10
Distance **220 yds** / Par **3**
Stroke Index **9**

33
203
67

Hole 11
Distance **359 yds** / Par **4**
Stroke Index **13**

30
71
134
150
191
209

Hole 12
Distance **430 yds** / Par **4**
Stroke Index **3**

32
71
109
150
173
186
208
257

Hole 13
Distance **361 yds** / Par **4**
Stroke Index **15**

27
117
131
168
193

Hole 14
Distance **507 yds** / Par **5**
Stroke Index **1**

33
73
105
136
148
183
225
280

6 Hole 6
Distance **536 yds** / Par **5**
Stroke Index **4**

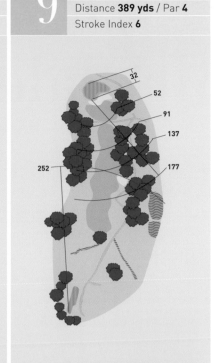

28
87
O.B.
150
178
216
260
275

7 Hole 7
Distance **161 yds** / Par **3**
Stroke Index **18**

144
34
O.B.

8 Hole 8
Distance **370 yds** / Par **4**
Stroke Index **10**

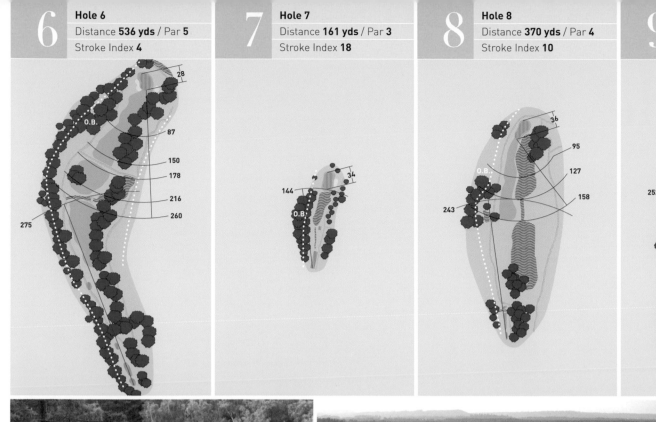

36
95
O.B.
127
158
243

9 Hole 9
Distance **389 yds** / Par **4**
Stroke Index **6**

32
52
91
137
252
177

CONTACT DETAILS

Address
Griggs Green, Liphook
GU30 7PE

Telephone
01428 724555

Website
www.oldthorns.com

15 Hole 15
Distance **268 yds** / Par **4**
Stroke Index **11**

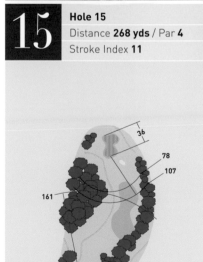

36
78
107
161

16 Hole 16
Distance **159 yds** / Par **3**
Stroke Index **17**

39
139
O.B.

17 Hole 17
Distance **492 yds** / Par **5**
Stroke Index **7**

23
74
122
182
205
234
263
287

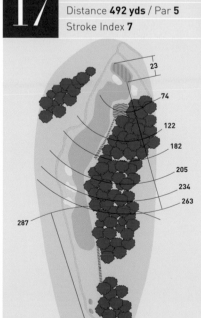

18 Hole 18
Distance **420 yds** / Par **4**
Stroke Index **5**

36
114
150
166
254
210

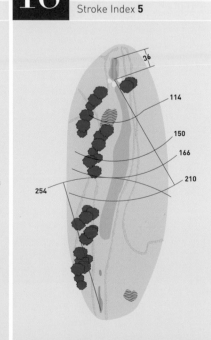

OLD THORNS COURSE

All distance measurements in
yards from the back tees.

Out	
Distance	**3255 yds**
Par	**36**
In	
Distance	**3216 yds**
Par	**36**
Totals	
Distance	**6471 yds**
Par	**72**

Royal Birkdale
MERSEYSIDE

Royal Birkdale, founded in 1889, is considered by many to be the ultimate championship venue, having staged the Walker and Curtis Cups, the Women's British Open, two Ryder Cups and eight Open championships. In 2008 it will host the Open for the ninth time.

The 1st hole provides an immediate taste of what is to come, requiring a well-placed drive to avoid a bunker, water hazard and out-of-bounds, to leave a reasonably clear view of the green. The 12th is the most spectacular of the short holes on the course, and is considered by Tom Watson to be one of the best par 3s in the world; tucked away in the sand hills, it continues to claim its fair share of disasters. Birkdale's longest hole is the 15th, which requires a shot straight down the middle off the tee to avoid the bunkers spread-eagled across the fairway. The approach on the monstrous final hole is arguably the most recognizable in golf, with the distinctive clubhouse designed to appear like an ocean cruise liner rising out of the sand hills, which provides a memorable finish to any round of golf.

Tour Notes

1951 On 11 November a notice is posted that reads "His Majesty The King has been graciously pleased to command that the club shall henceforth be known as Royal Birkdale Golf Club".

1969 Spectators witness a Ryder Cup match that ranks as one of the greatest. For the first time, a match is halved and Tony Jacklin's final missable putt on the 18th is conceded by Jack Nicklaus to halve the game and the match; a gesture of supreme sportsmanship that has never been forgotten.

1971 American Lee Trevino wins the 100th Open, joining immortals such as Bobby Jones, Gene Sarazen and Ben Hogan as golfers who have won both the US and British Opens in the same year.

Spain's Seve Ballesteros at the 1976 Open

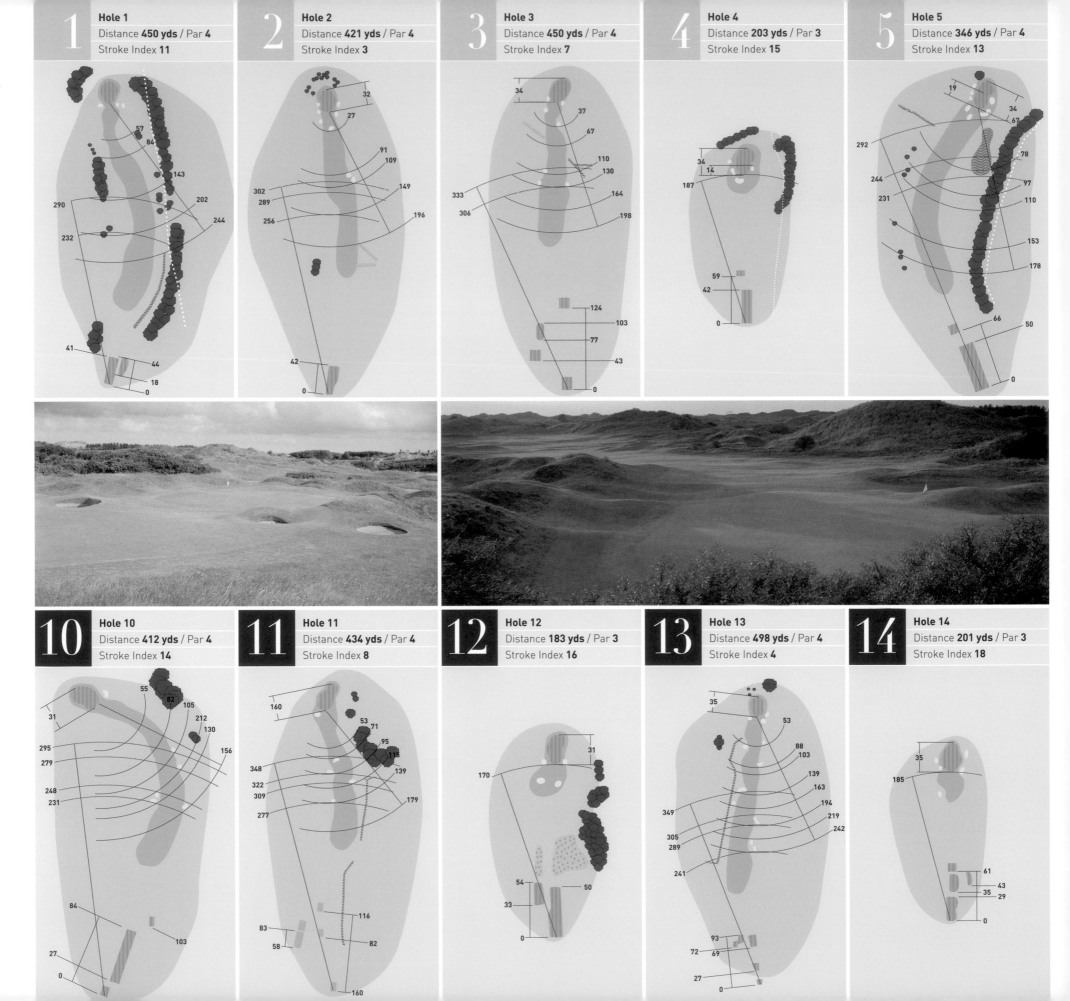

1 Hole 1
Distance **450 yds** / Par **4**
Stroke Index **11**

2 Hole 2
Distance **421 yds** / Par **4**
Stroke Index **3**

3 Hole 3
Distance **450 yds** / Par **4**
Stroke Index **7**

4 Hole 4
Distance **203 yds** / Par **3**
Stroke Index **15**

5 Hole 5
Distance **346 yds** / Par **4**
Stroke Index **13**

10 Hole 10
Distance **412 yds** / Par **4**
Stroke Index **14**

11 Hole 11
Distance **434 yds** / Par **4**
Stroke Index **8**

12 Hole 12
Distance **183 yds** / Par **3**
Stroke Index **16**

13 Hole 13
Distance **498 yds** / Par **4**
Stroke Index **4**

14 Hole 14
Distance **201 yds** / Par **3**
Stroke Index **18**

6 — Hole 6
Distance **509 yds** / Par **5**
Stroke Index **1**

7 — Hole 7
Distance **177 yds** / Par **3**
Stroke Index **17**

8 — Hole 8
Distance **458 yds** / Par **4**
Stroke Index **9**

9 — Hole 9
Distance **411 yds** / Par **4**
Stroke Index **5**

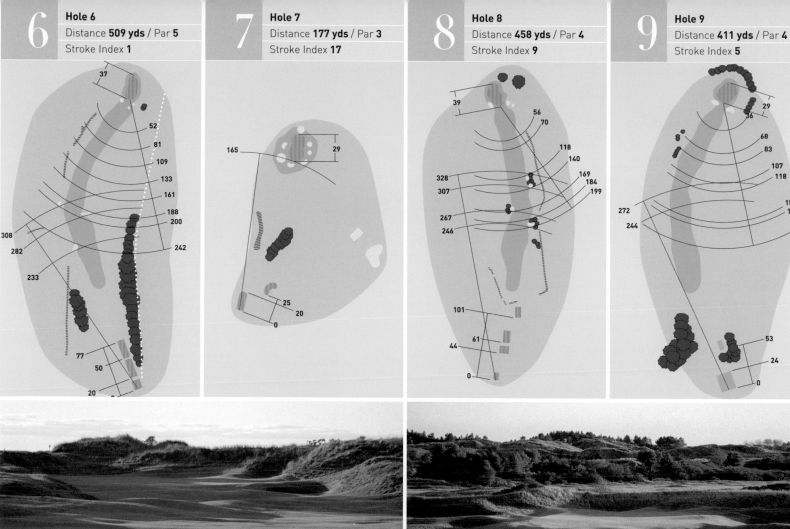

Royal Birkdale MERSEYSIDE

CONTACT DETAILS

Address
Waterloo Road, Birkdale,
Southport PR8 2LX

Telephone
01704 567920

Website
www.royalbirkdale.com

15 — Hole 15
Distance **544 yds** / Par **5**
Stroke Index **2**

16 — Hole 16
Distance **439 yds** / Par **4**
Stroke Index **12**

17 — Hole 17
Distance **572 yds** / Par **5**
Stroke Index **6**

18 — Hole 18
Distance **472 yds** / Par **4**
Stroke Index **10**

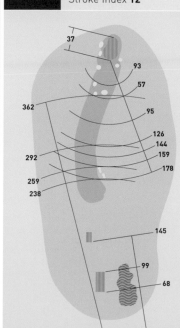

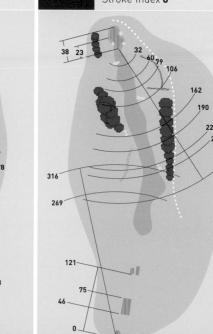

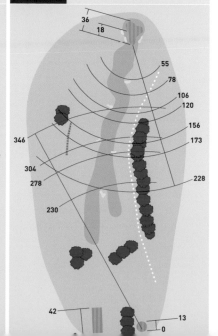

CHAMPIONSHIP COURSE

All distance measurements in yards from the blue tees.

All illustrations are based upon original Strokesaver artwork.

Out	
Distance	3425 yds
Par	35
In	
Distance	3755 yds
Par	36

Totals	
Distance	7180 yds
Par	71

THE GOLF TOUR

43

Royal Cinque Ports
KENT

Royal Cinque Ports, or Deal as it is more commonly known, was founded in 1892. Originally the course had nine holes, with a second nine added soon after. Following war damage in World War I, James Braid restored the almost obliterated links to open again in 1919. Sir Guy Campbell undertook further restoration in 1946 after World War II. The club assumed its royal title in 1910, coinciding with the election of King George V as patron; King George VI reconfirmed the title in 1949.

   This is a brute of a course and you need to achieve your score over the front nine, as the final seven holes are relentless, driving directly into the prevailing wind. Played by the legends—from Vardon, Taylor and Braid before the World War I to Nicklaus and Garcia in more recent times—Royal Cinque Ports has been the scene of two Opens, in 1909 and 1920, and since 1925 has been home to the Halford Hewitt Public Schools Championship: a treasured and welcomed reunion between public school old boys played over four days in April.

Tour Notes

1898 To celebrate the opening of an additional nine holes, amateur Freddie Tait, known to have an extremely powerful drive, plays a ball from St. George's clubhouse at Sandwich to the clubhouse at Deal. He manages easily to find the target, although his shot passes through a window along the way.

1905 HRH the Prince of Wales (later Edward VII), who played regularly on his visits to Deal, becomes president of the club for two years.

1909 Cinque Ports hosts the Open. Much controversy surrounds the use of the new rubber-cored ball, which is said to give significantly increased distance over the "guttie". J. H. Taylor's total of 295 wins him the Claret Jug, a gold medal, £20 and the fourth of his five Open victories.

2002 Prince Andrew, Duke of York, accepts patronage and his first function is to hand the winner the Queen Elizabeth the Queen Mother Cup, which Her Majesty had presented to the club in 2001.

1 Hole 1
Distance **387 yds** / Par **4**
Stroke Index **12**

2 Hole 2
Distance **401 yds** / Par **4**
Stroke Index **8**

3 Hole 3
Distance **510 yds** / Par **5**
Stroke Index **2**

4 Hole 4
Distance **152 yds** / Par **3**
Stroke Index **18**

5 Hole 5
Distance **542 yds** / Par **5**
Stroke Index **4**

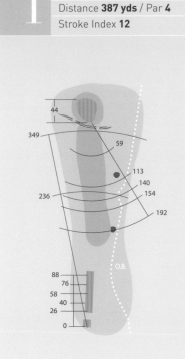

44
349
59
113
236
140
154
192
88
76
58
40
26
0
O.B.

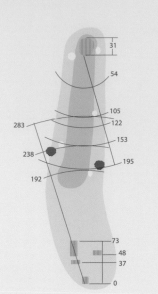

31
54
105
122
153
195
283
238
192
73
48
37
0

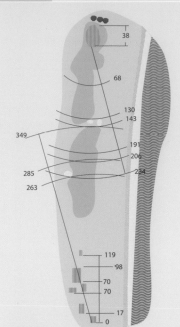

38
68
130
143
191
206
234
349
285
263
119
98
70
70
17
0

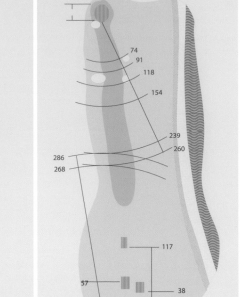

30
139
41
17
0

74
91
118
154
239
260
286
268
117
57
38
0

66 Golf is a game whose aim
is to hit a very small ball into
an even smaller hole, with
weapons singularly ill-designed
for the purpose 99

WINSTON CHURCHILL

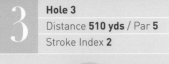

10 Hole 10
Distance **364 yds** / Par **4**
Stroke Index **11**

11 Hole 11
Distance **408 yds** / Par **4**
Stroke Index **5**

12 Hole 12
Distance **449 yds** / Par **4**
Stroke Index **1**

13 Hole 13
Distance **421 yds** / Par **4**
Stroke Index **13**

14 Hole 14
Distance **222 yds** / Par **3**
Stroke Index **7**

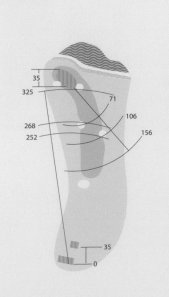

35
325
71
268
106
252
156
35
0

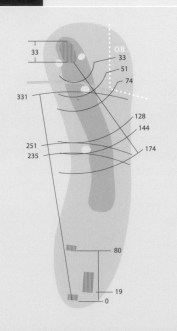

33
33
51
74
331
128
144
251
235
174
80
19
0
O.B.

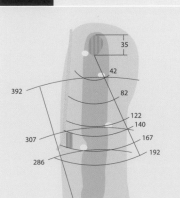

35
42
82
392
122
140
307
167
286
192
58
45
10
0

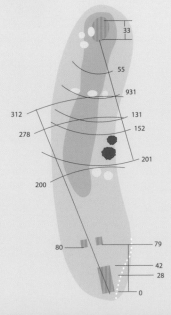

33
55
931
312
131
278
152
201
200
80
79
42
28
0

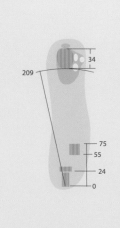

34
209
75
55
24
0

6 Hole 6
Distance **325 yds** / Par **4**
Stroke Index **14**

7 Hole 7
Distance **382 yds** / Par **4**
Stroke Index **6**

8 Hole 8
Distance **171 yds** / Par **3**
Stroke Index **16**

9 Hole 9
Distance **414 yds** / Par **4**
Stroke Index **10**

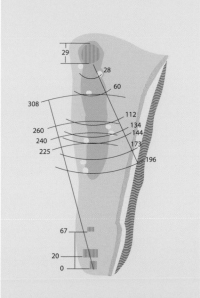
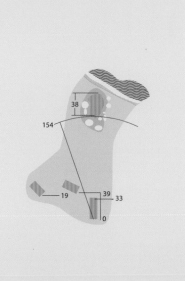
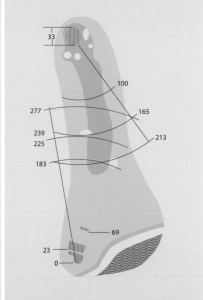

CONTACT DETAILS

Address
Golf Road, Deal CT14 6RF

Telephone
01304 374007

Website
www.royalcinqueports.com

15 Hole 15
Distance **451 yds** / Par **4**
Stroke Index **3**

16 Hole 16
Distance **507 yds** / Par **5**
Stroke Index **15**

17 Hole 17
Distance **397 yds** / Par **4**
Stroke Index **17**

18 Hole 1
Distance **457 yds** / Par **4**
Stroke Index **9**

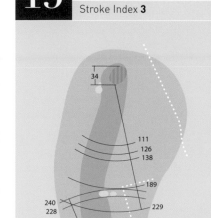
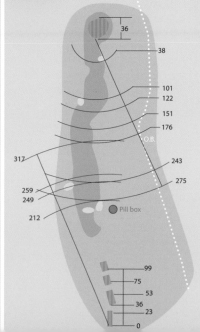
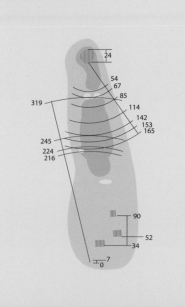

ROYAL CINQUE PORTS COURSE

All distance measurements in yards from the white tees.

All illustrations are based upon original Strokesaver artwork.

Out	
Distance	**3284 yds**
Par	**36**
In	
Distance	**3676 yds**
Par	**36**
Totals	
Distance	**6960 yds**
Par	**72**

Royal Liverpool
MERSEYSIDE

Constructed in 1869 on the land of the Liverpool Hunt Club, this world-famous championship course was one of the first seaside courses to be established in England. Over the years, golfing enthusiasts have come to Hoylake to witness no less than 11 Opens, 18 amateur championships and the 1992 ladies Curtis Cup. In 1921 the first amateur international US versus Great Britain challenge took place here, later known as the Walker Cup.

Visitors who play this historic course can expect an eventful round, with crosswinds, deep bunkers and hollows, all set against the backdrop of the stunning Welsh hills. Watch out for the 8th hole, which saw the great Bobby Jones take a seven on this par 5 on the way to his famous Grand Slam. The clubhouse has undergone an extensive and costly refurbishment; the original atmosphere and structure of the building has been retained, with the interior well equipped to meet the requirements of the 21st century.

Tour Notes

1871 The course is now extended to 18 holes and is bestowed with royal patronage by HRH the Duke of Connaught, Queen Victoria's youngest son.

1885–97 The first-ever Amateur Championships are held. Harold Hilton goes on to win the championship four times and the Open in 1892 and 1897, and Hoylake's own John Ball wins the championship an amazing eight times, as well as the Open in 1890.

1930 Bobby Jones secures a place in golf history by winning the Open and the Amateur championships on both sides of the Atlantic in the same year, retiring shortly afterwards aged 28 years.

2006 The Open returns to Hoylake for the first time in 39 years. A perfectly poised tournament sees Tiger Woods take his third Open with a magnificent display.

1 Course
Distance **429 yds** / Par **4**
Stroke Index **5**

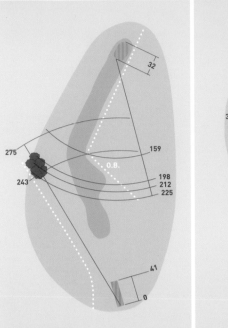

2 Road
Distance **372 yds** / Par **4**
Stroke Index **13**

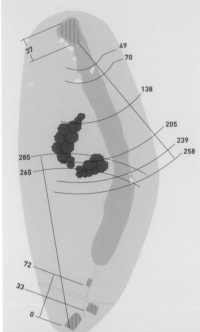

3 Long
Distance **528 yds** / Par **5**
Stroke Index **11**

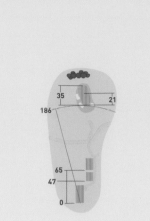

4 New
Distance **202 yds** / Par **3**
Stroke Index **7**

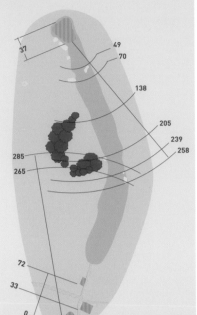

5 Telegraph
Distance **453 yds** / Par **4**
Stroke Index **1**

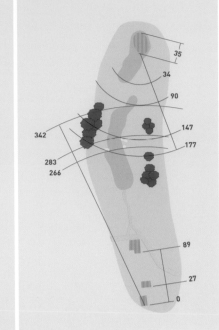

10 Dee
Distance **448 yds** / Par **4**
Stroke Index **8**

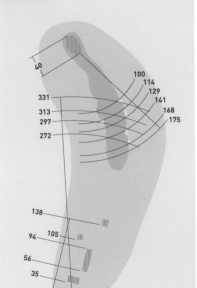

11 Alps
Distance **198 yds** / Par **3**
Stroke Index **14**

12 Hilbre
Distance **456 yds** / Par **4**
Stroke Index **4**

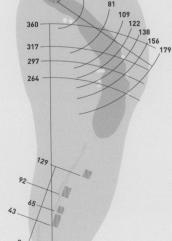

13 Rushes
Distance **161 yds** / Par **3**
Stroke Index **16**

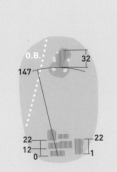

14 Field
Distance **554 yds** / Par **5**
Stroke Index **18**

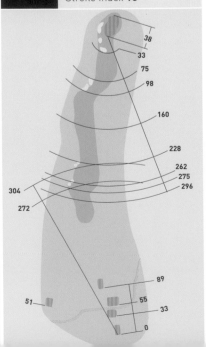

6 Briars
Distance **423 yds** / Par **4**
Stroke Index **9**

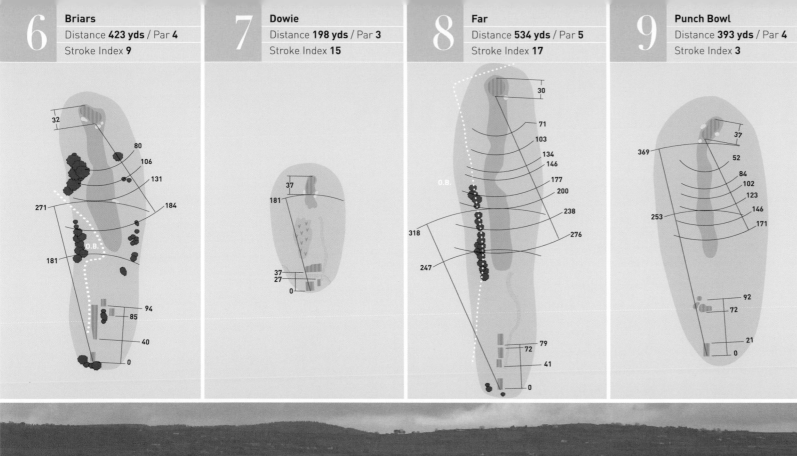

7 Dowie
Distance **198 yds** / Par **3**
Stroke Index **15**

8 Far
Distance **534 yds** / Par **5**
Stroke Index **17**

9 Punch Bowl
Distance **393 yds** / Par **4**
Stroke Index **3**

CONTACT DETAILS

Address
Meols Drive, Hoylake
CH47 4AL

Telephone
0151 632 3101

Website
www.royal-liverpool-golf.
com

15 Lake
Distance **459 yds** / Par **4**
Stroke Index **2**

16 Dun
Distance **560 yds** / Par **5**
Stroke Index **12**

17 Royal
Distance **454 yds** / Par **4**
Stroke Index **6**

18 Stand
Distance **436 yds** / Par **4**
Stroke Index **10**

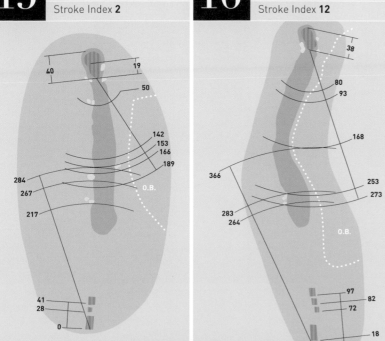

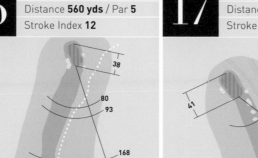

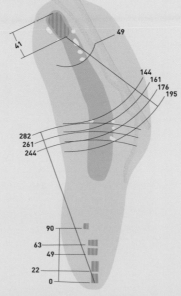

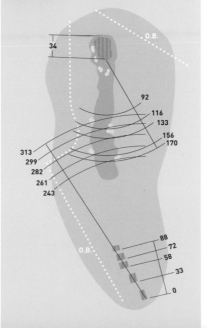

HOYLAKE COURSE

All distance measurements in
yards from the championship tees.

All illustrations are based upon
original Strokesaver artwork.

Out	
Distance	**3532 yds**
Par	**36**
In	
Distance	**3726 yds**
Par	**36**

Totals	
Distance	**7258 yds**
Par	**72**

Royal Lytham St. Annes
LANCASHIRE

Founded in 1886, this huge links course can be difficult, especially in windy conditions when the sea breeze will have an effect on your game. Though not a conventionally beautiful course, it has a character all of its own. It may not be the longest course in the country, but it is renowned for being difficult to achieve a good score as there are 200 bunkers flanking the fairways and greens. The nearby railway line and red-brick houses are distractions that add to the challenge.

Lytham has hosted two Ryder Cups and 10 Open championships, with some memorable victories. After hosting the first Ladies' Amateur Championship back in 1893, the club has continued to welcome women's championships, including the Curtis Cup and the Ladies' British Open, which will be played here again in 2009. The clubhouse walls are decked in history and memories of glory—from Seve's signed scorecard to Bobby Jones's portrait, the place is a living, breathing museum.

Tour Notes

1926 American Bobby Jones dramatically wins his first Open title as an amateur. A plaque in a bunker left of the 17th fairway commemorates his miracle shot out of the sand. Jones went on to become a legend, capturing 13 of the 21 major championships he entered before he retired at only 28.

1977 US dominance in the Ryder Cup now stretches to 20 years. This is the last time the Ryder Cup takes place with a Britain and Ireland team; in 1979 a united Europe faced the mighty Americans.

1988 Having already won the Open here in 1979, Ballesteros is back. Seve shoots a course-record 65 to win, and the crowd rises to acclaim what is acknowledged as the best round of the Spaniard's life.

2001 Former world number one David Duval finally proves he can win when it matters most. Duval is one of a handful of players to come to the Open looking to shake off the tag of "best player without a major title".

Dai Rees, Ryder Cup captain of Great Britain and Ireland, 1961

Hole 1
Distance **206 yds** / Par **3**
Stroke Index **13**

Hole 2
Distance **436 yds** / Par **4**
Stroke Index **5**

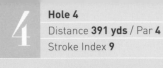

Hole 3
Distance **457 yds** / Par **4**
Stroke Index **1**

Hole 4
Distance **391 yds** / Par **4**
Stroke Index **9**

Hole 5
Distance **210 yds** / Par **3**
Stroke Index **15**

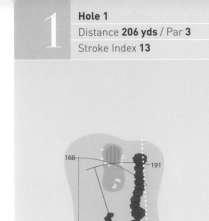

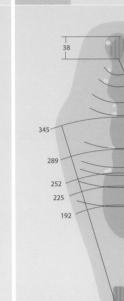

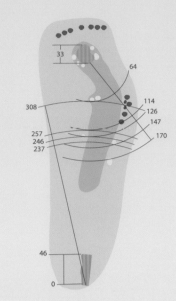

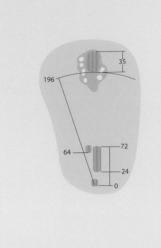

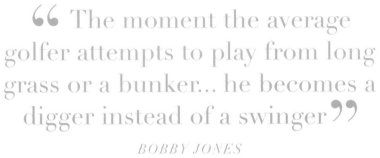

> 66 The moment the average golfer attempts to play from long grass or a bunker... he becomes a digger instead of a swinger 99
>
> *BOBBY JONES*

Hole 10
Distance **334 yds** / Par **4**
Stroke Index **10**

Hole 11
Distance **540 yds** / Par **5**
Stroke Index **4**

Hole 12
Distance **196 yds** / Par **3**
Stroke Index **14**

Hole 13
Distance **340 yds** / Par **4**
Stroke Index **18**

Hole 14
Distance **443 yds** / Par **4**
Stroke Index **6**

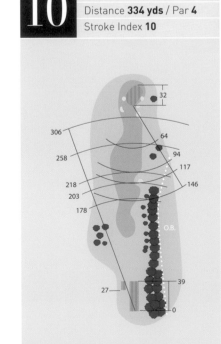

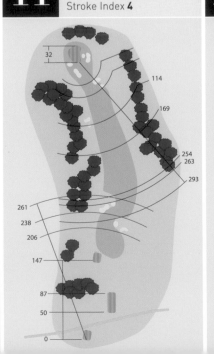

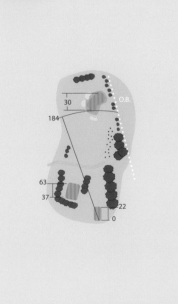

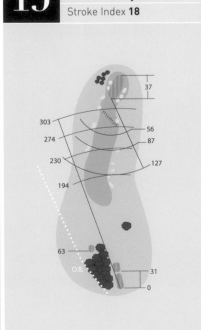

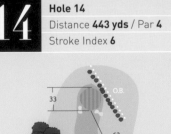

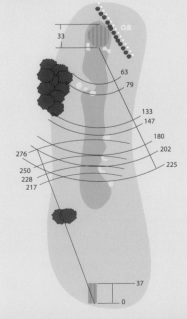

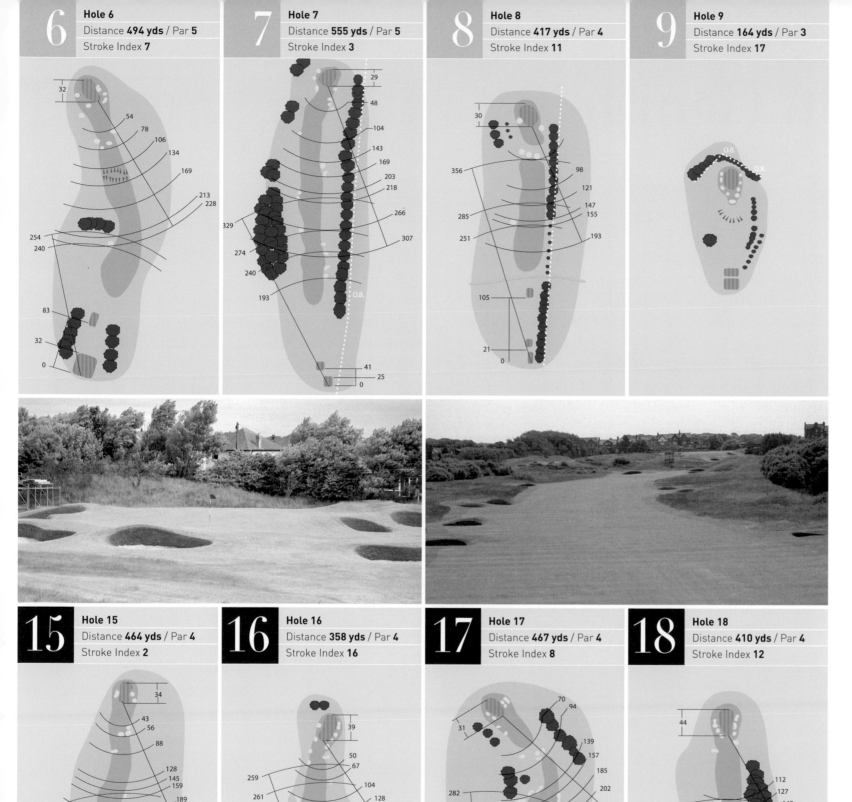

6 Hole 6
Distance **494 yds** / Par **5**
Stroke Index **7**

7 Hole 7
Distance **555 yds** / Par **5**
Stroke Index **3**

8 Hole 8
Distance **417 yds** / Par **4**
Stroke Index **11**

9 Hole 9
Distance **164 yds** / Par **3**
Stroke Index **17**

15 Hole 15
Distance **464 yds** / Par **4**
Stroke Index **2**

16 Hole 16
Distance **358 yds** / Par **4**
Stroke Index **16**

17 Hole 17
Distance **467 yds** / Par **4**
Stroke Index **8**

18 Hole 18
Distance **410 yds** / Par **4**
Stroke Index **12**

CONTACT DETAILS

Address
Links Gate, Lytham
St. Annes FY8 3LQ

Telephone
01253 724206

Website
www.royallytham.org

**ROYAL LYTHAM ST. ANNES
COURSE**

All distance measurements in
yards from the back tees.

All illustrations are based upon
original Strokesaver artwork.

Out	
Distance	**3330 yds**
Par	**35**
In	
Distance	**3552 yds**
Par	**36**

Totals	
Distance	**6882 yds**
Par	**71**

Royal St. George's
KENT

The course was designed and established in 1887 by Dr. Laidlaw Purves to serve the needs of London golfers, and was set to rival Scotland's St. Andrews. Consistently ranked among the leading golf courses in the world, Royal St. George's occupies a leading place in the history of golf. The club gained royal status in 1902, bestowed by King Edward VII, and the future Edward VIII became club captain in 1927. The club has hosted numerous major tournaments and many of golf's most famous names have played and triumphed here.

The combination of sea, cliffs and sand hills makes this a stunning venue. Set among the dunes of Sandwich Bay, the links provide a severe test for the greatest of golfers, with undulating fairways, borrows on the greens, strategically placed bunkers and prevailing winds that blow on all but the rarest of occasions. Only three Open winners—Bill Rogers, Greg Norman and Ben Curtis—have managed to under par after 72 holes.

Tour Notes

1894 After only 7 years of play, Sandwich is given the privilege of staging the very first Open outside Scotland, and goes on to host 12 more.

1967 Tony Jacklin makes the first-ever televised hole-in-one in the Dunlop Masters competition; a spectacular ace of 161 yards at the 16th hole.

1981 Following the introduction of a bypass easing traffic congestion in the small town, the 110th Open returns to

Sandwich after a break of over 30 years. American Bill Rogers shoots 276 to take the trophy in convincing style.

2003 The club hosts its 13th Open, won dramatically by the American outsider Ben Curtis after triumphing over the likes of Tiger Woods, Sergio Garcia and Nick Faldo.

1 Hole 1
Distance **440 yds** / Par **4**
Stroke Index **5**

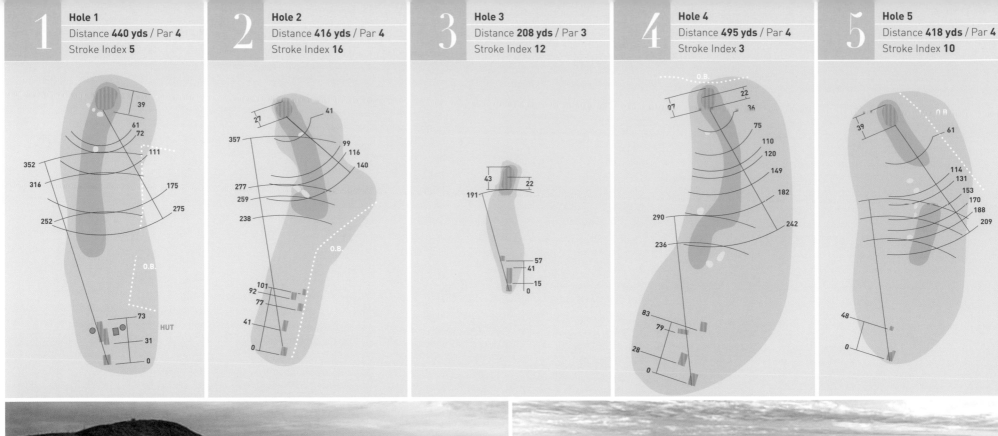

39
61
72
111
352
316
175
252
275
73
HUT
31
0

2 Hole 2
Distance **416 yds** / Par **4**
Stroke Index **16**

27
41
357
99
116
140
277
259
238
101
92
77
41
0
O.B.

3 Hole 3
Distance **208 yds** / Par **3**
Stroke Index **12**

43
22
191
57
41
15
0

4 Hole 4
Distance **495 yds** / Par **4**
Stroke Index **3**

O.B.
22
36
97
75
110
120
149
182
290
236
242
83
79
28
0

5 Hole 5
Distance **418 yds** / Par **4**
Stroke Index **10**

O.B.
39
61
114
131
153
170
188
209
48
0

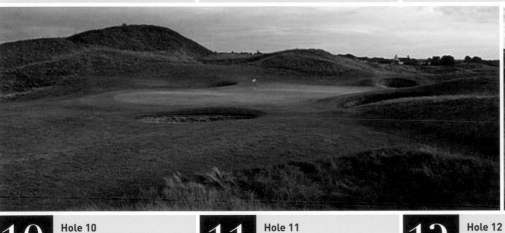

10 Hole 10
Distance **412 yds** / Par **4**
Stroke Index **8**

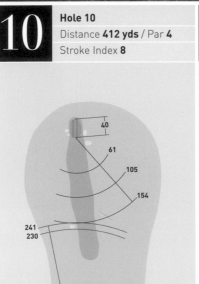

40
61
105
154
241
230
84
71
61
57
42
HUT
0

11 Hole 11
Distance **240 yds** / Par **3**
Stroke Index **15**

21
37
226
61
38
27
0

12 Hole 12
Distance **379 yds** / Par **4**
Stroke Index **13**

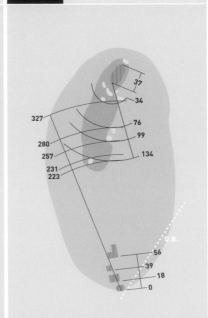

37
34
327
76
280
99
257
231
223
134
O.B.
56
39
18
0

13 Hole 13
Distance **457 yds** / Par **4**
Stroke Index **7**

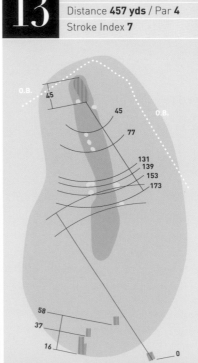

O.B.
45
45
O.B.
77
131
139
153
173
58
37
16
0

14 Hole 14
Distance **548 yds** / Par **5**
Stroke Index **2**

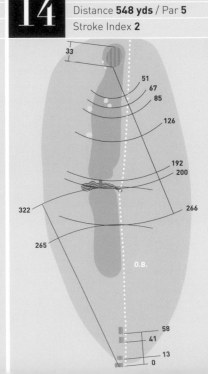

33
51
67
85
126
192
200
322
266
265
O.B.
58
41
13
0

6 Hole 6
Distance **170 yds** / Par **3**
Stroke Index **17**

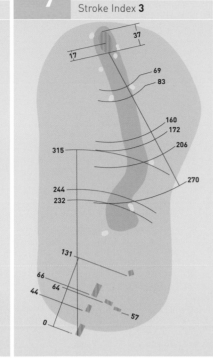

25   20   38
155

30
28
16
0

7 Hole 7
Distance **530 yds** / Par **5**
Stroke Index **3**

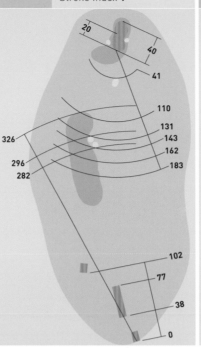

37
17
69
83
160
172
206
315   270
244
232
131
66
44   64
57
0

8 Hole 8
Distance **453 yds** / Par **4**
Stroke Index **1**

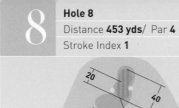
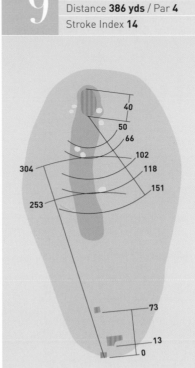

20
40
41
110
131
143
162
326   183
296
282

102
77
38
0

9 Hole 9
Distance **386 yds** / Par **4**
Stroke Index **14**

40
50
66
102
118
304   151
253

73
13
0

CONTACT DETAILS

Address
Sandwich CT13 9PB

Telephone
01304 613090

Website
www.royalstgeorges.com

66 I have a tip that will take
five strokes off anyone's game.
It's called an eraser 99

ARNOLD PALMER

15 Hole 15
Distance **473 yds** / Par **4**
Stroke Index **11**

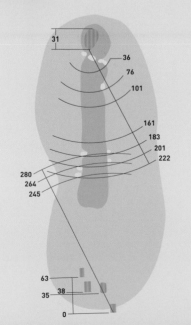

31
36
76
101
161
183
201
222
280
264
245

63
35   38
0

16 Hole 16
Distance **161 yds** / Par **3**
Stroke Index **18**

38
146
22
12   11
0

17 Hole 17
Distance **426 yds** / Par **4**
Stroke Index **4**

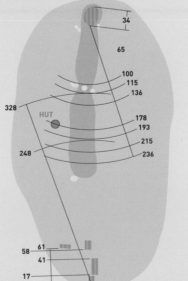

25
59
96
121
140
160
301   195
221
219
203
192

34
16
0

18 Hole 18
Distance **458 yds** / Par **4**
Stroke Index **9**

34
65
100
115
136
328   HUT   178
193
215
248   236

58   61
41
17
0

ROYAL ST. GEORGE'S COURSE

All distance measurements in yards from the championship tees.

All illustrations are based upon original Strokesaver artwork.

Out		
Distance	**3516 yds**	
Par	**35**	
In		
Distance	**3553 yds**	
Par	**35**	

Totals		
Distance	**7070 yds**	
Par	**70**	

13 St. Mellion
CORNWALL

Set among 450 acres of glorious Cornish countryside, St. Mellion, with its two outstanding courses, is heralded as the premier golf and country club in the southwest. The Old Course is perfect for golfers of all abilities. Complete with well-sited bunkers, strategically tiered greens and difficult water features, this is definitely not a course to be overlooked. The 12th hole is the most attractive, but can be intimidating, with its large lake beckoning the ball.

But if you really want to test your game, then head to the renowned Nicklaus Course (see plan page 62), designed by the great man himself. The spectacularly sculptured fairways and carpet greens of the Nicklaus are a challenge and an inspiration to all golfers. After a testing game you can relax in the Golfers' Bar that overlooks the 18th fairway of the Nicklaus Course.

Tour Notes

1976 St. Mellion Golf Club is founded and the Old Course, designed by H. Hamilton-Stutt, quickly gains a reputation as one of the finest courses in the UK.

1988 Officially opened in July, the Nicklaus Course is the first-ever course designed by Jack Nicklaus in the UK. His signature is all over this incredible course—water hazards, high tees and the requirement to place the ball in the correct position to score

well. When it opens Jack declares, "St. Mellion is potentially the finest golf course in Europe".

1990–95 The Benson and Hedges International Open is held 6 years running. Founded in 1971, this tournament ceased in 2003 because the British government introduced a ban on tobacco advertising and sponsorship. Seve Ballesteros was the most famous winner in 1994.

Hole 1
Distance **417 yds** / Par **4**
Stroke Index **5**

Hole 2
Distance **547 yds** / Par **5**
Stroke Index**10**

Hole 3
Distance **364 yds** / Par **4**
Stroke Index **3**

Hole 4
Distance **178 yds** / Par **3**
Stroke Index **15**

Hole 5
Distance **350 yds** / Par **4**
Stroke Index **11**

Hole 10
Distance **442 yds** / Par **4**
Stroke Index **12**

Hole 11
Distance **203 yds** / Par **3**
Stroke Index **14**

Hole 12
Distance **540 yds** / Par **5**
Stroke Index **6**

Hole 13
Distance **399 yds** / Par **4**
Stroke Index **8**

Hole 14
Distance **175 yds** / Par **3**
Stroke Index **17**

St. Mellion CORNWALL

6	**Hole 6** Distance **430 yds** / Par **4** Stroke Index **1**

7	**Hole 7** Distance **503 yds** / Par **5** Stroke Index **7**

8	**Hole 8** Distance **131 yds** / Par **3** Stroke Index **18**

9	**Hole 9** Distance **407 yds** / Par **4** Stroke Index **13**

CONTACT DETAILS

Address
Saltash PL12 6SD

Telephone
01579 351351

Website
www.st-mellion.co.uk

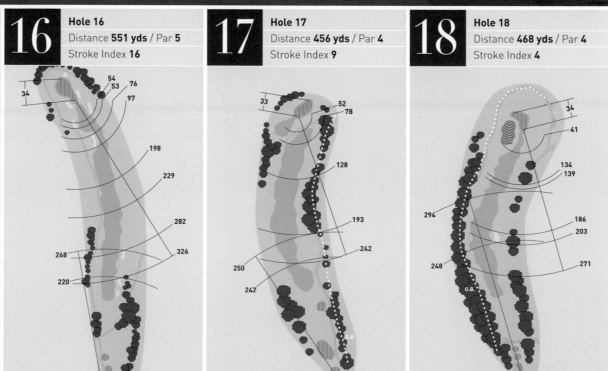

15	**Hole 15** Distance **428 yds** / Par **4** Stroke Index **2**

16	**Hole 16** Distance **551 yds** / Par **5** Stroke Index **16**

17	**Hole 17** Distance **456 yds** / Par **4** Stroke Index **9**

18	**Hole 18** Distance **468 yds** / Par **4** Stroke Index **4**

NICKLAUS COURSE

All distance measurements in yards from the blue tees.

Out	
Distance	**3327 yds**
Par	**36**
In	
Distance	**3662 yds**
Par	**36**
Totals	
Distance	**6989 yds**
Par	**72**

Sunningdale
BERKSHIRE

Sunningdale is blessed with two superbly conditioned championship courses, laid out on the most glorious piece of heathland. Both courses wind their way through heather, gorse and pine, but both display their own individual characteristics. The golf club has played host to many international competitions, including the Women's British Open on three occasions and the European Open on four.

The Old Course (see plan page 66) was founded in 1900 and was laid out by Willie Park, two-time winner of the Open (1887, 1889). It is a classic design, with immaculate turf and fairways lined with trees—most famous of these is the Sunningdale Oak, providing the club with its emblem. Pause at the 10th tee to take in the wonderful view across the valley to the woods on the horizon. The 5th is superb—the drive is downhill and the approach is played over a pond to the green. If it's a real challenge you want, the tougher New Course will severely test your golfing skills. Created by H. S. Colt in 1922 in direct response to a growing need for courses after World War I, it is a mixture of woodlands and open heath, with long carries and tight fairways.

Tour Notes

1926 Bobby Jones shoots what is hailed as the first and only "perfect round of golf" while qualifying for the Open Championship. In the days when shooting a 66 is out of the question, Jones does just that with 33 shots and 33 putts.

1934 The Sunningdale Foursomes is born. This traditional competition continues to be held annually, bringing together seasoned professionals and aspiring amateurs, men and women, in a good old-fashioned foursomes competition.

1987 Sunningdale stages the Walker Cup, the first time the competition has been held on an inland course in the UK. The Americans take the trophy home with them.

2000 Sunningdale celebrates its centenary year.

Hole 1
Distance **492 yds** / Par **5**
Stroke Index **8**

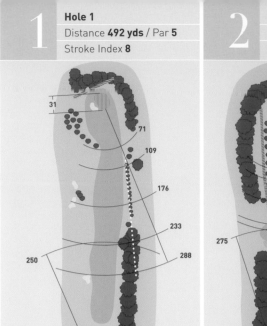

Hole 2
Distance **489 yds** / Par **4**
Stroke Index **4**

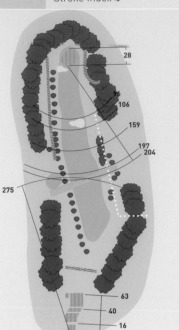

Hole 3
Distance **318 yds** / Par **4**
Stroke Index **12**

Hole 4
Distance **156 yds** / Par **3**
Stroke Index **16**

Hole 5
Distance **419 yds** / Par **4**
Stroke Index **2**

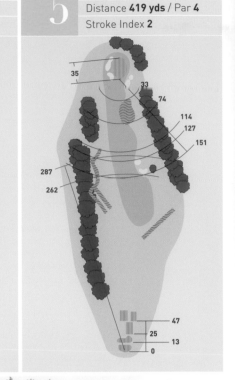

> 66 I still swing the way I used to, but when I look up the ball is going in a different direction 99
>
> *LEE TREVINO*

Hole 10
Distance **475 yds** / Par **4**
Stroke Index **7**

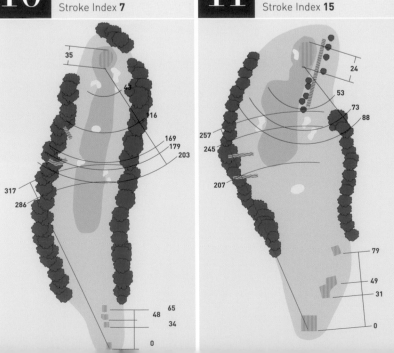

Hole 11
Distance **322 yds** / Par **4**
Stroke Index **15**

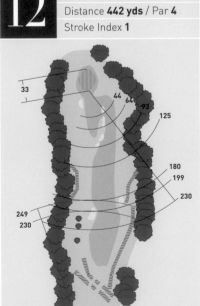

Hole 12
Distance **442 yds** / Par **4**
Stroke Index **1**

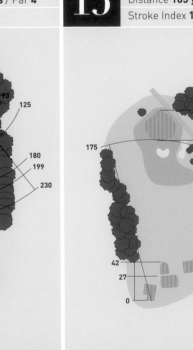

Hole 13
Distance **185 yds** / Par **3**
Stroke Index **17**

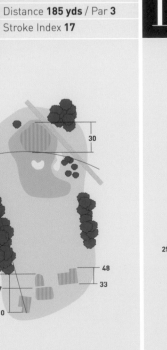

Hole 14
Distance **503 yds** / Par **5**
Stroke Index **5**

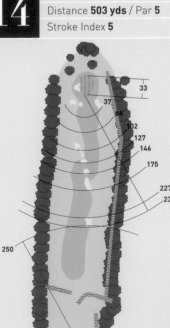

Sunningdale BERKSHIRE

6 Hole 6
Distance **433 yds** / Par **4**
Stroke Index **10**

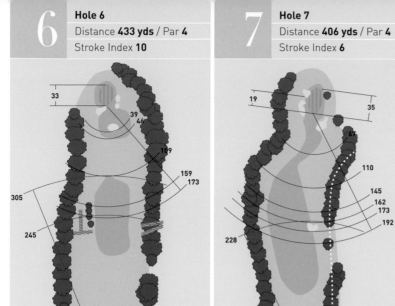
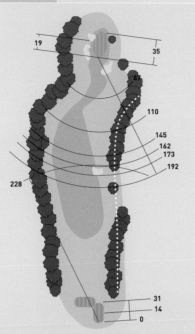

7 Hole 7
Distance **406 yds** / Par **4**
Stroke Index **6**

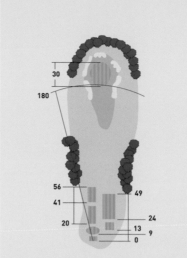

8 Hole 8
Distance **193 yds** / Par **3**
Stroke Index **18**

9 Hole 9
Distance **273 yds** / Par **4**
Stroke Index **14**

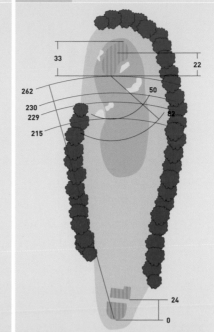

CONTACT DETAILS

Address
Ridgemount Road,
Sunningdale SL5 9RR

Telephone
01344 621681

Website
www.sunningdale-golfclub.
com

15 Hole 15
Distance **239 yds** / Par **3**
Stroke Index **11**

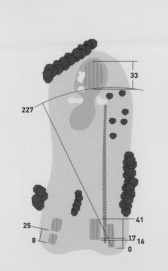

16 Hole 16
Distance **434 yds** / Par **4**
Stroke Index **3**

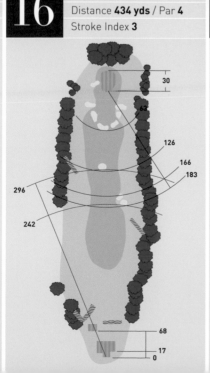

17 Hole 17
Distance **425 yds** / Par **4**
Stroke Index **13**

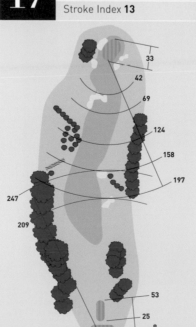

18 Hole 1
Distance **423 yds** / Par **4**
Stroke Index **9**

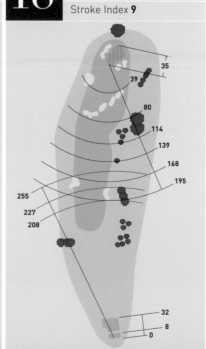

OLD COURSE

All distance measurements in
yards from the championship tees.

All illustrations are based upon
original Strokesaver artwork.

Out	
Distance	**3179 yds**
Par	**35**
In	
Distance	**3448 yds**
Par	**35**

Totals	
Distance	**6627 yds**
Par	**70**

15

Walton Heath
SURREY

Walton Heath's two extremely taxing courses enjoy an enviable international reputation. Both courses are intertwined and have a similar look and feel. The drainage is excellent, the turf crisp, the lies tight, the bunkers deep and the greens firm and quick. Walton Heath has played host to over 60 international amateur and professional championships, including the 1981 Ryder Cup. In 2007 the club was proud to be the choice for the US Open European Qualifying events.

The Old Course (see plan page 70) is tough. Some of the tee shots are long and require a solid drive to avoid the thick heather surrounding the fairway—otherwise wave goodbye to your ball. Some greens are amply protected by bunkers to the left and right. The 16th will probably linger longest in your memory; with a steep approach to the green, a weak shot will be swallowed by a troublesome bunker to the right. The New Course will also test your skills, requiring subtle shots to avoid straying from the fairway into thick gorse, bracken and heather.

Tour Notes

1904 The Old Course opens for play, marked by an exhibition match between Harry Vardon, J. H. Taylor and James Braid. This is designer Herbert Fowler's first golf-course venture, from which he goes on to become one of the leading golf-course architects of the era.

1912 James Braid becomes the club professional, remaining in that capacity until his death in 1950. For much of his life Braid lived at Walton-on-the-Hill close to his beloved golf course.

1935–36 Walton Heath claims the distinction of being the only English club to have a reigning monarch as club captain, when the Prince of Wales becomes king in January 1936.

1981 The Ryder Cup takes place, won by an American team considered to be one of the best line-ups ever seen in the tournament—between them, the players have won 36 major championships.

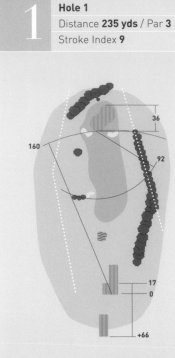

Hole 1
Distance **235 yds** / Par **3**
Stroke Index **9**

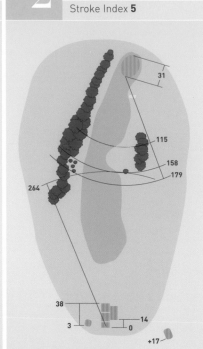

Hole 2
Distance **458 yds** / Par **4**
Stroke Index **5**

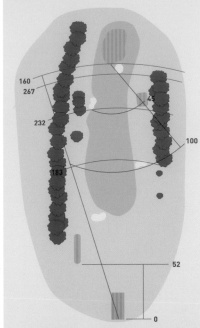

Hole 3
Distance **289 yds** / Par **4**
Stroke Index **17**

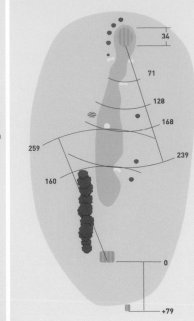

Hole 4
Distance **441 yds** / Par **4**
Stroke Index **1**

Hole 5
Distance **391 yds** / Par **4**
Stroke Index **11**

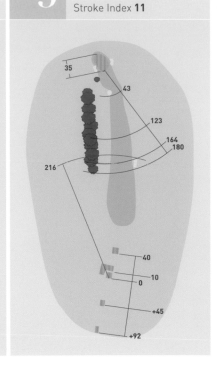

> **❝** Golf is a difficult game, but it's a little easier if you trust your instincts. It's too hard a game to try and play like someone else **❞**
>
> *NANCY LOPEZ*

10 Hole 10
Distance **399 yds** / Par **4**
Stroke Index **4**

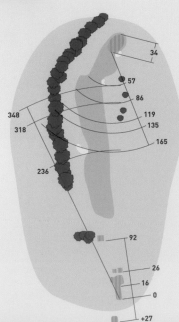

11 Hole 11
Distance **189 yds** / Par **3**
Stroke Index **16**

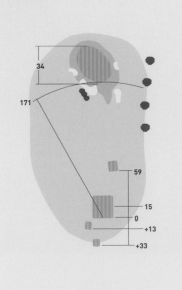

12 Hole 12
Distance **371 yds** / Par **4**
Stroke Index **14**

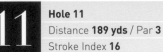

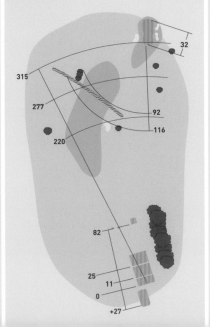

13 Hole 13
Distance **548 yds** / Par **5**
Stroke Index **6**

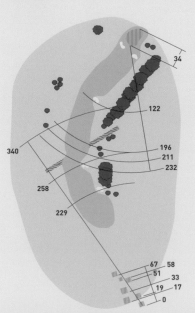

14 Hole 14
Distance **517 yds** / Par **5**
Stroke Index **12**

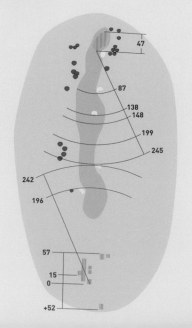

6 — Hole 6
Distance **427 yds** / Par **4**
Stroke Index **7**

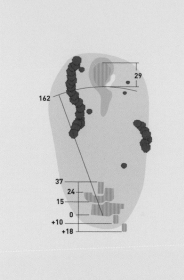

7 — Hole 7
Distance **174 yds** / Par **3**
Stroke Index **15**

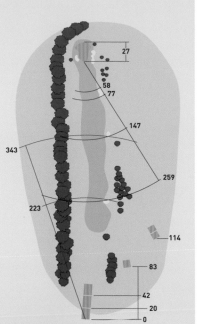

8 — Hole 8
Distance **494 yds** / Par **5**
Stroke Index **3**

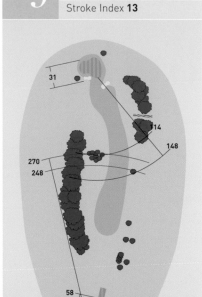

9 — Hole 9
Distance **400 yds** / Par **4**
Stroke Index **13**

CONTACT DETAILS

Address
Deans Lane, Walton-on-the-Hill KT20 7TP

Telephone
01737 812380

Website
www.whgc.co.uk

15 — Hole 15
Distance **408 yds** / Par **4**
Stroke Index **2**

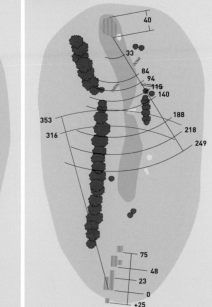

16 — Hole 16
Distance **510 yds** / Par **5**
Stroke Index **8**

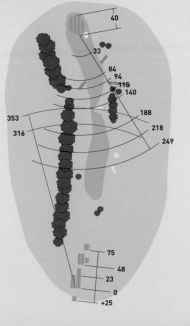

17 — Hole 17
Distance **181 yds** / Par **3**
Stroke Index **18**

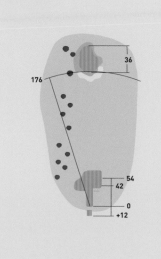

18 — Hole 18
Distance **404 yds** / Par **4**
Stroke Index **10**

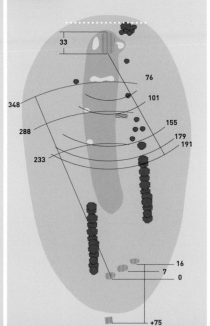

OLD COURSE

All distance measurements in yards from the white tees.

All illustrations are based upon original Strokesaver artwork.

Out	
Distance	**3309 yds**
Par	**35**
In	
Distance	**3527 yds**
Par	**37**

Totals	
Distance	**6836 yds**
Par	**72**

16

Wentworth
SURREY

At the end of a rhododendron-lined drive, Wentworth's famous castellated clubhouse proudly looks out over lush fairways and beautifully manicured greens. Internationally acclaimed, Wentworth Golf Club has been home of the World Matchplay—the European Tour's flagship event—since 1964 and the PGA Championship since 1984. The three courses are laid out over glorious heathland with pine woods, oak and birch, where golfers tread in the footsteps of the game's great players from the last 80 years.

Familiar to millions of television viewers who have followed championships held here, the West Course (see plan page 74) has a place in the hearts of golfers all over the world. Architect Harry Colt's 1926 design is a stern classic layout that requires golfers to examine every part of their game. Fairways turn both ways and there is a wonderful flow to the course, with pleasing elevation changes and a variety of different length par 3s, 4s and 5s. Recent modifications to bring the course into the 21st century have involved extensive re-bunkering and lengthening of certain holes. The other courses, the East Course (opened 1924) and the Edinburgh Course (opened 1990 by John Jacobs, with input from Gary Player and Bernard Gallacher), also have an illustrious pedigree.

1926 The first unofficial match between the American and British/Irish professionals—what was to become the Ryder Cup—takes place on the East Course; a landslide victory for the euphoric Great Britain and Ireland team.

1953 The Ryder Cup puts Wentworth on the golfing world map with the most fiercely contested competition since 1933. The Americans gain victory in the waning hour.

1956 Wentworth hosts the Canada Cup, the forerunner to golf's World Cup; it's won by the US dream team of Ben Hogan and Sam Snead.

1975 Prolific golfer Bernard Gallacher takes over as club professional while combining his duties with a successful tournament career. In December 1996 Gallacher retires from his position.

Ben Hogan competing in the Canada Cup, 1956

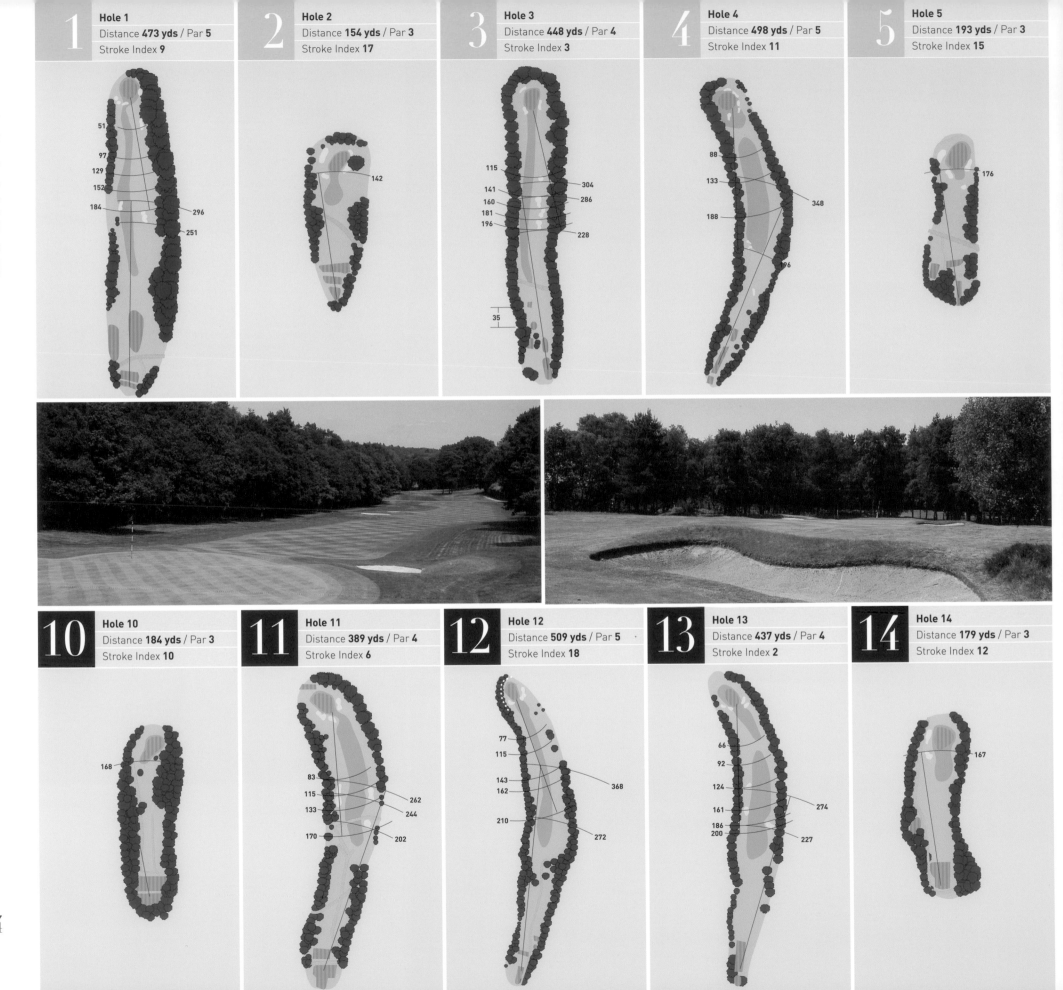

1 Hole 1
Distance **473 yds** / Par **5**
Stroke Index **9**

51
97
129
152
184
296
251

2 Hole 2
Distance **154 yds** / Par **3**
Stroke Index **17**

142

3 Hole 3
Distance **448 yds** / Par **4**
Stroke Index **3**

115
141
160
181
196
304
286
228
35

4 Hole 4
Distance **498 yds** / Par **5**
Stroke Index **11**

88
133
188
348
196

5 Hole 5
Distance **193 yds** / Par **3**
Stroke Index **15**

176

10 Hole 10
Distance **184 yds** / Par **3**
Stroke Index **10**

168

11 Hole 11
Distance **389 yds** / Par **4**
Stroke Index **6**

83
115
133
170
262
244
202

12 Hole 12
Distance **509 yds** / Par **5**
Stroke Index **18**

77
115
143
162
210
368
272

13 Hole 13
Distance **437 yds** / Par **4**
Stroke Index **2**

66
92
124
161
186
200
274
227

14 Hole 14
Distance **179 yds** / Par **3**
Stroke Index **12**

167

6 Hole 6
Distance **351 yds** / Par **4**
Stroke Index **13**

37
64
298
115
242
216
152
182

7 Hole 7
Distance **396 yds** / Par **4**
Stroke Index **5**

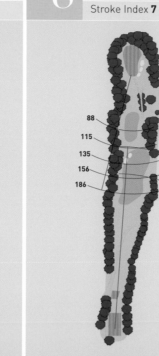

30
87
95
293
126
247
161
214

8 Hole 8
Distance **391 yds** / Par **4**
Stroke Index **7**

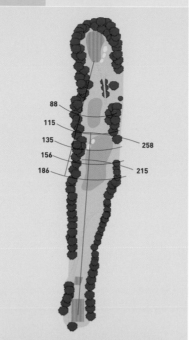

88
115
135
258
156
186
215

9 Hole 9
Distance **449 yds** / Par **4**
Stroke Index **1**

76
112
147
178
264
270
238

CONTACT DETAILS

Address
Wentworth Drive,
Virginia Water GU25 4LS

Telephone
01344 842201

Website
www.wentworthclub.com

15 Hole 15
Distance **477 yds** / Par **4**
Stroke Index **4**

79
131
167
184
297
210
233
241

16 Hole 16
Distance **383 yds** / Par **4**
Stroke Index **16**

65
305
87
105
275
118
135
245
167
217

17 Hole 17
Distance **566 yds** / Par **5**
Stroke Index **8**

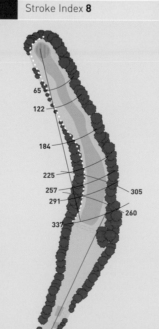

65
122
184
225
257
305
291
260
337

18 Hole 18
Distance **521 yds** / Par **5**
Stroke Index **14**

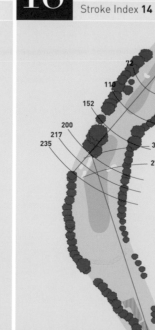

72
110
152
200
217
321
235
279

WEST COURSE

All distance measurements in
yards from the white tees.

Out	
Distance	**3353 yds**
Par	**36**
In	
Distance	**3645 yds**
Par	**37**

Totals	
Distance	**6998 yds**
Par	**73**

17 Woburn

BUCKINGHAMSHIRE

Easily accessible from the M1 motorway, Woburn is famed not only for its golf courses but also for the magnificent stately home and wildlife park that share the beautiful surrounding countryside. Charles Lawrie, of the golf design firm Cotton Pennink, designed two of the great courses here, beautifully set among mature trees.

The Duke's Course, opened in 1976, is a tough challenge for golfers at all levels, with its natural hazards and the combination of heather, gorse and bracken. The relatively easier Duchess Course, opened 1978, still demands a high level of skill to negotiate the fairways that are guarded by towering pines. A third course, the Marquess (see plan page 78), which uses one of the best pieces of land on the estate, opened in June 2000. It has been praised worldwide as a superior tournament course.

Tour Notes

1974 The 14th Duke of Bedford decides that the game of golf should be brought to Woburn Abbey in an attempt to rejuvenate this wonderful home and estate.

1979 The Duke's Course hosts the British Masters for the first time and is thereafter chosen for a further 13 tournaments; the last British Masters on this course takes place in 2000.

1990s Long before the course eventually opens, plans are set in motion to develop a course that will be considered one of the best in Europe, the Marquess. Based on designs by Peter Alliss, Clive Clark, Ross McMurray and Alex Hay, the course breaks with the tradition of the other courses—enhanced by an area of mixed woodland rather than dominant pines.

2001 The British Masters is switched to the brand new Marquess. Frenchman Thomas Levet takes the title, and the following year, England's young new talent Justin Rose claims glory and his first professional win on British soil.

Hole 1
Distance **395 yds** / Par **4**
Stroke Index **12**

Hole 2
Distance **506 yds** / Par **5**
Stroke Index **8**

Hole 3
Distance **473 yds** / Par **4**
Stroke Index **2**

Hole 4
Distance **425 yds** / Par **4**
Stroke Index **14**

Hole 5
Distance **415 yds** / Par **4**
Stroke Index **4**

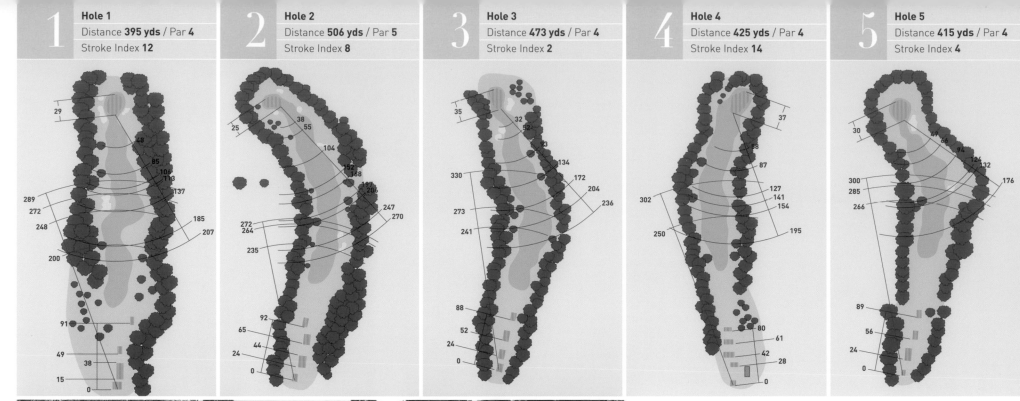

> 66 Be decisive. A wrong
> decision is generally less
> disastrous than indecision 99
>
> *BERNHARD LANGER*

10 Hole 10
Distance **374 yds** / Par **4**
Stroke Index **11**

11 Hole 11
Distance **579 yds** / Par **5**
Stroke Index **5**

12 Hole 12
Distance **343 yds** / Par **4**
Stroke Index **15**

13 Hole 13
Distance **467 yds** / Par **4**
Stroke Index **1**

14 Hole 14
Distance **219 yds** / Par **3**
Stroke Index **7**

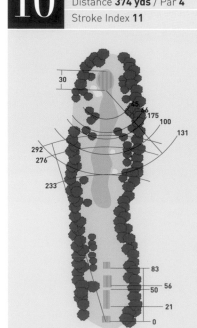

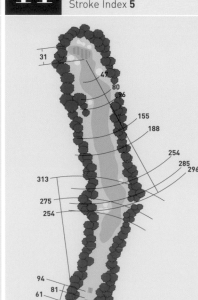

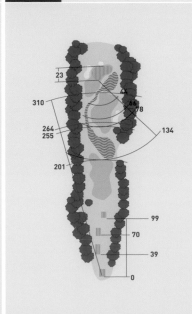

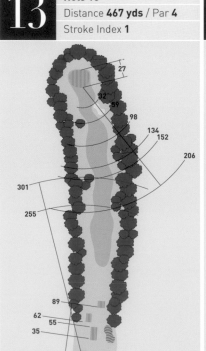

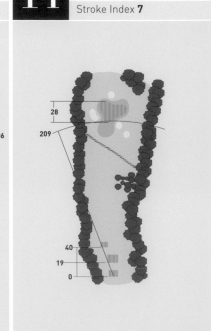

Hole 6
Distance **159 yds** / Par **3**
Stroke Index **18**

Hole 7
Distance **538 yds** / Par **5**
Stroke Index **6**

Hole 8
Distance **188 yds** / Par **3**
Stroke Index **16**

Hole 9
Distance **473 yds** / Par **4**
Stroke Index **10**

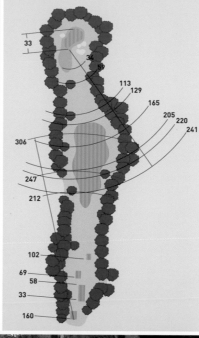

CONTACT DETAILS

Address
Little Brickhill MK17 9LJ

Telephone
01908 370356

Website
www.golf.discoverwoburn.co.uk

Hole 15
Distance **575 yds** / Par **5**
Stroke Index **13**

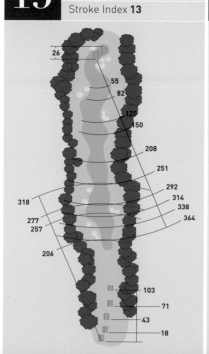

Hole 16
Distance **450 yds** / Par **4**
Stroke Index **3**

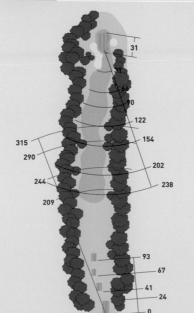

Hole 17
Distance **176 yds** / Par **3**
Stroke Index **17**

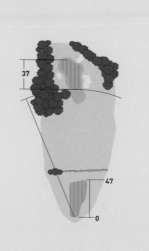

Hole 18
Distance **459 yds** / Par **4**
Stroke Index **9**

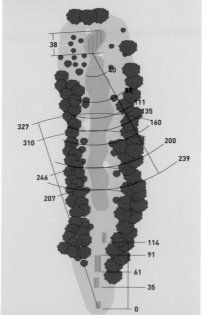

MARQUESS COURSE

All distance measurements in yards from the back tees.

All illustrations are based upon original Strokesaver artwork.

Out	
Distance	**3572 yds**
Par	**36**
In	
Distance	**3642 yds**
Par	**36**

Totals	
Distance	7214 yds
Par	72

SCOTLAND

⑱ **Carnoustie** 82
Angus

⑲ **Duke's Course** 86
Fife

⑳ **Fairmont St. Andrews** 90
Fife

㉑ **Gleneagles Hotel** 94
Perth & Kinross

㉒ **Marriott Dalmahoy** 98
Edinburgh

㉓ **Prestwick** 102
South Ayrshire

㉔ **Royal Dornoch** 106
Highland

㉕ **Royal Troon** 110
South Ayrshire

㉖ **St. Andrews Links** 114
Fife

㉗ **Westerwood Hotel** 118
North Lanarkshire

㉘ **Westin Turnberry Resort** 122
South Ayrshire

18 Carnoustie
ANGUS

Carnoustie may not be the prettiest golf course but it has been voted the top course in Britain by many golfing greats and described as Scotland's ultimate golfing challenge. The course has its origins in the 1560s, but the present course dates from 1850, designed by Allan Robertson. Some 20 years later the legendary Old Tom Morris improved and extended the course to 18 holes and in 1926 famous architect James Braid redesigned the Championship Course (see plan page 84) by adding new bunkers, greens and tees. This is one mean golf course and most of the world's top players have struggled to tame the monster. You have to cross the snaking burn no less than five times while playing the closing two holes. In addition, there are some of the most formidable bunkers to contend with.

The Burnside Course is enclosed on three sides by the Championship Course and has been used for the Open qualifying rounds. The Buddon Links has been extensively remodelled, making it ideal for mid to high handicappers. The Open has been held on the Championship Course seven times in 1931, 1937, 1953, 1968, 1975, 1999 and, with a dramatic conclusion, in 2007.

Tour Notes

1931 Carnoustie stages its first Open. Edinburgh-born Tommy Armour, who emigrated to America, is a popular winner. Armour lost an eye in a mustard gas attack while fighting in the British Army during World War I.

1937 Englishman Henry Cotton wins the Open again. Cotton seems oblivious to the conditions as he returns an amazing 71 in torrential rain on a water-logged course—one of his greatest achievements.

1999 Frenchman Jean Van de Velde, needing to make only a six on the 18th hole to win the Open, squanders his chances in excruciating fashion shooting a triple-bogey seven—which includes his famous barefoot paddle in the Barry Burn to recover the ball. Local hero Paul Lawrie goes on to win after a play off.

2007 In one of the most exciting climaxes in the history of the Open, Ireland's Padraig Harrington clinches a win over the course leader, Sergio Garcia of Spain, in a nail-biting play off. Also at the Open an emotional Seve Ballesteros annouces his retirement from golf at the course where he made his Open debut in 1975. It ends one of the most glittering careers in the modern game.

Left: Ben Hogan, winner of the Open in 1953

Below: Padraig Harrington, 2007 Open winner

1 **Cup**
Distance **400 yds** / Par **4**
Stroke Index **10**

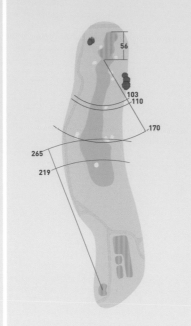

35

116
137

268
248

172

2 **Gulley**
Distance **459 yds** / Par **4**
Stroke Index **4**

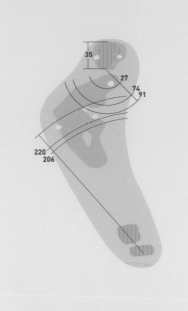

56

103
110

170

265
219

3 **Jockie's Burn**
Distance **355 yds** / Par **4**
Stroke Index **14**

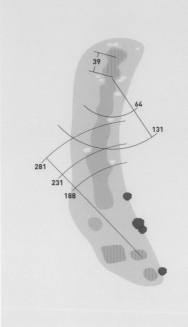

35

27
74
91

220
206

4 **Hillocks**
Distance **375 yds** / Par **4**
Stroke Index **16**

39

64

131

281
231
188

5 **Brae**
Distance **408 yds** / Par **4**
Stroke Index **12**

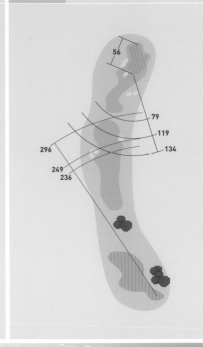

56

79
119
134

296
249
236

> 66 *A good caddie is more than a mere assistant. He is guide, philosopher and friend* 99
>
> *HENRY LONGHURST*

10 **South America**
Distance **465 yds** / Par **4**
Stroke Index **3**

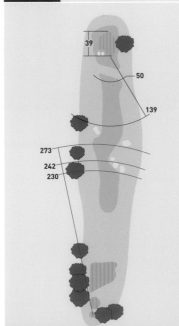

39

50

139

273
242
230

11 **Dyke**
Distance **380 yds** / Par **4**
Stroke Index **15**

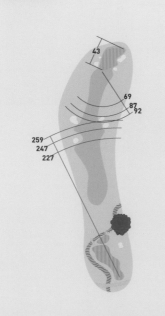

43

69
87
92

259
247
227

12 **Southward Ho**
Distance **504 yds** / Par **5**
Stroke Index **9**

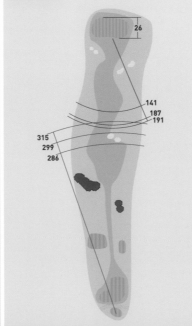

26

141
187
191

315
299
286

13 **Whins**
Distance **171 yds** / Par **3**
Stroke Index **17**

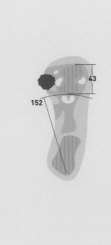

43

152

14 **Spectacles**
Distance **510 yds** / Par **5**
Stroke Index **1**

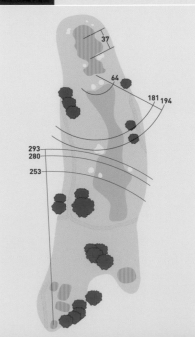

37

64

181 194

293
280

253

6 Hogan's Ally
Distance **573 yds** / Par **5**
Stroke Index **2**

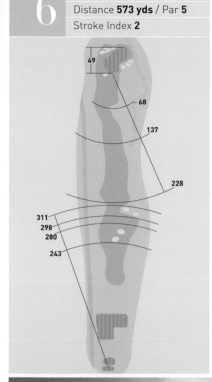

7 Plantation
Distance **409 yds** / Par **4**
Stroke Index **8**

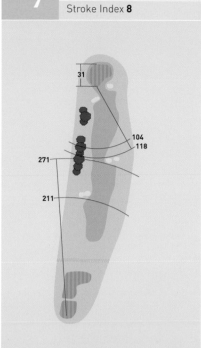

8 Short
Distance **181 yds** / Par **3**
Stroke Index **18**

9 Railway
Distance **474 yds** / Par **4**
Stroke Index **6**

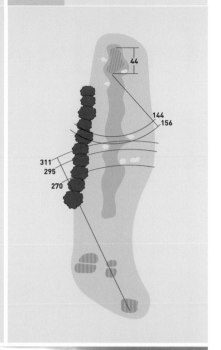

CONTACT DETAILS

Address
20 Links Parade, Carnoustie
DD7 7JF

Telephone
01241 802280

Website
www.carnoustiegolflinks.
co.uk

15 Lucky Slap
Distance **471 yds** / Par **4**
Stroke Index **7**

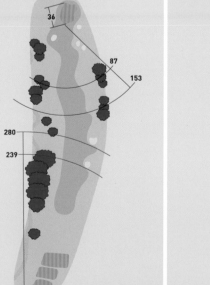

16 Barry Burn
Distance **249 yds** / Par **3**
Stroke Index **13**

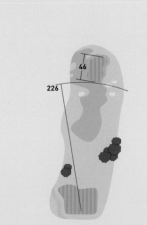

17 Island
Distance **460 yds** / Par **4**
Stroke Index **5**

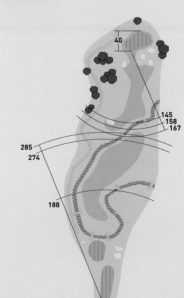

18 Home
Distance **510 yds** / Par **4**
Stroke Index **11**

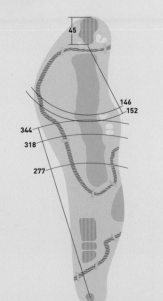

CHAMPIONSHIP COURSE

All distance measurements in
yards from the blue tees.

Out	
Distance	**3634 yds**
Par	**36**
In	
Distance	**3720 yds**
Par	**36**
Totals	
Distance	**7354 yds**
Par	**72**

Duke's Course
FIFE

Designed by five times Open champion Peter Thompson, Duke's commands a spectacular setting above St. Andrews. Competing with 10 courses in the immediate area and another 30 within a 30-minute drive, Duke's is regarded as one of the best heathland courses in the country.

Blending the characteristics of a links course with an inland course, it offers rolling fairways, undulating greens and a testing woodland section, plus magnificent views over St. Andrews Bay towards Carnoustie. There are five separate tees at every hole, which caters for every level of golfer, and paved buggy paths twist throughout the course to enable year-round cart use. It is hard not to be distracted by some of the truly stupendous views, particularly at the 6th, 7th, 13th and 14th holes. The attractive clubhouse overlooks the closing holes and offers a nice retreat after a hard day's golf.

Tour Notes

1995 Encouraged by the increasing need for tee times in the area, the Duke's Course is opened in July. Prince Andrew, HRH The Duke of York, marks the occasion by playing an inaugural round with the British Lions rugby team.

2004 Duke's Course and the Old Course Hotel are sold to the Kohler Company as part of a long-term development programme for the resort. Kohler Company make a significant investment to modify the golf course.

2006 With the intension of taking the Duke's to a new height of all-round excellence, the course is renovated, adding five completely new holes designed by Tim Liddy. His plans incorporate many of the features of the heathland courses of the 1920s, blending and sculpting the course with the natural surroundings.

1 Highland
Distance **528 yds** / Par **5**
Stroke Index **6**

2 Drumcarrow
Distance **451 yds** / Par **4**
Stroke Index **2**

3 Denhead
Distance **171 yds** / Par **3**
Stroke Index **18**

4 Roundel
Distance **433 yds** / Par **4**
Stroke Index **12**

5 Beeches
Distance **374 yds** / Par **4**
Stroke Index **14**

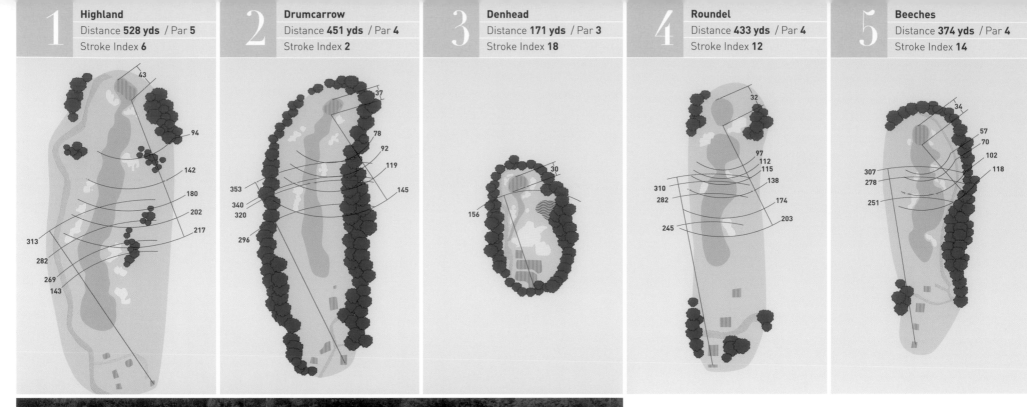

> 66 The terrible beauty is that
> in the brotherhood of golf we
> are all the same—certifiable 99
>
> *SEAN CONNERY*

10 Burn Brig
Distance **448 yds** / Par **4**
Stroke Index **5**

11 Winthank
Distance **640 yds** / Par **5**
Stroke Index **1**

12 Double Dyke
Distance **224 yds** / Par **3**
Stroke Index **17**

13 Braw View
Distance **424 yds** / Par **4**
Stroke Index **13**

14 Well
Distance **472 yds** / Par **4**
Stroke Index **3**

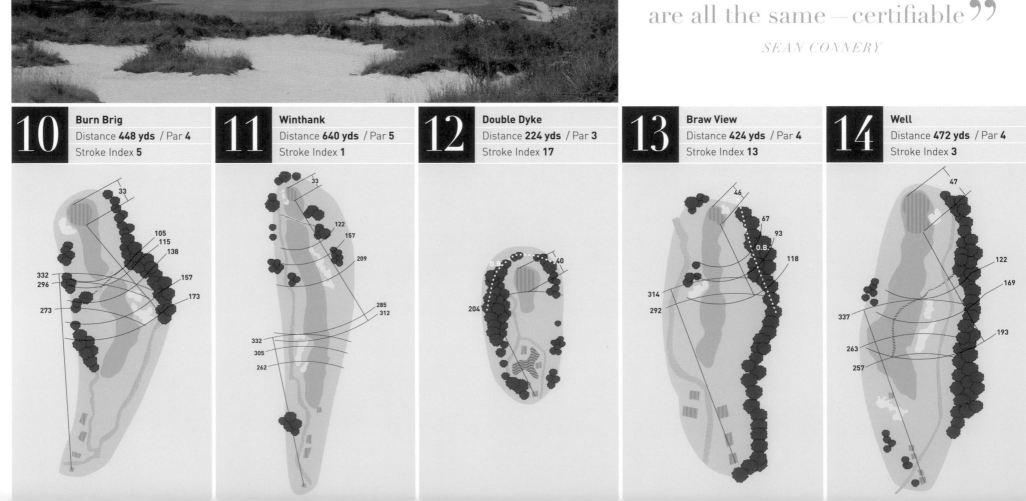

6 Badgers
Distance **596 yds** / Par **5**
Stroke Index **4**

7 Debrae
Distance **513 yds** / Par **4**
Stroke Index **8**

8 Fair Dunt
Distance **250 yds** / Par **3**
Stroke Index **16**

9 Craigtoun
Distance **417 yds** / Par **4**
Stroke Index **10**

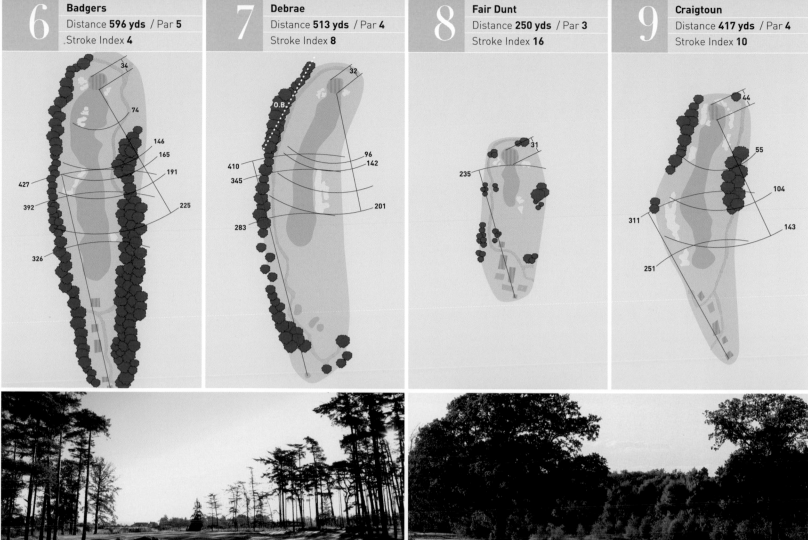

CONTACT DETAILS

Address
Craigtoun, St. Andrews
KY16 8NS

Telephone
01334 474371

Website
www.oldcoursehotel.co.uk

15 Steading
Distance **453 yds** / Par **4**
Stroke Index **7**

16 Melville
Distance **231 yds** / Par **3**
Stroke Index **15**

17 Strath
Distance **429 yds** / Par **4**
Stroke Index **11**

18 Ice House
Distance **458 yds** / Par **4**
Stroke Index **9**

DUKE'S COURSE

All distance measurements in
yards from the back tees.

Out	
Distance	3733 yds
Par	36
In	
Distance	3779 yds
Par	35
Totals	
Distance	7512 yds
Par	71

Fairmont St. Andrews
FIFE

In the face of so much history there was inevitably an air of expectation when this new course was built so close to the "home of golf". But one look will convince you that Fairmont St. Andrews will complement rather than compete with the ancient course. Sweeping dramatically down to the rugged coastline, within sight of the old town's skyline, the five-star resort has two magnificent golf courses, the Torrance (see plan page 92) and the Devlin. Both are chequered with ancient stone walls overrun in season by flowering yellow gorse and broom, white quince, red campion and delicate bluebells, while stone bridges span the burn running through the Torrance.

The Torrance Course, chosen as an Open qualifying course for 2010, has a traditional Scottish layout, which works its way around the hotel before bursting open to reveal a cross section of the remaining 12 holes, which wind down towards the coastal edge. There are no dull holes on the Torrance, but the back nine has the most spectacular ocean holes. The Devlin is a stunning cliff-top course with unique characteristics and requiring a well-devised strategy of play—it's one of the longest courses in the UK. At the heart of the two courses is a £2 million clubhouse, with a balcony facing the sea.

Tour Notes

1990s American entrepreneur Donald Panoz's wisdom is questioned when he plows an estimated £58 million into building St. Andrews Bay Resort (as it was first known) 3 miles south of the mighty "auld grey toon".

2001 Panoz's dream comes to fruition when his friend, the late Gene Sarazen, hooks up with victorious 2002 European Ryder Cup captain Sam Torrance to create the Torrance Course. The course finally opens in June.

2002 The Devlin Course opens for play to a rapturous standing ovation. It was designd by Australian Bruce Devlin, with Sarazen as his consultant.

Hole 1
Distance **418 yds** / Par **4**
Stroke Index **10**

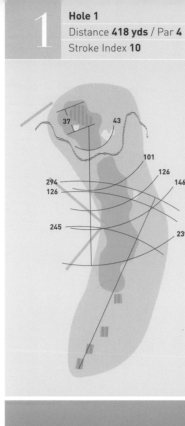

37 43
101
126
146
294
126
245
239

Hole 2
Distance **335 yds** / Par **4**
Stroke Index **14**

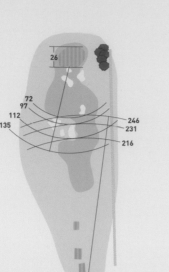

26
72
97
112
135
246
231
216

Hole 3
Distance **211 yds** / Par **3**
Stroke Index **8**

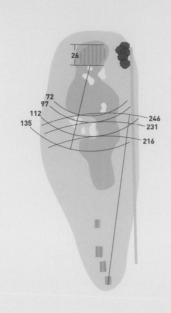

43
192

Hole 4
Distance **498 yds** / Par **5**
Stroke Index **4**

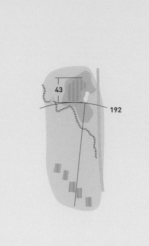
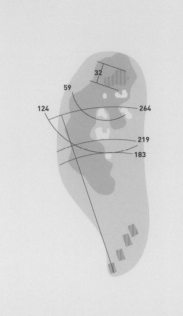

160
O.B.
104
124
200
245
276
262
230

Hole 5
Distance **339 yds** / Par **4**
Stroke Index **18**

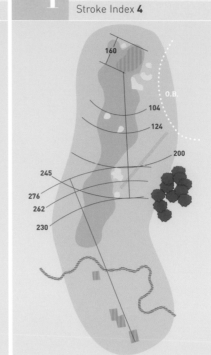

32
59
264
124
219
183

Hole 10
Distance **537 yds** / Par **5**
Stroke Index **9**

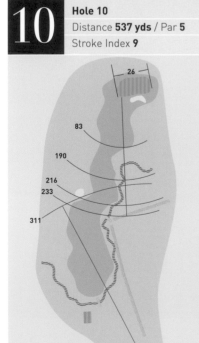

26
83
190
216
233
311

Hole 11
Distance **176 yds** / Par **3**
Stroke Index **17**

44
155

Hole 12
Distance **434 yds** / Par **4**
Stroke Index **5**

41
68
129
136
174
268
279
243
228

Hole 13
Distance **357 yds** / Par **4**
Stroke Index **15**

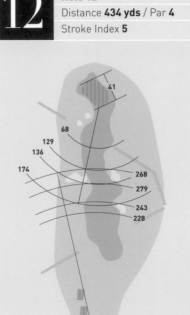

24
68
122
154
221
197

Hole 14
Distance **426 yds** / Par **4**
Stroke Index **3**

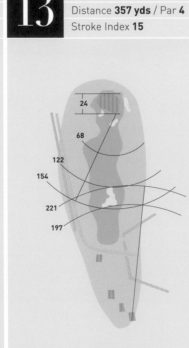
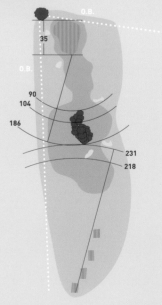
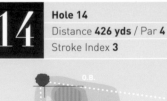

O.B.
35
O.B.
90
104
186
231
218

6 Hole 6
Distance **220 yds** / Par **3**
Stroke Index **16**

7 Hole 7
Distance **461 yds** / Par **4**
Stroke Index **2**

8 Hole 8
Distance **546 yds** / Par **5**
Stroke Index **6**

9 Hole 9
Distance **376 yds** / Par **4**
Stroke Index **12**

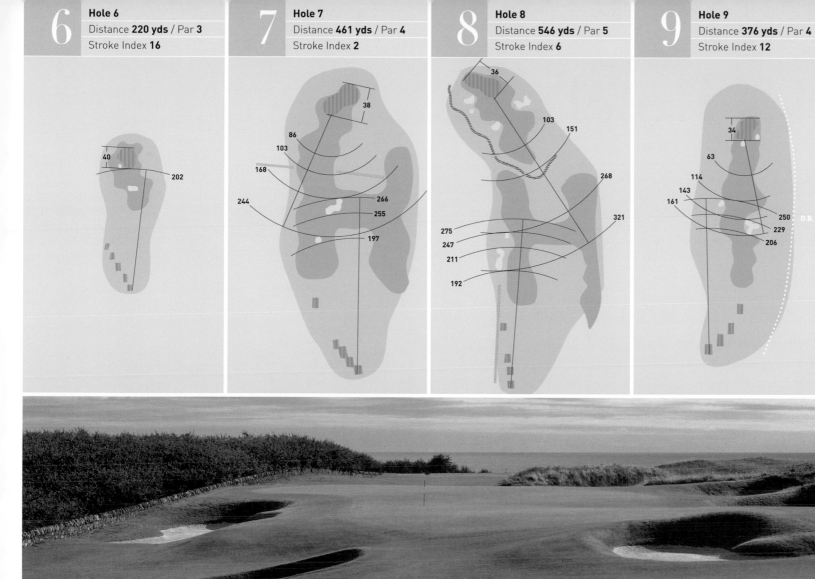

CONTACT DETAILS

Address
St. Andrews KY16 8PN

Telephone
01334 837000

Website
www.www.fairmont.com/
standrews/recreation/golf

15 Hole 15
Distance **221 yds** / Par **3**
Stroke Index **13**

16 Hole 16
Distance **465 yds** / Par **4**
Stroke Index **7**

17 Hole 17
Distance **448 yds** / Par **4**
Stroke Index **1**

18 Hole 18
Distance **569 yds** / Par **5**
Stroke Index **11**

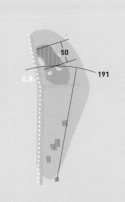
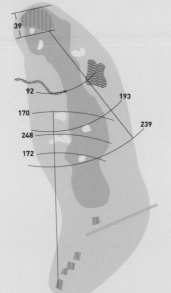
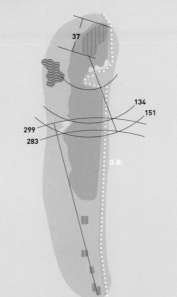
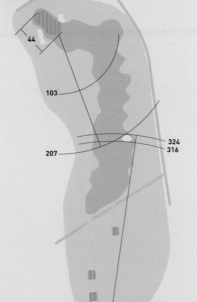

TORRANCE COURSE

All distance measurements in
yards from the blue tees.

Out		
Distance		**3404 yds**
Par		**36**
In		
Distance		**3633 yds**
Par		**36**
Totals		
Distance		**7037 yds**
Par		**72**

Gleneagles Hotel
PERTH & KINROSS

Gleneagles is truly a golfer's paradise and ranks among the best in the world, boasting three magnificent 18-hole courses—two designed by James Braid, one by Jack Nicklaus—plus a fine nine-hole called the Wee Course that enables both the beginner and more experienced golfer to get some useful practice.

The King's Course (see plan page 96), with the Grampian Mountains spectacularly in view to the north, has an abundance of heather, gorse, raised greens and plateau tees. Considered an easier test of golf, the shorter Queen's Course features fairways lined with Scots pines and water hazards set in a softer landscape. Another course, Glendevon, was opened in 1980 but was incorporated into the most recent addition, the PGA Centenary Course. Gleneagles' jewel in the crown, the PGA Centenary, has an American-Scottish layout fraught with water hazards, elevated tees and raised contoured greens. It has a five-tier tee structure, making it both the longest and shortest playable course.

Tour Notes

1919 The King's Course opens, leading the way in championship golf at Gleneagles, soon followed by the Queen's Course, both designed and created by James Braid.

1928 A third course, the Wee Course by George Alexander, is unveiled; lengthened to 18 holes in 1974 and renamed Princes.

Early 1990s Jack Nicklaus creates the Monarch Course, which includes the existing Glendevon and some holes of the Princes. The remaining holes are used for a new nine-hole course, recalling the Wee Course of the 1920s.

2001 To celebrate the centenary year of the Professional Golfer's Association, the Monarch is renamed the PGA Centenary Course, and is selected as the venue for the 2014 Ryder Cup.

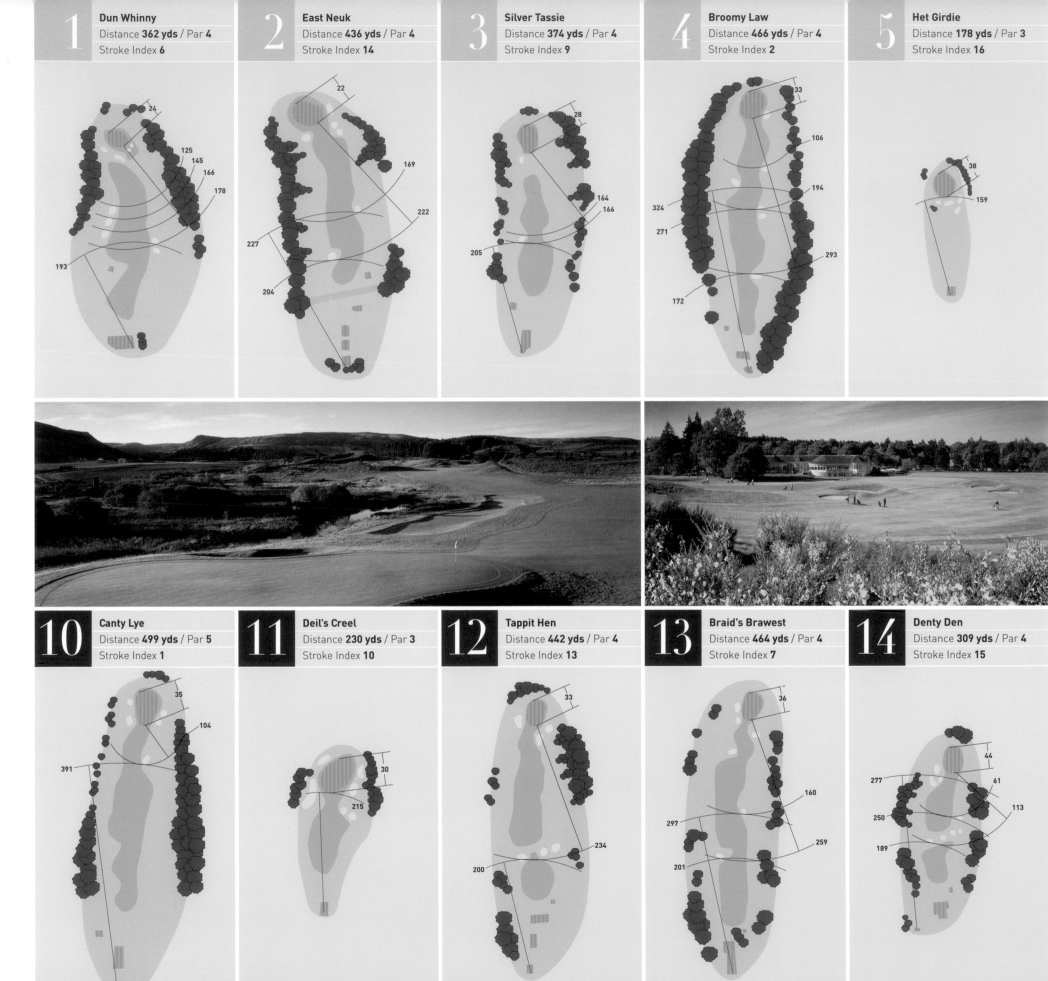

1 Dun Whinny
Distance **362 yds** / Par **4**
Stroke Index **6**

2 East Neuk
Distance **436 yds** / Par **4**
Stroke Index **14**

3 Silver Tassie
Distance **374 yds** / Par **4**
Stroke Index **9**

4 Broomy Law
Distance **466 yds** / Par **4**
Stroke Index **2**

5 Het Girdie
Distance **178 yds** / Par **3**
Stroke Index **16**

10 Canty Lye
Distance **499 yds** / Par **5**
Stroke Index **1**

11 Deil's Creel
Distance **230 yds** / Par **3**
Stroke Index **10**

12 Tappit Hen
Distance **442 yds** / Par **4**
Stroke Index **13**

13 Braid's Brawest
Distance **464 yds** / Par **4**
Stroke Index **7**

14 Denty Den
Distance **309 yds** / Par **4**
Stroke Index **15**

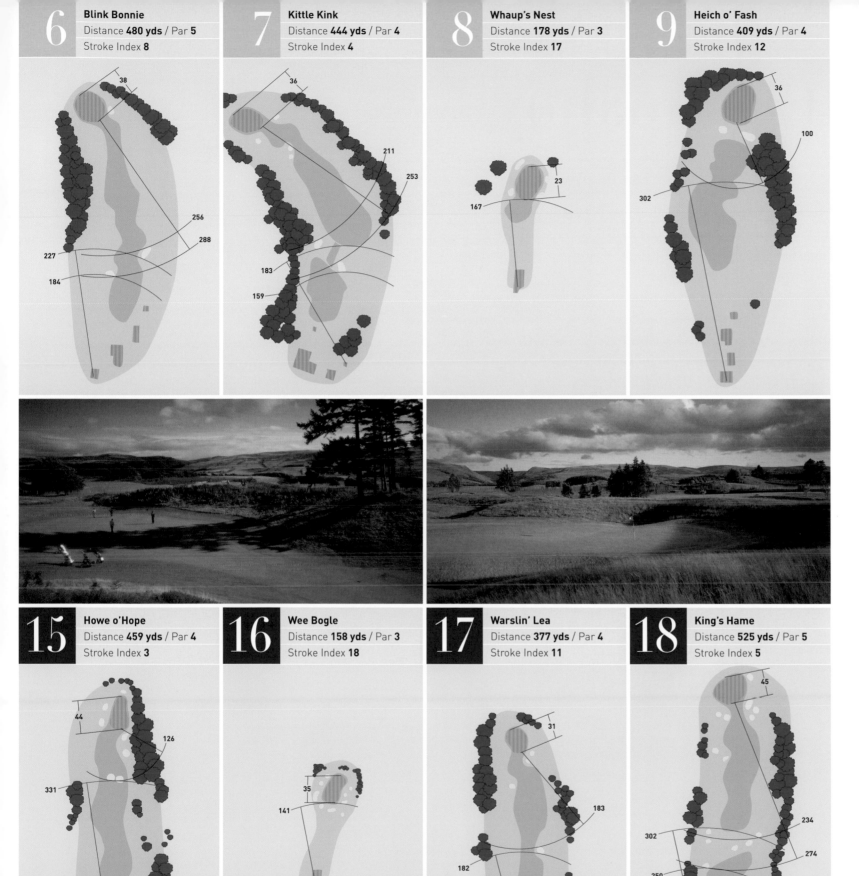

6 Blink Bonnie
Distance **480 yds** / Par **5**
Stroke Index **8**

7 Kittle Kink
Distance **444 yds** / Par **4**
Stroke Index **4**

8 Whaup's Nest
Distance **178 yds** / Par **3**
Stroke Index **17**

9 Heich o' Fash
Distance **409 yds** / Par **4**
Stroke Index **12**

15 Howe o'Hope
Distance **459 yds** / Par **4**
Stroke Index **3**

16 Wee Bogle
Distance **158 yds** / Par **3**
Stroke Index **18**

17 Warslin' Lea
Distance **377 yds** / Par **4**
Stroke Index **11**

18 King's Hame
Distance **525 yds** / Par **5**
Stroke Index **5**

CONTACT DETAILS

Address
Auchterarder PH3 1NF

Telephone
01764 662231

Website
www.gleneagles.com

KING'S COURSE

All distance measurements in
yards from the blue tees.

Out		
Distance	**3327 yds**	
Par	**35**	
In		
Distance	**3463 yds**	
Par	**36**	
Totals		
Distance	**6471 yds**	
Par	**71**	

Marriott Dalmahoy
EDINBURGH

Set in over 1,000 acres of superb Scottish landscape, Dalmahoy is surrounded by woodland and lochs, and has striking views of the Pentland Hills. The East Course (see plan page 100) has hosted many major events, including the Solheim Cup and the Charles Church Seniors PGA Championship of Scotland.

The course has long sweeping fairways and generous greens protected by strategic bunkers. Many of the long par-4 holes can be problematic to any golfer. The 9th hole is the longest and has a ha-ha wall 80 yards short of the putting green; the 17th, known as the 'Wee Wrecker', is a heavily bunkered par 3, which tests a golfer's skill to the limit; the signature 18th hole has the green set in front of Dalmahoy's historic hotel, with a testing approach over a wide ravine. The shorter West Course presents a different test, with tighter fairways requiring more accuracy from the tee. The finishing holes incorporate the Golgar burn meandering through the fairway to create a tough finish.

Tour Notes

1927 The golf club is established; both courses are designed and laid out by James Braid, former Open champion turned golf-course designer.

1992 On the East Course, the European ladies record a memorable first-time victory over the United States in the Solheim Cup. Britain's Laura Davies puts in a fine performance, with some spectacular putting.

2004 The East Course undergoes a £1 million redevelopment. A couple of cracking new holes are added and, as a result, the layout is lengthened to 7,475 yards making it the longest golf course in Scotland.

1
Hole 1
Distance **532 yds** / Par **5**
Stroke Index **8**

32
71
106
120
202
232
248
272
245
227
94
9
0
+36

2
Hole 2
Distance **454 yds** / Par **4**
Stroke Index **4**

33
58
102
148
186
274
232
95
21
0
+25

3
Hole 3
Distance **451 yds** / Par **4**
Stroke Index **2**

34
138
162
196
266
241
216
72
29
14
0

4
Hole 4
Distance **144 yds** / Par **3**
Stroke Index **18**

34
129
19
0

5
Hole 5
Distance **324 yds** / Par **4**
Stroke Index **16**

30
59
70
287
264
243
155
15
0

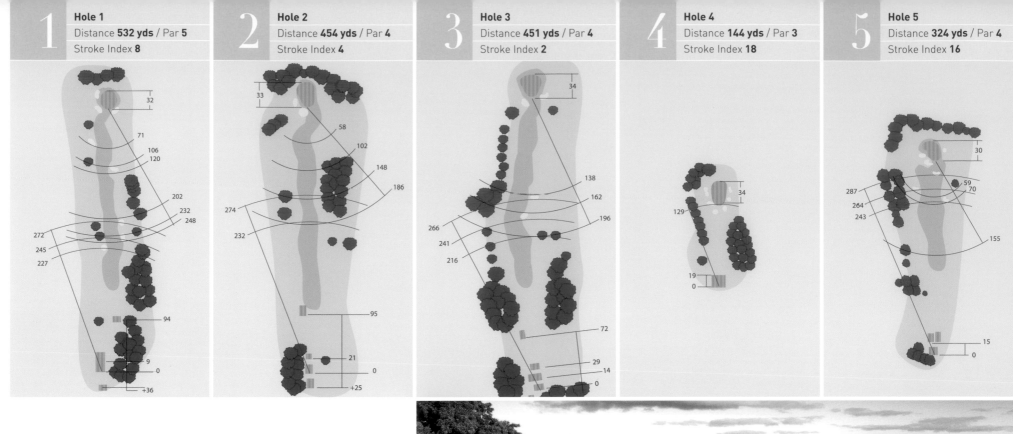

> 66 Keep on hitting it
> straight until the wee ball
> goes in the hole 99
>
> *JAMES BRAID*

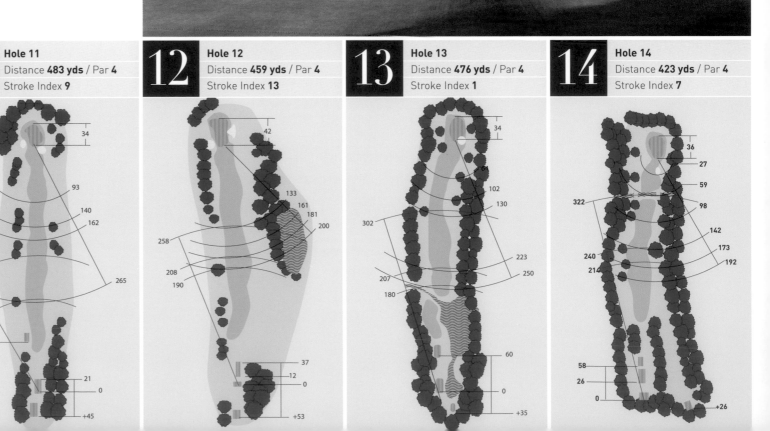

10
Hole 10
Distance **540 yds** / Par **5**
Stroke Index **15**

38
37
108
135
151
194
243
285
246
116
48
28
0
+37

11
Hole 11
Distance **483 yds** / Par **4**
Stroke Index **9**

34
93
140
162
235
265
165
88
21
0
+45

12
Hole 12
Distance **459 yds** / Par **4**
Stroke Index **13**

42
133
161
181
200
258
208
190
37
12
0
+53

13
Hole 13
Distance **476 yds** / Par **4**
Stroke Index **1**

34
61
102
130
302
223
250
207
180
60
0
+35

14
Hole 14
Distance **423 yds** / Par **4**
Stroke Index **7**

36
27
59
98
322
142
173
192
240
214
58
26
0
+26

6
Hole 6
Distance **406 yds** / Par **4**
Stroke Index **6**

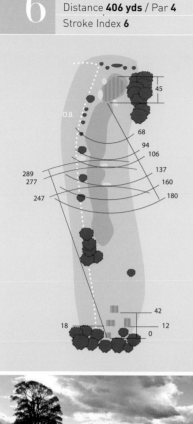

45
68
94
106
137
160
180
289
277
247
18
42
12
0
O.B.

7
Hole 7
Distance **204 yds** / Par **3**
Stroke Index **10**

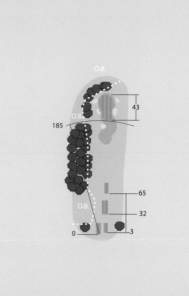

O.B.
43
185
O.B.
O.B.
65
32
0
3

8
Hole 8
Distance **354 yds** / Par **4**
Stroke Index **12**

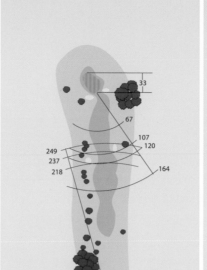

33
67
107
120
164
249
237
218
17
0

9
Hole 9
Distance **487 yds** / Par **4**
Stroke Index **14**

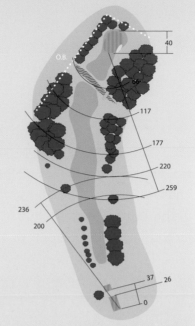

O.B.
40
117
177
220
259
236
200
37
26
0

22

Marriott Dalmahoy EDINBURGH

CONTACT DETAILS

Address
Kirknewton EH27 8EB

Telephone
0131 335 1845

Website
www.marriott.com/edigs

15
Hole 15
Distance **428 yds** / Par **4**
Stroke Index **11**

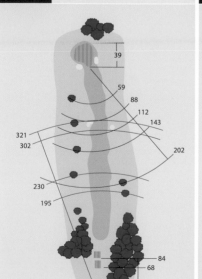

39
59
88
112
143
202
321
302
230
195
84
68
18
0

16
Hole 16
Distance **605 yds** / Par **5**
Stroke Index **3**

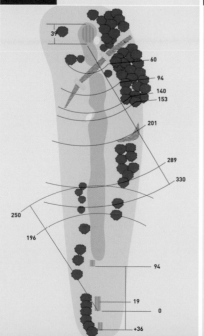

39
60
94
140
153
201
289
330
250
196
94
19
0
+36

17
Hole 17
Distance **245 yds** / Par **3**
Stroke Index **17**

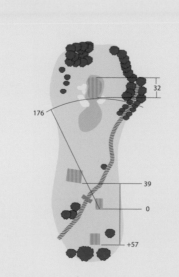

32
176
39
0
+57

18
Hole 18
Distance **460 yds** / Par **4**
Stroke Index **5**

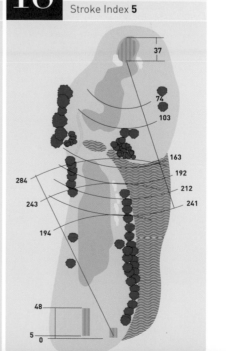

37
74
103
163
192
212
241
284
243
194
48
5
0

EAST COURSE

All distance measurements in
yards from the blue tees.

Out	
Distance	**3356 yds**
Par	**35**
In	
Distance	**4119 yds**
Par	**37**
Totals	
Distance	**7475 yds**
Par	**72**

THE GOLF TOUR

101

23 Prestwick
SOUTH AYRSHIRE

If you appreciate the game of yesteryear then this traditional monument to golf is a place you'll embrace with passion. Founded in 1851, the club where Young Tom Morris learned the game is laced with charming, one-of-a kind holes designed by his father, Old Tom Morris. A stone cairn to the west of the clubhouse marks the first tee of the original 12-hole course from which the first-ever Open was played. It has since been played here no fewer than 24 times. The links course snakes through tight, rippled fairways, many shots are blind, and the fast undulating greens can be impossible.

Seven of the original greens are still played on today. Perhaps the most famous of these is the Alps (17th). It is a menace of a hole, played through a gorse-lined amphitheatre with a blind approach and the giant Sahara bunker that swallows any shot not solidly struck. The 3rd hole is famous for the fearsome Cardinal, a deep bunker propped up by railway sleepers that protects the upper fairway.

Tour Notes

1860 The first Open is held at Prestwick, organized by the members who subscribe £25 to purchase a Challenge Belt (a red leather belt with silver clasps), which was won by Willie Park.

1870 Young Tom Morris is allowed to keep the Challenge Belt after winning the Open at Prestwick for three successive years. His first-round score of 47 over 12 holes has never been equalled or bettered. At the age of 24, Young Tom dies from a lung haemorrhage on Christmas Day 1895.

1914 Harry Vardon wins the Open for a record sixth time, three victories of which are at Prestwick.

1925 Prestwick hosts the Open for the last time as it becomes obvious there is insufficient room to handle the crowds, and safety is a concern.

2001 A major refurbishment to the clubhouse is completed ready for the club's 150th anniversary celebrations. The Amateur Championships are held as part of the celebrations.

1 Railway
Distance **346 yds** / Par **4**
Stroke Index **11**

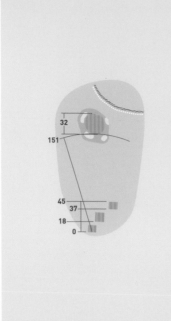

30
29
99
289
136
203
66
34
0

2 Tunnel
Distance **167 yds** / Par **3**
Stroke Index **17**

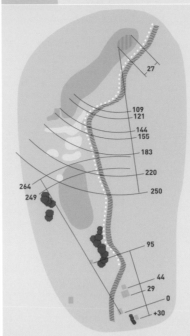

32
151
45
37
18
0

3 Cardinal
Distance **502 yds** / Par **5**
Stroke Index **3**

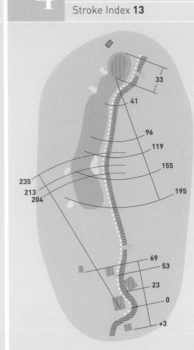

27
109
121
144
155
183
220
250
264
249
95
44
29
0
+30

4 Bridge
Distance **417 yds** / Par **4**
Stroke Index **13**

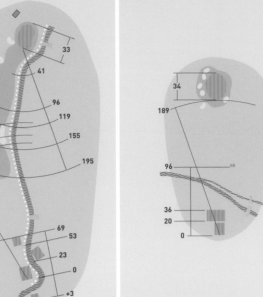

33
41
96
119
155
195
235
213
204
69
53
23
0
+3

5 Himalayas
Distance **206 yds** / Par **3**
Stroke Index **5**

34
189
96
36
20
0

10 Arran
Distance **454 yds** / Par **4**
Stroke Index **4**

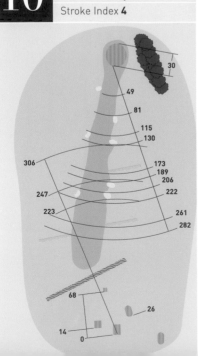

30
49
81
115
130
306
173
189
206
222
247
223
261
282
68
26
14
0

11 Carrick
Distance **215 yds** / Par **3**
Stroke Index **16**

35
179
45
20
+17

12 Wall
Distance **552 yds** / Par **5**
Stroke Index **8**

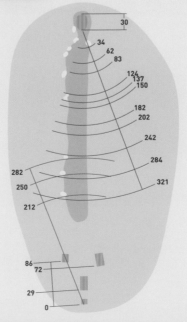

30
34
62
83
124
137
150
182
202
242
284
282
250
321
212
86
72
29
0

13 Sea Headrig
Distance **460 yds** / Par **4**
Stroke Index **2**

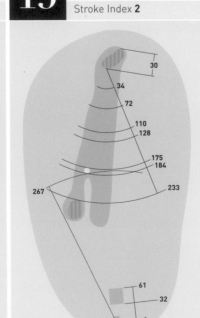

30
34
72
110
128
175
184
267
233
61
32
0

14 Goosedubs
Distance **362 yds** / Par **4**
Stroke Index **14**

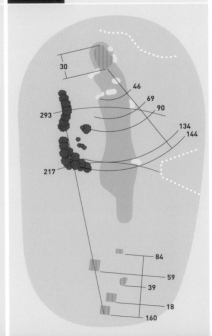

30
46
69
90
293
134
144
217
84
59
39
18
160

6 Elysian Fields
Distance **407 yds** / Par **4**
Stroke Index **15**

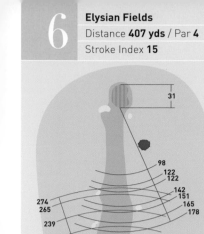

31
98
122
122
142
151
165
178
274
265
239
219

73
40
0

7 Monkton Miln
Distance **488 yds** / Par **4**
Stroke Index **1**

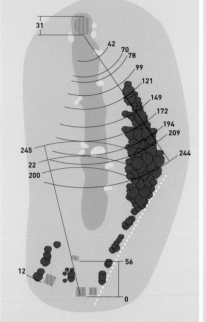

29
44
52
91
120
133
164
178
198
212
221
251
315
267
249
221

100
81
56
0

8 End
Distance **431 yds** / Par **4**
Stroke Index **9**

31
42
70
78
99
121
149
172
194
209
244
245
22
200

56
12
0

9 Eglinton
Distance **461 yds** / Par **4**
Stroke Index **7**

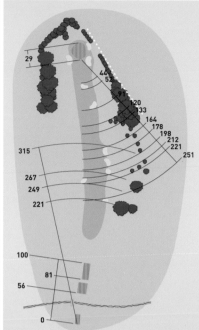

32
47
96
120
177
208
226
257
273
246
198

67
37
20
7
0

Prestwick SOUTH AYRSHIRE

CONTACT DETAILS

Address
2 Links Road, Prestwick
KA9 1QG

Telephone
01292 477404

Website
www.prestwickgc.com

15 Narrows
Distance **347 yds** / Par **4**
Stroke Index **10**

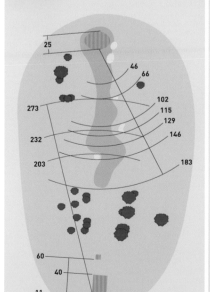

25
46
66
102
115
129
146
183
273
232
203

60
40
11
0

16 Cardinals Back
Distance **288 yds** / Par **4**
Stroke Index **18**

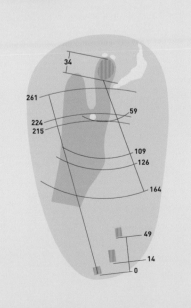

34
59
109
126
164
261
224
215

49
14
0

17 Alps
Distance **391 yds** / Par **4**
Stroke Index **6**

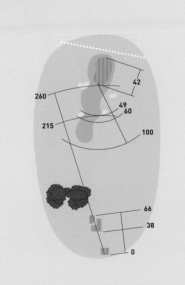

22
41
84
113
124
158
182
191
302
228

23
0

18 Clock
Distance **284 yds** / Par **4**
Stroke Index **12**

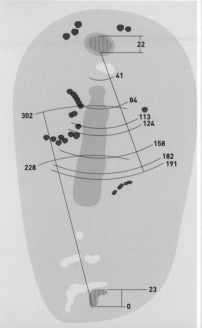

42
49
60
100
260
215

66
38
0

PRESTWICK COURSE

All distance measurements in yards from the back tees.

All illustrations are based upon original Strokesaver artwork.

Out	
Distance	3425 yds
Par	35
In	
Distance	3353 yds
Par	36
Totals	
Distance	**6778 yds**
Par	**71**

Royal Dornoch
HIGHLAND

Wild, isolated and mesmerizing, every golfer should make at least one pilgrimage to this timeless setting. A pure white sandy beach dividing the links from the Dornoch Firth and splashes of bright yellow gorse in spring add to the beauty. The design for the Championship Course (see plan page 108) fell to Old Tom Morris, who used the unique linksland features to create a subtle course that offers a magical golfing experience. Over the years the course has been tweaked and enhanced. It appears amicable but proves very challenging in play, with stiff breezes and tight lies. Golfers are forced to play by feel and instinct and let go of charts and mechanical thinking. Come prepared to be rewarded for good shots and punished for bad.

The 18-hole Struie links course provides, in a gentler style, an enjoyable test of a golfer's accuracy. As Dornoch is rather isolated from the main centres of population it has never been selected to stage the more major championships. Nevertheless it has been chosen to hold the prestigious British Amateur, Northern Open, the Scottish Ladies and the Home Internationals.

1877 Dornoch Golf Club is founded. Records show that golf was played here in 1616, making it the world's third oldest golf course behind St. Andrews and Leith.

1906 At the request of Millicent, Duchess of Sutherland, the club is granted a royal charter by King Edward VII and takes on its new title, the Royal Dornoch Golf Club, ensuring the highest of standards.

2000–2007 The Donald Ross Junior Invitational Golf Tournament is played annually as a celebration of junior golf in the highlands. It is in memory of the famous Dornoch greenkeeper and professional, Donald Ross (1872–1948).

107

1 First
Distance **331 yds** / Par **4**
Stroke Index **7**

2 Ord
Distance **184 yds** / Par **3**
Stroke Index **15**

3 Earl's Cross
Distance **414 yds** / Par **4**
Stroke Index **11**

4 Achinchanter
Distance **427 yds** / Par **4**
Stroke Index **3**

5 Hilton
Distance **354 yds** / Par **4**
Stroke Index **9**

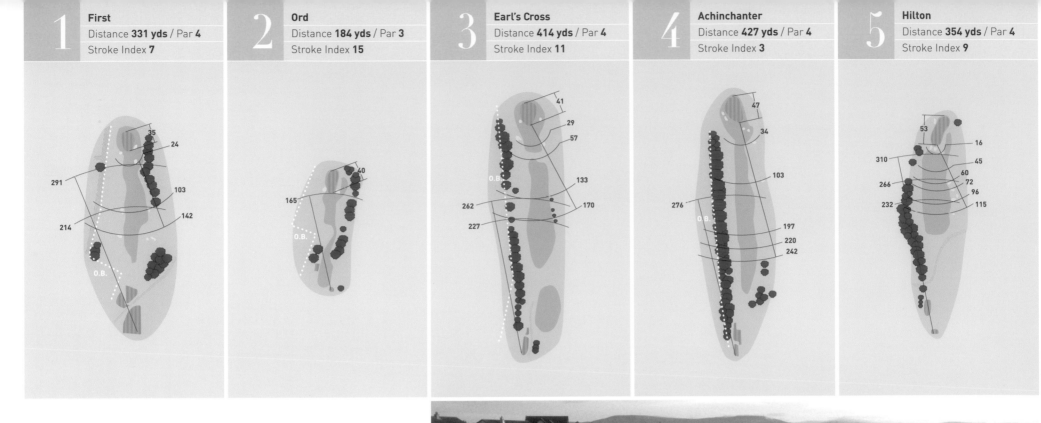

> " There are no absolutes
> in golf. Golf is such an
> individual game, and no two
> people swing alike "
>
> *KATHY WHITWORTH*

10 Fuaran
Distance **177 yds** / Par **3**
Stroke Index **16**

11 A'chlach
Distance **450 yds** / Par **4**
Stroke Index **4**

12 Sutherland
Distance **507 yds** / Par **5**
Stroke Index **12**

13 Bents
Distance **180 yds** / Par **3**
Stroke Index **18**

14 Foxy
Distance **445 yds** / Par **4**
Stroke Index **2**

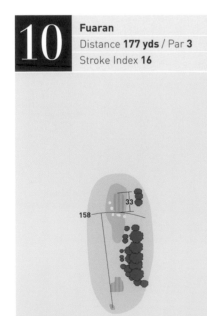

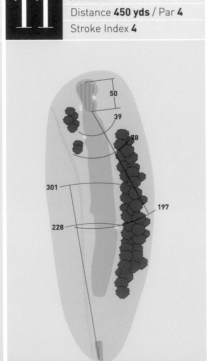

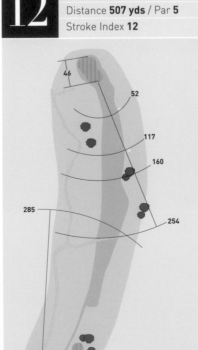

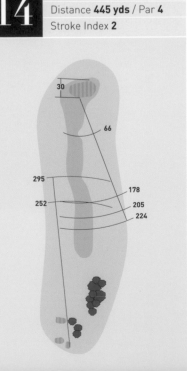

6 Whinny Brae
Distance **163 yds** / Par **3**
Stroke Index **17**

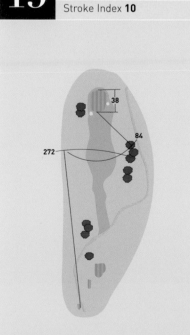

150 — 33

7 Pier
Distance **463 yds** / Par **4**
Stroke Index **1**

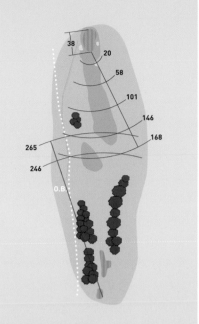

40
56
317
0.B.
205
226

8 Dunrobin
Distance **437 yds** / Par **4**
Stroke Index **5**

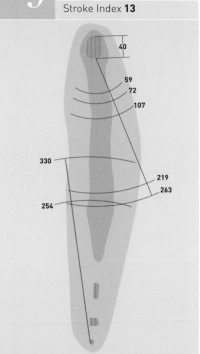

38
20
58
101
146
168
265
246
0.B.

9 Craiglaith
Distance **529 yds** / Par **5**
Stroke Index **13**

40
59
72
107
330
219
263
254

CONTACT DETAILS

Address
Golf Road, Dornoch
IV25 3LW

Telephone
01862 810219

Website
www.royaldornoch.com

15 Stulaig
Distance **358 yds** / Par **4**
Stroke Index **10**

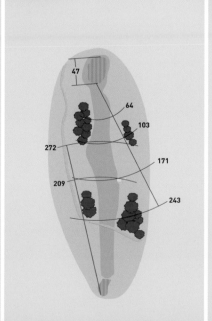

38
84
272

16 High Hole
Distance **402 yds** / Par **4**
Stroke Index **6**

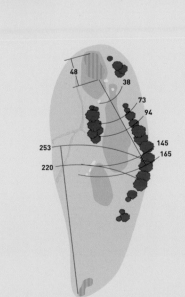

47
64
103
272
171
209
243

17 Valley
Distance **405 yds** / Par **4**
Stroke Index **8**

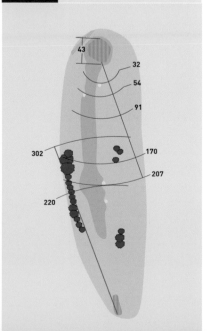

48
38
73
94
253
145
165
220

18 Home
Distance **456 yds** / Par **4**
Stroke Index **14**

43
32
54
91
302
170
207
220

CHAMPIONSHIP COURSE

All distance measurements in
yards from the blue tees.

Out	
Distance	**3302 yds**
Par	**35**
In	
Distance	**3380 yds**
Par	**35**
Totals	
Distance	**6682 yds**
Par	**70**

Royal Troon
SOUTH AYRSHIRE

Troon was founded in March 1878 with just five holes on linksland. In its first decade it grew from five holes to six, then 12, and finally 18. The Old Course (see plan page 110) is one of the great links courses in Scotland. Its reputation is based on its combination of rough and sandy hills, bunkers and a severity of finish that has diminished the championship hopes of many. With a prevailing north-westerly wind on the back nine to contend with as well, accurate shots are essential. The most successful players have relied on an equal blend of finesse and power.

The Open has been played here eight times and Royal Troon has the shortest hole of all the courses hosting the Open. Ten new bunkers and four new tees were added after the 1997 competition. Other courses include the shorter Portland, which is a little more sheltered, and the nine-hole Craigend.

1915 Club captain, Adam Wood, gifts Troon a set of golf clubs, which are considered to be the oldest in existence, thought to date back to the Stuart kings. The originals are now in the British Golf Museum in St. Andrews but replicas are proudly displayed in Royal Troon's clubhouse.

1923 It is with great pride that Troon welcomes its first Open championship, where 222 entrants start their quest for the Claret Jug.

1950 Bobby Locke wins the Open with a score of 279, becoming the first player to score less than 280 in an Open championship.

1978 On its 100th anniversary, the Troon Golf Club is proud to receive the royal accolade and today remains the most recent club to be so acclaimed.

2004 Long-shot American Todd Hamilton holds off the best players in the world without blinking, to win the 133rd British Open in a stunning four-hole play off over three-time major winner Ernie Els.

Arnold Palmer

Jack Nicklaus putting in the 1973 Open

1 Seal
Distance **370 yds** / Par **4**
Stroke Index **16**

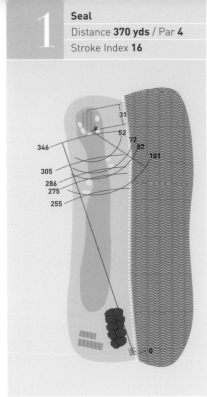

346
305
286
275
255
31
52
72
82
101
0

2 Black Rock
Distance **391 yds** / Par **4**
Stroke Index **7**

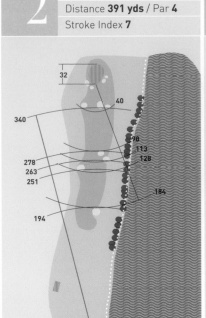

32
40
340
278
263
251
194
98
113
128
184
26
0

3 Gyaws
Distance **379 yds** / Par **4**
Stroke Index **11**

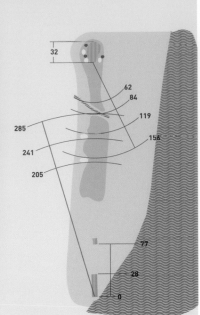

32
62
84
119
156
285
241
205
77
28
0

4 Dunure
Distance **560 yds** / Par **5**
Stroke Index **4**

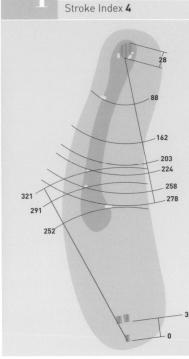

28
88
162
203
224
258
278
321
291
252
36
0

5 Greenan
Distance **210 yds** / Par **3**
Stroke Index **14**

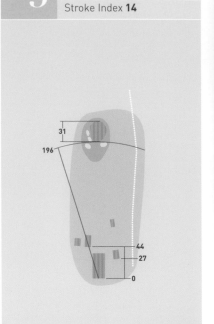

31
196
44
27
0

> ❝ Sudden success in golf is like the sudden acquisition of wealth. It is apt to unsettle and deteriorate the character ❞
>
> *P. G. WODEHOUSE*

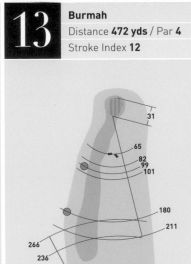
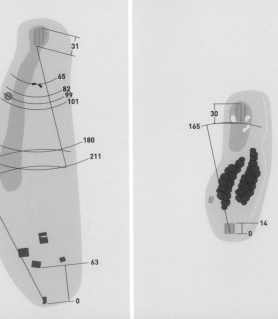

10 Sandhills
Distance **438 yds** / Par **4**
Stroke Index **10**

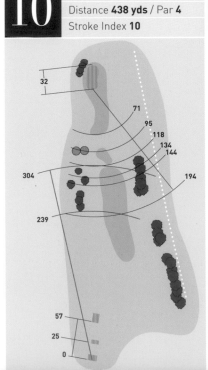

32
71
95
118
134
137
144
304
239
194
57
25
0

11 The Railway
Distance **490 yds** / Par **4**
Stroke Index **1**

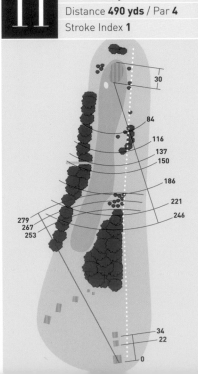

30
84
116
137
150
186
221
246
279
267
253
34
22
0

12 The Fox
Distance **431 yds** / Par **4**
Stroke Index **6**

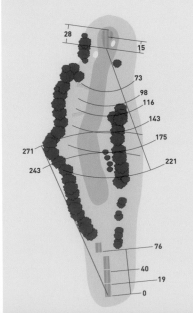

28
15
73
98
116
143
175
221
271
243
76
40
19
0

13 Burmah
Distance **472 yds** / Par **4**
Stroke Index **12**

31
65
82
99
101
180
211
266
236
63
0

14 Alton
Distance **178 yds** / Par **3**
Stroke Index **15**

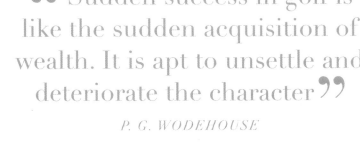

30
165
14
0

6 Turnberry
Distance **601 yds** / Par **5**
Stroke Index **2**

33	
27	
55	
153	
175	
160	
282	
299	
311	
306	
278	
95	86
59	
25	
2	

7 Tel-el-Kebir
Distance **405 yds** / Par **4**
Stroke Index **9**

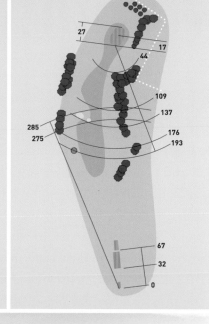

32
63
85
327
309
113
124
148
267
240
51
48
17
0

8 Postage Stamp
Distance **123 yds** / Par **3**
Stroke Index **18**

18	30
110	
38	
22	
12	
0	

9 The Monk
Distance **423 yds** / Par **4**
Stroke Index **5**

27	17
44	
109	
137	
285	176
275	193
67	
32	
0	

CONTACT DETAILS

Address
Craigend Road, Troon
KA10 6EP

Telephone
01292 311555

Website
www.royaltroon.com

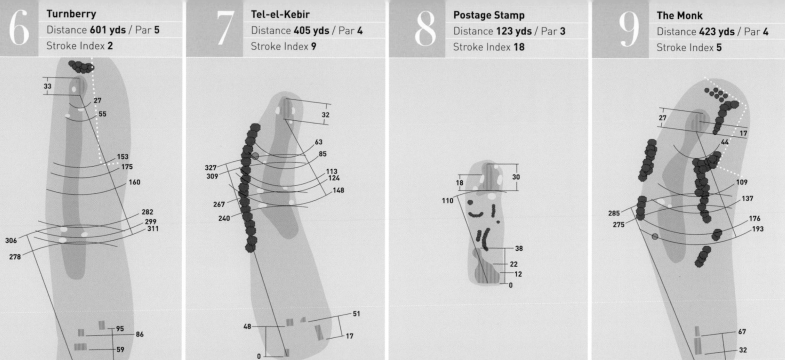

15 Crosbie
Distance **483 yds** / Par **4**
Stroke Index **3**

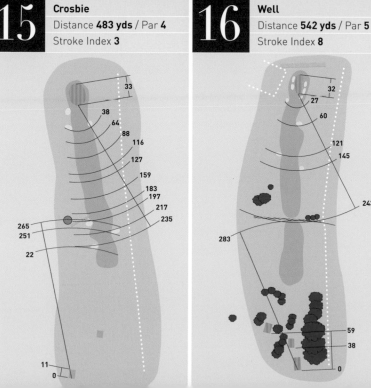

33	
38	
64	
88	
116	
127	
159	
183	
197	
217	
235	
265	
251	
22	
11	
0	

16 Well
Distance **542 yds** / Par **5**
Stroke Index **8**

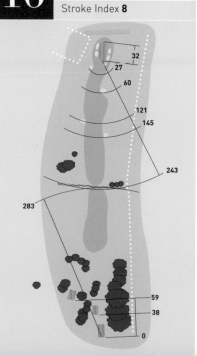

32
27
60
121
145
243
283
59
38
0

17 Rabbit
Distance **222 yds** / Par **3**
Stroke Index **13**

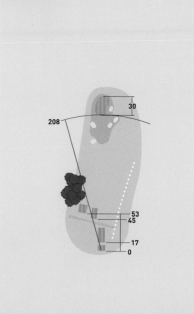

30	
208	
30	
53	
45	
17	
0	

18 Craigend
Distance **457 yds** / Par **4**
Stroke Index **17**

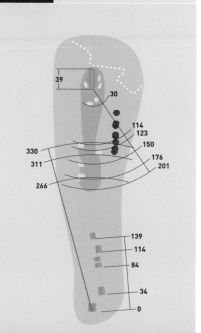

39	
30	
114	
123	
150	
330	176
311	201
266	
139	
114	
84	
34	
0	

OLD COURSE

All distance measurements in
yards from the back tees.

All illustrations are based upon
original Strokesaver artwork.

Out	
Distance	**3462 yds**
Par	**36**
In	
Distance	**3713 yds**
Par	**35**
Totals	
Distance	**7175 yds**
Par	**71**

St. Andrews Links
FIFE

The six 18-hole courses and one nine-hole course at St. Andrews Links make it the largest golf complex in Europe. The Old Course (see plan page 116), the oldest in the world, is acknowledged as the home of golf and has seen many great golfers walk its hallowed ground and witnessed some of golf's most dramatic moments. The course has 112 bunkers, many of them world famous. Another feature is the double greens, where the outward and inward holes are cut on the same putting surface. With the layout entrusted to the legendary Old Tom Morris, the New Course opened in 1895. Although always standing in the shadows of the Old Course, this classic links is still an exciting test of skill. In 1897 the Jubilee was added. By 1914, the pressure for play on the existing courses founded the need for the Eden, and the Strathtyrum followed in 1993; in the same year, the nine-hole Balgrove was upgraded. The Castle Course is due to open for play in 2008.

Tour Notes

1457 Golf is banned by King James II of Scotland as it is distracting young men from archery practice.

1552 The first written record of golf at St. Andrews confirms the rights of local townspeople to play golf over the links.

1754 The Society of St. Andrews Golfers is founded, later changing its name to the Royal & Ancient Golf Club.

2000 Tiger Woods wins the 26th Open with a record 19 under par. In June the biggest event in golfing history—the World Shotgun 2000—is held, with golfers around the world hitting a ball simultaneously in a global celebration of six centuries of golf and the new millennium.

2005 The Open returns to St. Andrews; Tiger Woods triumphs, to join an elite list of two-time winners. Jack Nicklaus bids farewell to competitive golf.

2007 The Women's British Open takes place on the Old Course for the first time, after many years of amateur ladies' golf on the famous links.

Left: Bobby Jones, 1927 Open

1 Burn
Distance **370 yds** / Par **4**
Stroke Index **10**

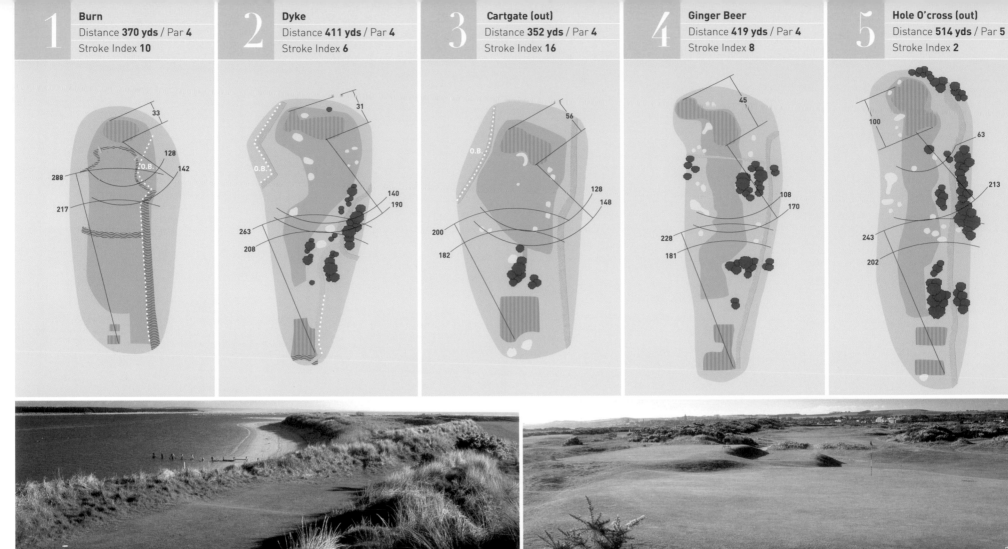

2 Dyke
Distance **411 yds** / Par **4**
Stroke Index **6**

3 Cartgate (out)
Distance **352 yds** / Par **4**
Stroke Index **16**

4 Ginger Beer
Distance **419 yds** / Par **4**
Stroke Index **8**

5 Hole O'cross (out)
Distance **514 yds** / Par **5**
Stroke Index **2**

10 Bobby Jones
Distance **318 yds** / Par **4**
Stroke Index **15**

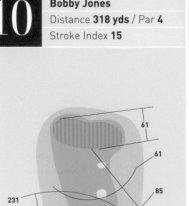

11 High (in)
Distance **172 yds** / Par **3**
Stroke Index **7**

12 Heathery (in)
Distance **316 yds** / Par **4**
Stroke Index **3**

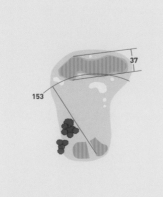

13 Hole O'cross (in)
Distance **398 yds** / Par **4**
Stroke Index **11**

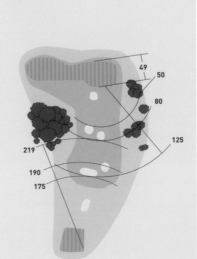

14 Long
Distance **523 yds** / Par **5**
Stroke Index **1**

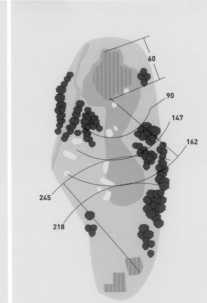

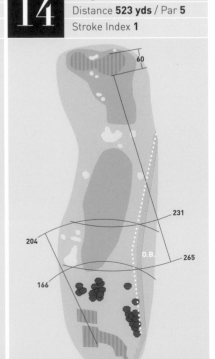

6 Heathery (out)
Distance **374 yds** / Par **4**
Stroke Index **12**

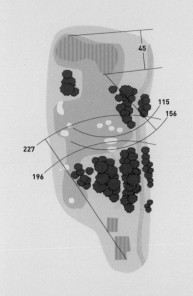

7 High (out)
Distance **359 yds** / Par **4**
Stroke Index **4**

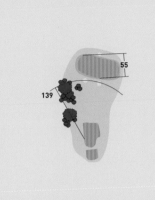

8 Short
Distance **166 yds** / Par **3**
Stroke Index **14**

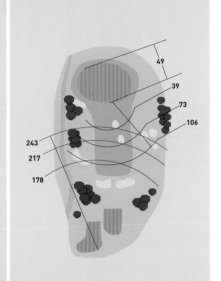

9 End
Distance **307 yds** / Par **4**
Stroke Index **18**

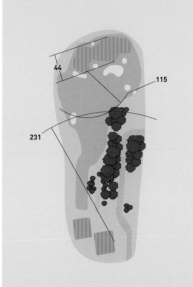

CONTACT DETAILS

Address
Pilmour House, St. Andrews
KY16 9SF

Telephone
01334 479555

Website
www.standrews.org.uk

15 Cartgate (in)
Distance **414 yds** / Par **4**
Stroke Index **9**

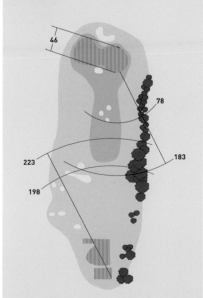

16 Corner Of The Dyke
Distance **381 yds** / Par **4**
Stroke Index **13**

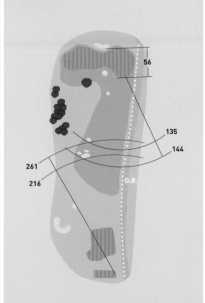

17 Road
Distance **461 yds** / Par **4**
Stroke Index **5**

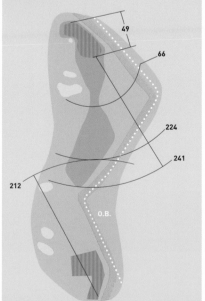

18 Tom Morris
Distance **354 yds** / Par **4**
Stroke Index **17**

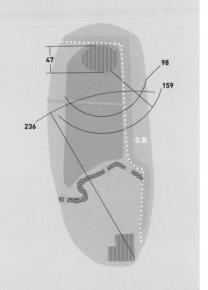

OLD COURSE

All distance measurements in
yards from the medal tees.

Out	
Distance	**3272 yds**
Par	**36**
In	
Distance	**3337 yds**
Par	**36**

Totals	
Distance	**6609 yds**
Par	**72**

Westerwood Hotel
NORTH LANARKSHIRE

This combination of golfers' heaven and purpose-built luxury hotel is set in a 400-acre estate nestling at the foot of the Campsie Hills. The undulating parkland and woodland course is a challenging 18 holes for both experts and beginners. Holes meander through silver birch, firs, heaths and heather. You must be solid with your tee shot to deal with direction, wind and distance. The spectacular 15th, the Waterfall, is not for the faint-hearted, with its green set against a 60ft rock face.

Sitting on the clubhouse patio looking out over the course to the stunning backdrop of the hills beyond, it's hard to believe that you're only 12 miles out of town. Leisure facilities include a state-of-the-art indoor pool and gymnasium, and for the less energetic, the steam-room, Jacuzzi and beauty salon are the perfect place to be pampered. Corporate Golf Days are a specialty, with experienced staff on hand to help with the arrangements.

Tour Notes

1991 The Westerwood course opens for play. The rolling American style is the joint venture of one of golf's all-time greats, Spaniard Seve Ballesteros, and Dave Thomas.

2000 Morton Hotels purchases the resort and makes major investment in both the hotel and course as part of an ongoing development plan.

2003 The British Amputee Golf Open is held at Westerwood, an event open to any golfer who has lost a limb. This is the first time the championship has been held in Scotland, and the event attracts competitors from all over the world, including Sweden, South Africa, the United States and Australia.

2006 Q Hotels takes on the running of Westerwood and plans a massive £5 million investment for the future.

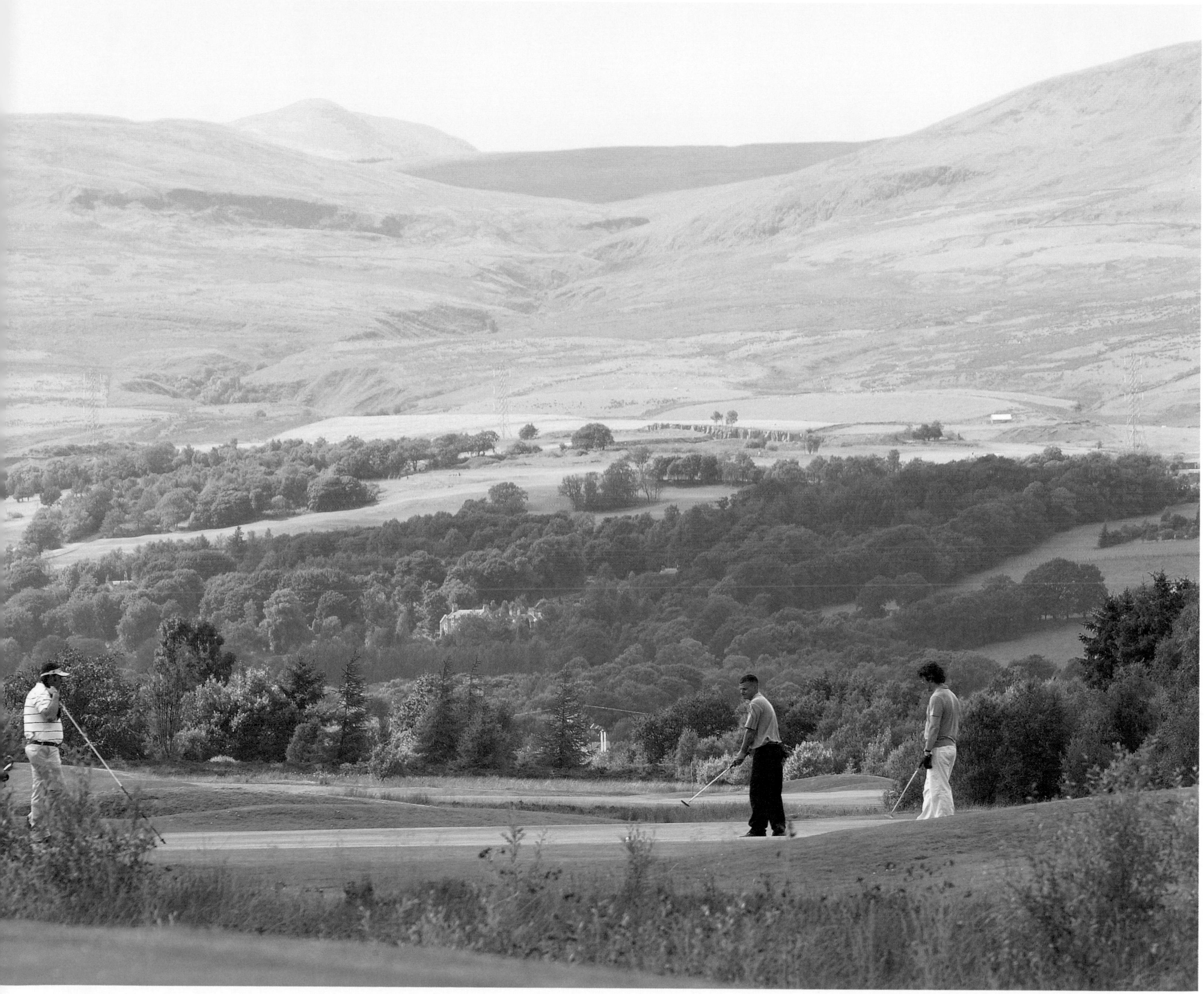

1	**Antonine**
	Distance **499 yds** / Par **5**
	Stroke Index **9**

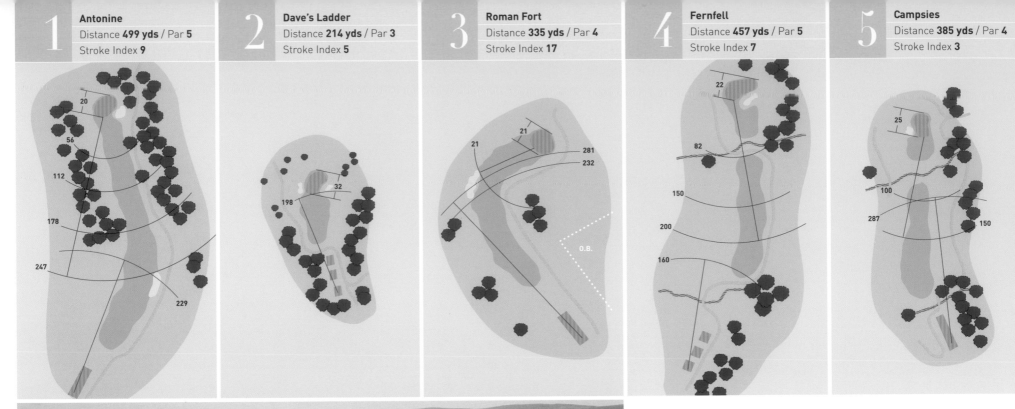

2	**Dave's Ladder**
	Distance **214 yds** / Par **3**
	Stroke Index **5**

3	**Roman Fort**
	Distance **335 yds** / Par **4**
	Stroke Index **17**

4	**Fernfell**
	Distance **457 yds** / Par **5**
	Stroke Index **7**

5	**Campsies**
	Distance **385 yds** / Par **4**
	Stroke Index **3**

> " As far as swing and techniques
> are concerned, I don't know
> diddly squat. When I'm playing
> well, I don't even take aim "
>
> *FRED COUPLES*

10	**Old Inns**
	Distance **330 yds** / Par **4**
	Stroke Index **12**

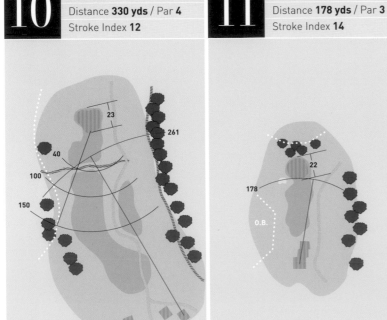

11	**Carrickstone**
	Distance **178 yds** / Par **3**
	Stroke Index **14**

12	**Abby's Way**
	Distance **305 yds** / Par **4**
	Stroke Index **18**

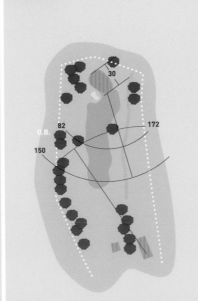

13	**Laura's Pond**
	Distance **175 yds** / Par **3**
	Stroke Index **2**

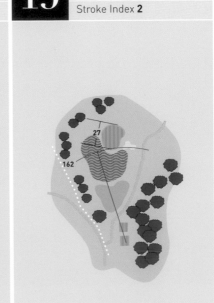

14	**Quarry**
	Distance **522 yds** / Par **5**
	Stroke Index **6**

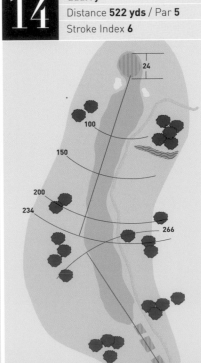

6 Seve's Trap
Distance **335 yds** / Par **4**
Stroke Index **13**

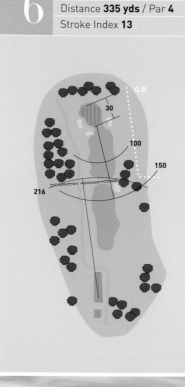

7 Waterways
Distance **390 yds** / Par **4**
Stroke Index **1**

8 Little Grove
Distance **172 yds** / Par **3**
Stroke Index **15**

9 Drum Cap
Distance **527 yds** / Par **5**
Stroke Index **11**

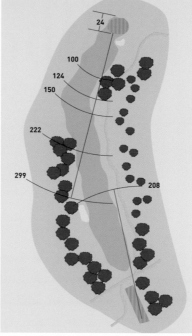

CONTACT DETAILS

Address
St. Andrews Drive,
Westerwood G68 0EW

Telephone
01236 725281

Website
www.qhotels.co.uk

15 Waterfall
Distance **164 yds** / Par **3**
Stroke Index **16**

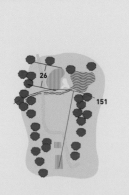

16 High Cliff
Distance **400 yds** / Par **4**
Stroke Index **8**

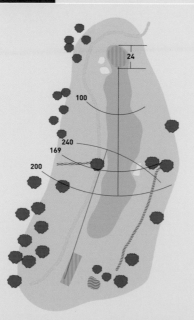

17 Fallen Oak
Distance **374 yds** / Par **4**
Stroke Index **10**

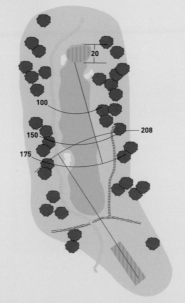

18 Murrayshall
Distance **501 yds** / Par **5**
Stroke Index **4**

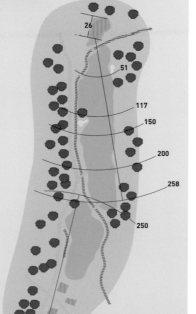

WESTERWOOD COURSE

All distance measurements in
yards from the white tees.

Out	
Distance	**3314 yds**
Par	**37**
In	
Distance	**2949 yds**
Par	**35**
Totals	
Distance	**6263 yds**
Par	**72**

Westin Turnberry Resort
SOUTH AYRSHIRE

Turnberry is considered one of the finest of all golf destinations in the world, where some of the most remarkable moments in Open history have taken place. The coastal scenery is breathtaking, with views out over the Mull of Kintyre, Arran, the majestic Ailsa Craig and the Turnberry lighthouse.

The acclaimed Ailsa Course is now rivalled by the highly praised Kintyre Course (see plan page 124) opened in 2001, while the nine-hole Arran, created by Donald Steel and Colin Montgomerie, has similar challenges, such as undulating greens, tight tee shots, pot bunkers and thick Scottish rough. With the famous hotel on the left and the magnificent Ailsa Craig away to the right, there are few vistas in the world of golf to match the first tee here. That said, Turnberry's trademark must be the 9th. This remote tee, on a rocky promontory on the edge of the sea, provides an awesome experience that is not recommended to those of a nervous disposition.

Tour Notes

1947 Course designer Mackenzie Ross superbly transforms a former airfield into one of the world's most exciting golf courses.

1977 Turnberry hosts its first Open, famous for its head-to-head between Jack Nicklaus and Tom Watson. Watson claims a one-stroke victory over his great rival, and the memorable contest is named the "Duel in the Sun".

2000 The Colin Montgomerie Links Golf Academy is opened alongside the luxurious and extensive clubhouse. It features 12 driving bays, four short-game bays, two dedicated teaching rooms and a group teaching room.

2009 Another name will be added to the Open's winners at Turnberry, when the competition returns to the Ailsa Course in the summer.

1	**Barley Rigs** Distance **530 yds** / Par **5** Stroke Index **7**
2	**Cosie Neuk** Distance **176 yds** / Par **3** Stroke Index **13**
3	**Leerie Licht** Distance **323 yds** / Par **4** Stroke Index **15**
4	**Sandy Loo** Distance **392 yds** / Par **4** Stroke Index **5**
5	**Friar's Carse** Distance **456 yds** / Par **4** Stroke Index **1**

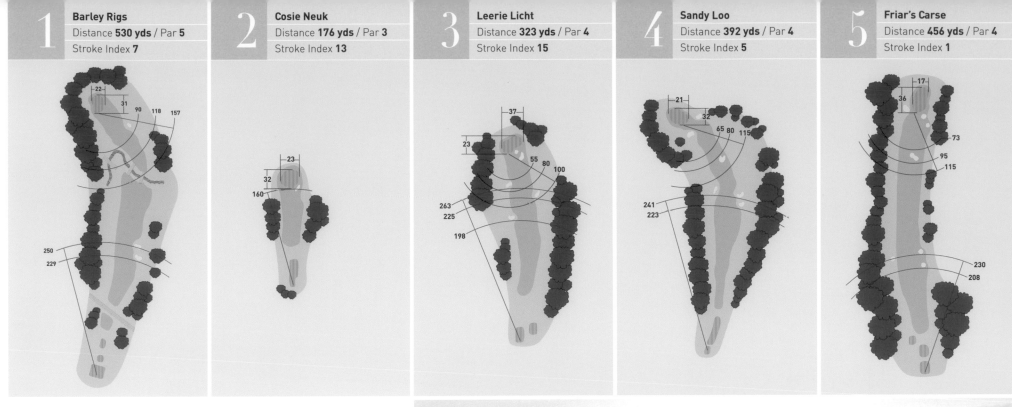

10	**Bains Hill** Distance **437 yds** / Par **4** Stroke Index **8**
11	**Doon N'roon** Distance **428 yds** / Par **4** Stroke Index **12**
12	**Dinna Shy** Distance **203 yds** / Par **3** Stroke Index **16**
13	**The Misk** Distance **462 yds** / Par **4** Stroke Index **2**
14	**Drum Adoon** Distance **529 yds** / Par **5** Stroke Index **10**

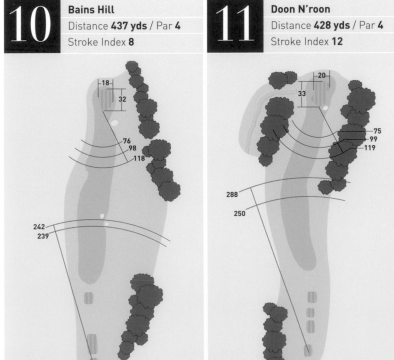
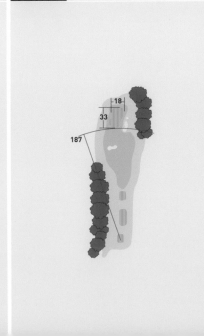
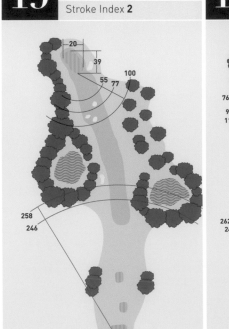
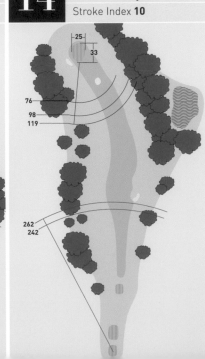

6 Holy Isle
Distance **184 yds** / Par **3**
Stroke Index **11**

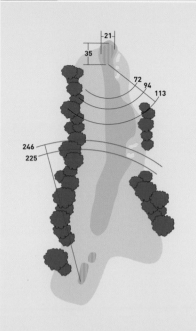

7 Roon The Ben
Distance **376 yds** / Par **4**
Stroke Index **3**

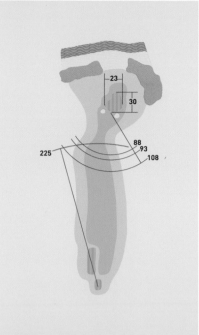

8 Kintyre's Cove
Distance **306 yds** / Par **4**
Stroke Index **17**

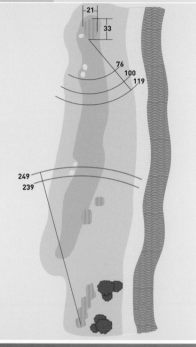

9 Windy Brae
Distance **480 yds** / Par **5**
Stroke Index **9**

Westin Turnberry Resort SOUTH AYRSHIRE

15 Scurdy
Distance **473 yds** / Par **4**
Stroke Index **6**

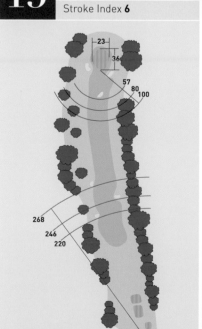

16 Paddy's Milestane
Distance **141 yds** / Par **3**
Stroke Index **18**

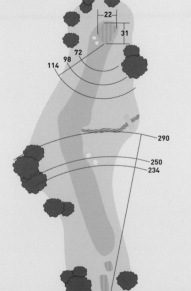

17 Lea Rig
Distance **451 yds** / Par **4**
Stroke Index **4**

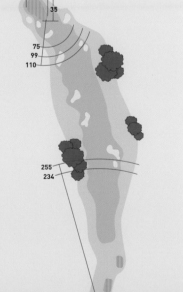

18 Kintyre Hame
Distance **514 yds** / Par **5**
Stroke Index **14**

CONTACT DETAILS

Address
Turnberry KA26 9LT

Telephone
01655 331000

Website
www.turnberry.co.uk

KINTYRE COURSE

All distance measurements in
yards from the blue tees.

Out	
Distance	**3223 yds**
Par	**36**
In	
Distance	**3638 yds**
Par	**36**

Totals	
Distance	**6861 yds**
Par	**72**

WALES

㉙ **Aberdovey**   128
Gwynedd

㉚ **Celtic Manor Resort**   132
Newport

㉛ **Marriott St. Pierre**   136
Monmouthshire

㉜ **Royal St. David's**   140
Gwynedd

㉝ **Royal Porthcawl**   144
Mid-Glamorgan

29 Aberdovey
GWYNEDD

Golf was first played at Aberdovey in 1886, with the club founded six years later. The links has since developed into one of the finest championship courses in Wales, and has hosted many prestigious events over the years. Golfers will appreciate easy flat walking alongside the dunes of this characteristic seaside links.

The wind can play an important role, being unpredictable, with anything from a gentle breeze to a strong blow to bend the ball. Memorable holes include the 3rd, 11th and a good short hole at the 12th, with great views of Cardigan Bay. There are other stunningly beautiful views of Snowdonia National Park and your concentration may be disturbed by the cries of buzzards, kites and seabirds. The late Bernard Darwin was a former president and captain at the club, and a golf correspondent for *The Times*. Aberdovey was a personal favourite of his and many of his writings featured the course, which he referred to as "the course that my soul loves best of all the courses in the world".

Tour Notes

1892 Aberdovey Golf Club is founded. Legend suggests that the first course was laid out on the natural turf, using flowerpots for holes. The design is by the Ruck family, but the new links grows rapidly, with improvements by James Braid and Herbert Fowler.

1998 With the help of a Lottery grant, a new championship-standard clubhouse opens, following a fire that destroyed the historic old clubhouse in 1995. HRH Prince Andrew, The Duke of York, performs the official opening.

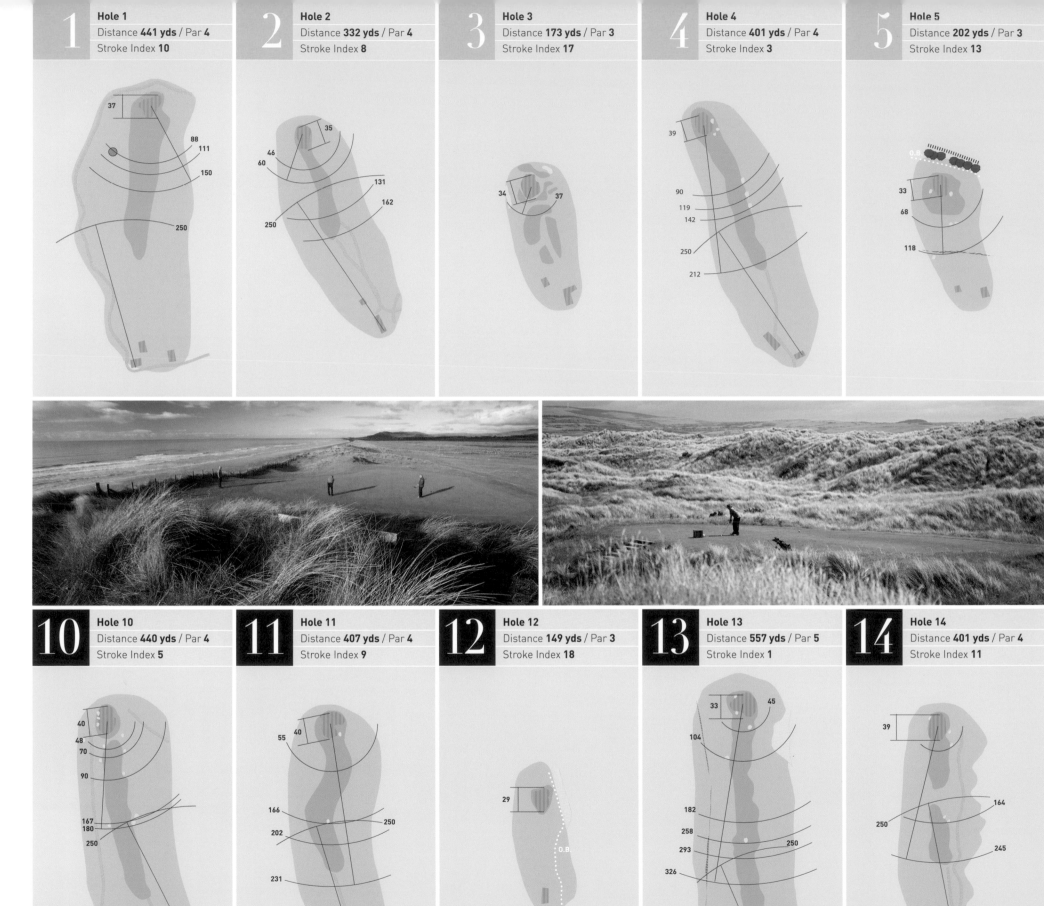

Hole 1
Distance **441 yds** / Par **4**
Stroke Index **10**

37
88
111
150
250

Hole 2
Distance **332 yds** / Par **4**
Stroke Index **8**

35
46
60
131
162
250

Hole 3
Distance **173 yds** / Par **3**
Stroke Index **17**

34
37

Hole 4
Distance **401 yds** / Par **4**
Stroke Index **3**

39
90
119
142
250
212

Hole 5
Distance **202 yds** / Par **3**
Stroke Index **13**

0.B.
33
68
118

Hole 10
Distance **440 yds** / Par **4**
Stroke Index **5**

40
48
70
90
167
180
250

Hole 11
Distance **407 yds** / Par **4**
Stroke Index **9**

40
55
166
202
250
231

Hole 12
Distance **149 yds** / Par **3**
Stroke Index **18**

29
0.B.

Hole 13
Distance **557 yds** / Par **5**
Stroke Index **1**

33
45
104
182
258
293
250
326

Hole 14
Distance **401 yds** / Par **4**
Stroke Index **11**

39
164
250
245

6 Hole 6
Distance **431 yds** / Par **4**
Stroke Index **6**

7 Hole 7
Distance **518 yds** / Par **5**
Stroke Index **2**

8 Hole 8
Distance **335 yds** / Par **4**
Stroke Index **15**

9 Hole 9
Distance **160 yds** / Par **3**
Stroke Index **12**

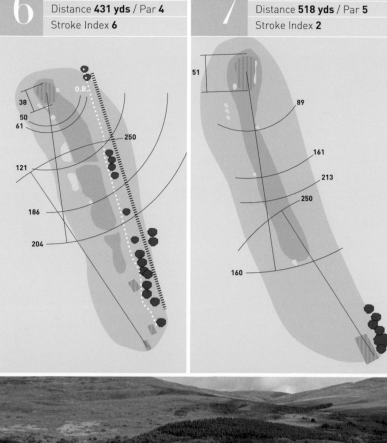

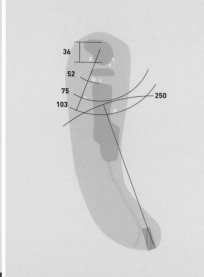

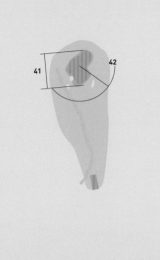

Aberdovey GWYNEDD

CONTACT DETAILS

Address
Aberdyfi LL35 0RT

Telephone
01654 767493

Website
www.aberdoveygolf.co.uk

15 Hole 15
Distance **509 yds** / Par **5**
Stroke Index **7**

16 Hole 16
Distance **288 yds** / Par **4**
Stroke Index **16**

17 Hole 17
Distance **428 yds** / Par **4**
Stroke Index **4**

18 Hole 18
Distance **443 yds** / Par **4**
Stroke Index **14**

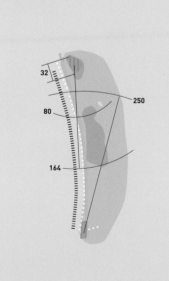

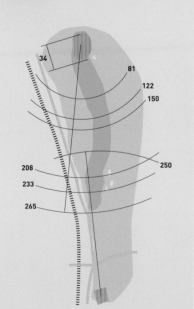

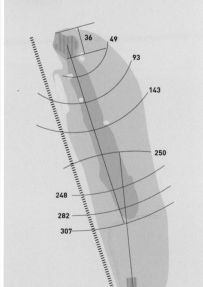

ABERDOVEY COURSE

All distance measurements in
yards from the back tees.

Out	
Distance	**2993 yds**
Par	**34**
In	
Distance	**3622 yds**
Par	**37**
Totals	
Distance	**6615 yds**
Par	**71**

30 Celtic Manor Resort
NEWPORT

This relatively new resort has quickly become a world-renowned venue for golf, set in 1,400 acres of beautiful, unspoiled parkland at the southern gateway to Wales. Boasting three championship courses, Celtic Manor offers a challenge for all levels of play, complemented by a golf school and one of the largest clubhouses in Europe, as well as extensive leisure facilities.

The Roman Road Course, opened in 1995, has hosted the Celtic Manor Wales Open every year since 2000 and the All*Star Cup. The Montgomerie Course, designed by golfing legend Colin Montgomerie, opened in 2007; it has dramatic tee shots overlooking the valleys, plus there are some breathtaking downhill shots to be played. In 2010, the Celtic Manor Resort will host the Ryder Cup on the world's first ever course to be specifically designed for this prestigious tournament, The Ryder Cup Course (see plan page 134). This new course, which opened in 2007, features nine holes from the original Wentwood Hills course and nine spectacular new holes in the valley of the River Usk.

Tour Notes

2001 Following a commitment from Celtic Manor Resort to build a course specifically designed for the occasion, the Ryder Cup Committee announces that the 38th Ryder Cup will be held here in 2010. This will be the first time the prestigious tournament has been held in Wales.

2005–2006 For two consecutive years, the All*Star Cup is staged on the Roman Road Course, featuring a long list of celebrities that includes Catherine Zeta Jones, Michael Douglas, Alice Cooper, Jane Seymour, William Baldwin and Bruce Forsyth.

Above and left: Players at the Wales Open Championship

1 Hole 1
Distance **465 yds** / Par **4**
Stroke Index **11**

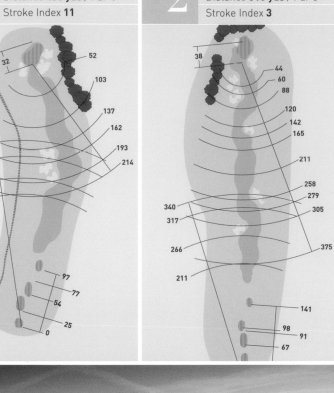

32
52
103
137
162
193
214
300
274
246
221

97
77
54
25
0

2 Hole 2
Distance **610 yds** / Par **5**
Stroke Index **3**

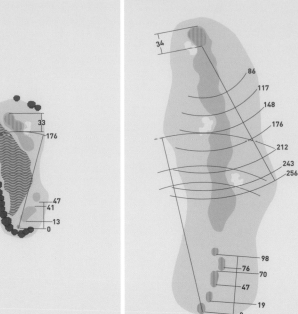

38
44
60
88
120
142
165
211
258
279
305
340
317
266
211
375

141
98
91
67

3 Hole 3
Distance **189 yds** / Par **3**
Stroke Index **13**

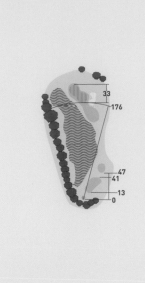

33
176
47
41
13
0

4 Hole 2
Distance **461 yds** / Par **4**
Stroke Index **15**

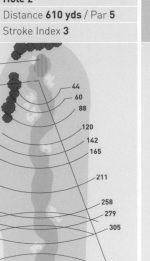

34
86
117
148
176
212
243
256

98
76
70
47
19
0

5 Hole 5
Distance **457 yds** / Par **4**
Stroke Index **1**

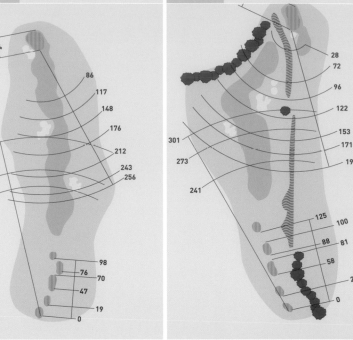

28
72
96
122
153
171
195
301
273
241

125 100
88 81
58
24
0

10 Hole 10
Distance **210 yds** / Par **3**
Stroke Index **18**

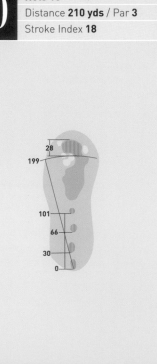

28
199
101
66
30
0

11 Hole 11
Distance **562 yds** / Par **5**
Stroke Index **8**

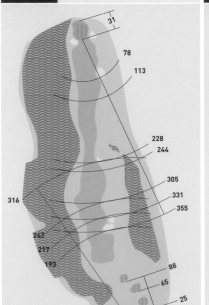

31
78
113
228
244
305
331
355
316
242
217
193
88
65
25
0

12 Hole 12
Distance **458 yds** / Par **4**
Stroke Index **4**

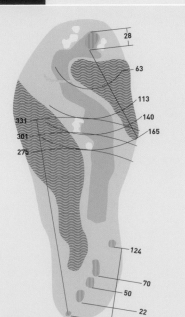

28
63
113
140
165
331
301
275
124
70
50
22
0

13 Hole 13
Distance **189 yds** / Par **3**
Stroke Index **14**

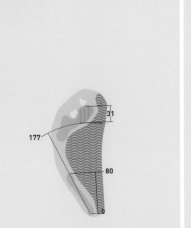

31
177
80
0

14 Hole 2
Distance **413 yds** / Par **4**
Stroke Index **2**

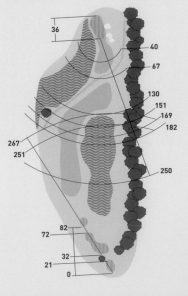

36
40
67
130
151
169
182
267
251
250
82
72
32
21
0

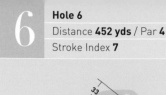

6 | Hole 6
Distance **452 yds** / Par **4**
Stroke Index **7**

7 | Hole 7
Distance **213 yds** / Par **3**
Stroke Index **17**

8 | Hole 8
Distance **439 yds** / Par **4**
Stroke Index **9**

9 | Hole 9
Distance **666 yds** / Par **5**
Stroke Index **5**

CONTACT DETAILS

Address
Coldra Woods,
The Usk Valley NP18 1HQ

Telephone
01633 413000

Website
www.celtic-manor.com

15 | Hole 15
Distance **377 yds** / Par **4**
Stroke Index **12**

16 | Hole 16
Distance **508 yds** / Par **4**
Stroke Index **6**

17 | Hole 17
Distance **211 yds** / Par **3**
Stroke Index **16**

18 | Hole 18
Distance **613 yds** / Par **5**
Stroke Index **10**

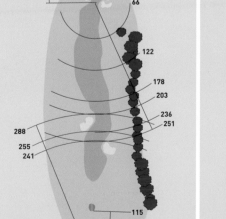

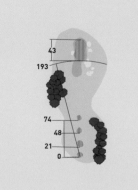

RYDER CUP COURSE

All distance measurements in
yards from the blue tees.

All illustrations are based upon
original Strokesaver artwork.

Out	
Distance	**3952 yds**
Par	**36**
In	
Distance	**3541 yds**
Par	**35**

Totals	
Distance	**7493 yds**
Par	**71**

Marriott St. Pierre
MONMOUTHSHIRE

Nestled in 400 acres of beautiful parkland, Marriott St. Pierre's two 18-hole courses are built around a graceful 14th-century manor house and 11th-century Norman church. The Old Course (see plan page 138) is considered one of the finest in the country and has been a fantastic host to no fewer than 14 European Tour events. Some of the world's most illustrious players have succeeded here, including such legends as Seve Ballesteros, Greg Norman and Bernhard Langer.

The 18th hole is famous for its tee shot over the huge lake to an elevated green, and it has been known to take 11 shots to finish the round. Meandering through the Monmouthshire countryside, the much shorter Mathern Course, opened in 1975, has its own challenges and is highly enjoyable for golfers of all abilities. The complex also offers a 13-bay floodlit driving range with a video analysis room, putting and chipping greens, and a short game practice area.

Tour Notes

1961 Plans get underway for the first 18-hole course at St. Pierre. Architect Ken Cotton lays it out over an existing deer park around an 11-acre lake surrounded by trees. The impressive course opens for play the following year.

1980 Bernhard Langer wins the British Masters, the first German to win a major tournament. St. Pierre has held the British Masters eight times; the last champion being Ian Woosnam in 1983.

1996 The Americans retain the fourth Solheim Cup on the Old Course, overpowering the European team by 17 to 11. The US team become the first team to win the Solheim Cup on foreign soil.

1 Hole 1
Distance **575 yds** / Par **5**
Stroke Index **3**

2 Hole 2
Distance **364 yds** / Par **4**
Stroke Index **9**

3 Hole 3
Distance **167 yds** / Par **3**
Stroke Index **15**

4 Hole 4
Distance **377 yds** / Par **4**
Stroke Index **13**

5 Hole 5
Distance **407 yds** / Par **4**
Stroke Index **1**

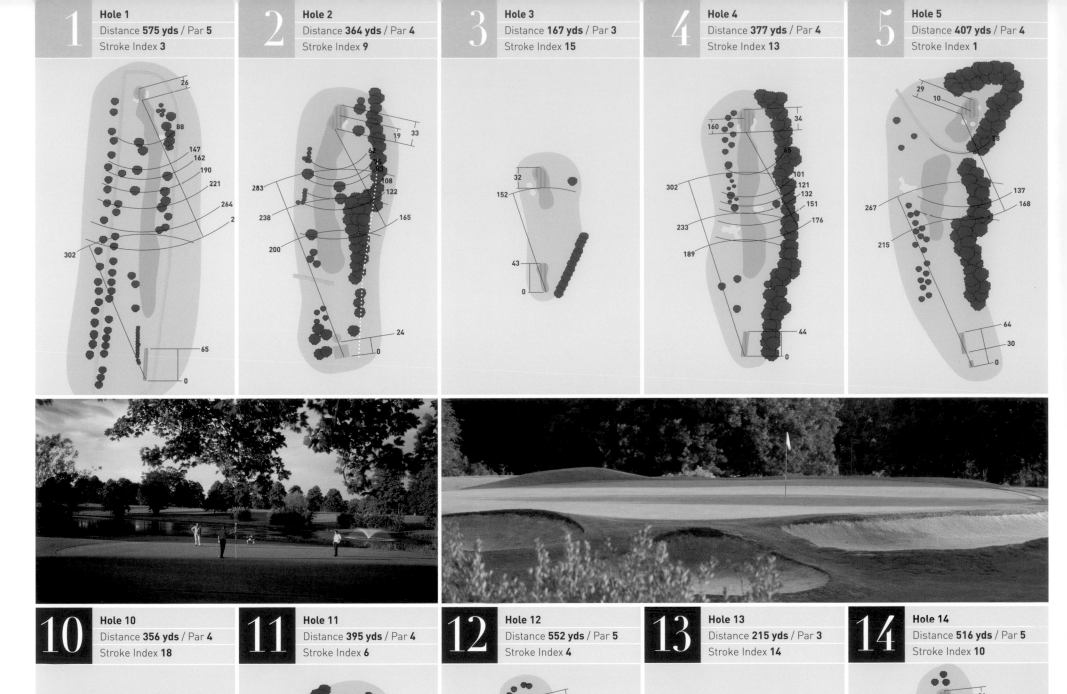

10 Hole 10
Distance **356 yds** / Par **4**
Stroke Index **18**

11 Hole 11
Distance **395 yds** / Par **4**
Stroke Index **6**

12 Hole 12
Distance **552 yds** / Par **5**
Stroke Index **4**

13 Hole 13
Distance **215 yds** / Par **3**
Stroke Index **14**

14 Hole 14
Distance **516 yds** / Par **5**
Stroke Index **10**

6 Hole 6
Distance **164 yds** / Par **3**
Stroke Index **11**

7 Hole 7
Distance **443 yds** / Par **4**
Stroke Index **5**

8 Hole 8
Distance **306 yds** / Par **4**
Stroke Index **17**

9 Hole 9
Distance **443 yds** / Par **4**
Stroke Index **7**

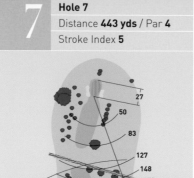

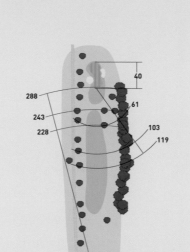

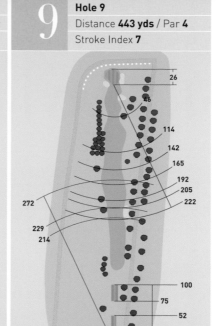

31

Marriott St. Pierre
MONMOUTHSHIRE

CONTACT DETAILS

Address
St. Pierre Park, Chepstow
NP16 6YA

Telephone
01291 625261

Website
www.marriotstpierre.co.uk

66 *Always remember that however good you may be, the game is your master* **99**

J. H TAYLOR

15 Hole 15
Distance **363 yds** / Par **4**
Stroke Index **16**

16 Hole 16
Distance **425 yds** / Par**4**
Stroke Index **2**

17 Hole 17
Distance **430 yds** / Par **4**
Stroke Index **12**

18 Hole 18
Distance **235 yds** / Par **3**
Stroke Index **8**

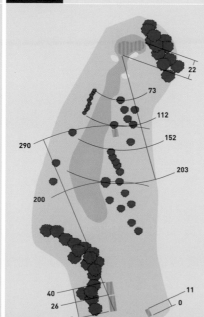

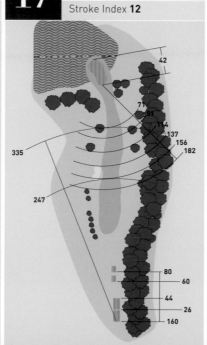

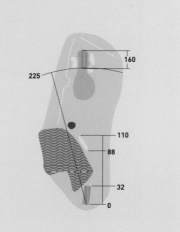

OLD COURSE

All distance measurements in yards from the white tees.

All illustrations are based upon original Strokesaver artwork.

Out	
Distance	**3246 yds**
Par	**35**
In	
Distance	**3487 yds**
Par	**36**

Totals	
Distance	**6733 yds**
Par	**71**

THE GOLF TOUR

139

Royal St. David's
GWYNEDD

One of the finest traditional championship links courses in the world, Royal St. David's lies beneath the constant gaze of Harlech Castle, with its magnificent backdrop of the Snowdonia mountains. The course is recognized as one of the world's toughest par 69s, with its natural hazards, zigzags and prevailing westerly wind. The battle with the elements demands strength and accuracy. Founded in 1894, the club was granted its royal title by King Edward VII in 1908. The link with royalty continued when, in 1934, the future Duke of Windsor captained the club while he was Prince of Wales.

The opening holes of the course provide relatively flat and easy walking but on reaching the 14th the ground becomes undulating. One of the most outstanding holes is the 15th, with a long drive across the dunes and a narrow fairway approach to the green; from here the magnificent Mount Snowdon is visible in the distance. The 16th hole has some fine views of Lyn peninsula and across Tremadog Bay. The club has welcomed numerous amateur championships, home internationals and Welsh national tournaments.

Tour Notes

Early 1890s On his return from Australia, author and sportsman Harold Finch-Hatton is said to have first used the site of the future St. David's Golf Club as an area for boomerang practice. He later joins forces with local William Henry Moore to design the links.

1903 St. David's holds its first professional tournament, won by the renowned James Braid.

2009 The popular Ladies British Open Amateur Championships will be held at Royal St. David's for the sixth time in the championship's history and the first time since 1987.

Hole 1
Distance **443 yds** / Par **4**
Stroke Index **9**

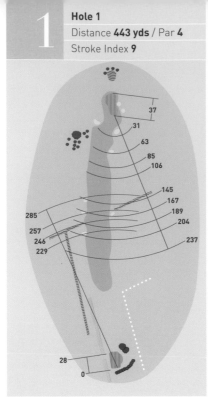

37
31
63
85
106
145
167
189
204
237
285
257
246
229
28
0

Hole 2
Distance **376 yds** / Par **4**
Stroke Index **14**

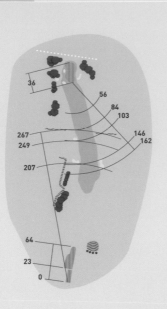

36
56
84
103
146
162
267
249
207
64
23
0

Hole 3
Distance **468 yds** / Par **4**
Stroke Index **2**

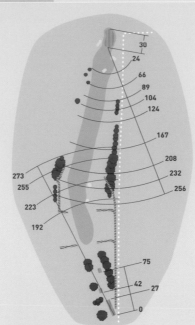

30
24
66
89
104
124
167
208
232
256
273
255
223
192
75
42
27
0

Hole 4
Distance **188 yds** / Par **3**
Stroke Index **13**

25
177
47
2
0

Hole 5
Distance **378 yds** / Par **4**
Stroke Index **8**

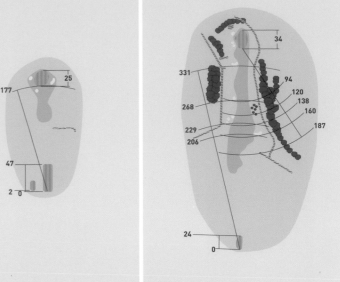

34
331
94
120
138
160
268
187
229
206
24
0

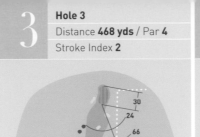
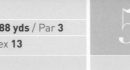

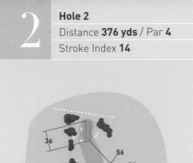

Hole 10
Distance **453 yds** / Par **4**
Stroke Index **1**

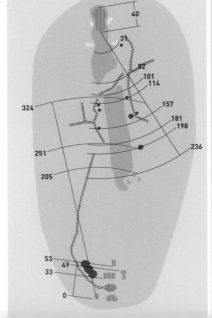
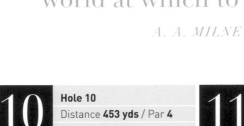

40
31
82
101
114
157
181
198
324
251
236
205
53
49
33
0

Hole 11
Distance **153 yds** / Par **3**
Stroke Index **17**

28
141
48
0

Hole 12
Distance **436 yds** / Par **4**
Stroke Index **10**

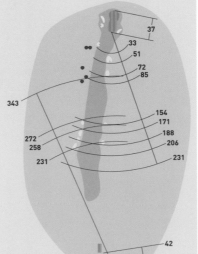
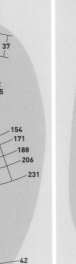

37
33
51
72
85
154
171
188
206
231
343
272
258
231
42
13
0

Hole 13
Distance **450 yds** / Par **4**
Stroke Index **7**

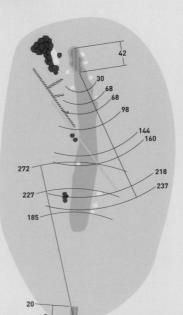

42
30
68
68
98
144
160
272
218
227
237
185
20
0

Hole 14
Distance **222 yds** / Par **3**
Stroke Index **12**

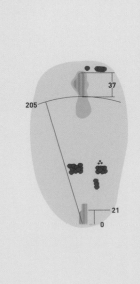

42
37
205
21
0

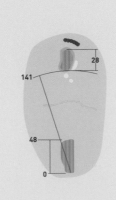

6
Hole 6
Distance **403 yds** / Par **4**
Stroke Index **11**

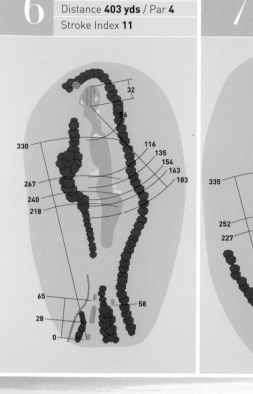

7
Hole 7
Distance **514 yds** / Par **5**
Stroke Index **4**

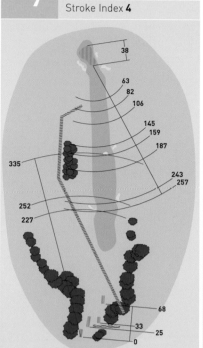

8
Hole 8
Distance **517 yds** / Par **5**
Stroke Index **6**

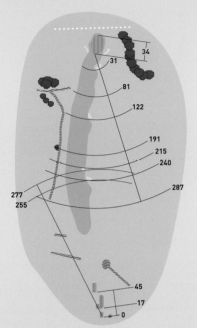

9
Hole 9
Distance **185 yds** / Par **3**
Stroke Index **16**

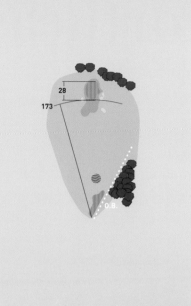

CONTACT DETAILS

Address
Harlech LL46 2UB

Telephone
01776 780361

Website
www.royalstdavids.co.uk

15
Hole 15
Distance **432 yds** / Par **4**
Stroke Index **3**

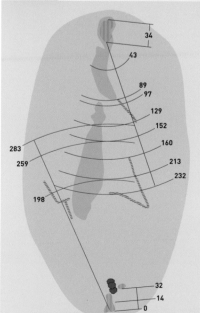

16
Hole 16
Distance **354 yds** / Par **4**
Stroke Index **14**

17
Hole 17
Distance **428 yds** / Par **4**
Stroke Index **5**

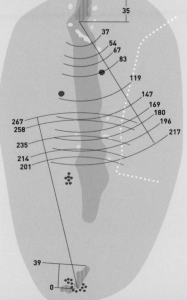

18
Hole 18
Distance **201 yds** / Par **3**
Stroke Index **18**

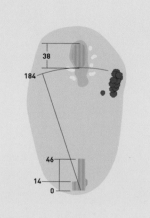

ROYAL ST. DAVID'S COURSE

All distance measurements in yards from the blue tees.

All illustrations are based upon original Strokesaver artwork.

Out	
Distance	**3462 yds**
Par	**36**
In	
Distance	**3129 yds**
Par	**33**
Totals	
Distance	**6601 yds**
Par	**69**

Royal Porthcawl
MID-GLAMORGAN

One of the great links courses, Royal Porthcawl is unique in that the sea is in full view from every single hole. The club was founded in 1896 and the course designed by Ramsey Hunter, with substantial modifications by Harry Colt in 1913 and by Tom Simpson in 1933. Edward VII bestowed royal patronage on the club in 1909.

The opening four and the last six holes present the golfer with a classic links course but in the middle the ground rises and there are stunning views over the Bristol Channel. With exposure to the prevailing Atlantic gales and the lack of dunes and trees to give protection, this course demands accuracy, concentration and careful club selection. The 18th is fascinating as it plays downhill towards the sea and from the tee you feel as if you are hitting straight into the water. Porthcawl has been host to many prestigious professional and amateur events during its illustrious history.

1964 Royal Porthcawl is chosen as the venue for the Curtis Cup. The US ladies team secures victory over the Great Britain and Ireland ladies with a three point lead.

1995 The biennial Walker Cup takes place at Porthcawl. Nineteen-year-old Tiger Woods constantly overdrives his opponent, 44-year-old Gary Wolstenholme, but fails to win the match as the Englishman steals a one-stroke victory at the final hole. This proves vital as Great Britain and Ireland go on to clinch the Cup by 14 points to 10.

2005 Porthcawl hosts one of the most important tournaments for amateur boys' teams, the Jacques Leglise Trophy. The best young golfers from the British Isles challenge the cream of Continental Europe and in this year Europe lifts the trophy. Golfing legends such as Sergio Garcia have cut their teeth on this tournament.

Hole 1
Distance **324 yds** / Par **4**
Stroke Index **15**

Hole 2
Distance **451 yds** / Par **4**
Stroke Index **3**

Hole 3
Distance **445 yds** / Par **4**
Stroke Index **7**

Hole 4
Distance **212 yds** / Par **3**
Stroke Index **11**

Hole 5
Distance **611 yds** / Par **5**
Stroke Index **13**

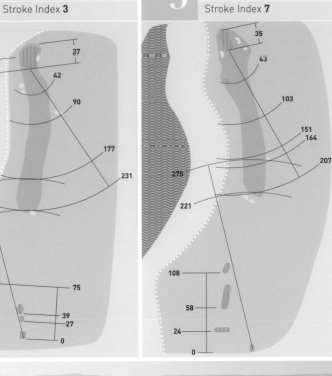
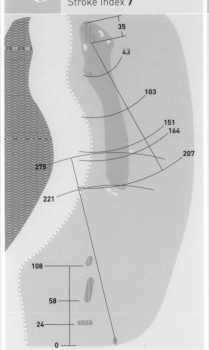
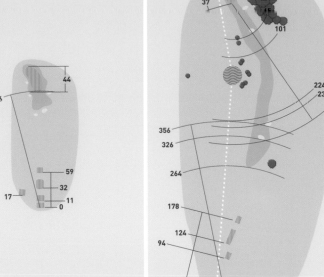

34

7

60
77
97
293
252
235
218
8 14
0

37
21
42
90
177
231
260
208
75
39
27
0

35
43
103
151
164
207
275
221
108
58
24
0

44
196
59
32
17
11
0

37
101
224
235
270
356
326
264
178
124
94
0

Hole 10
Distance **336 yds** / Par **4**
Stroke Index **16**

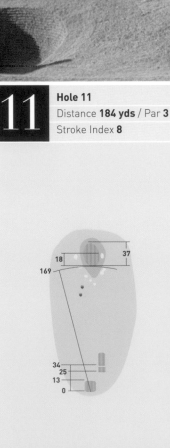

Hole 11
Distance **184 yds** / Par **3**
Stroke Index **8**

Hole 12
Distance **467 yds** / Par **5**
Stroke Index **12**

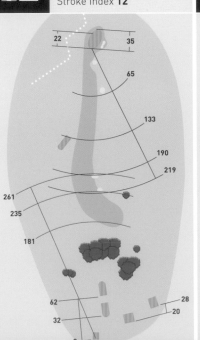

Hole 13
Distance **475 yds** / Par **4**
Stroke Index **4**

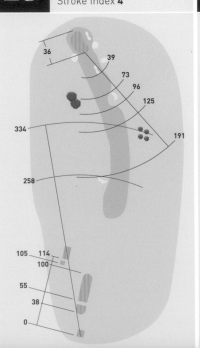

Hole 14
Distance **149 yds** / Par **3**
Stroke Index **18**

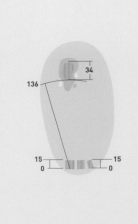
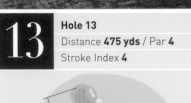

43

47
86
269

33
18
9
0

18
37
169
34
25
13
0

22
35
65
133
190
219
261
235
181
62
28
32
20
0

36
39
73
96
125
334
191
258
105 114
100
55
38
0

34
136
15
0
15

6 Hole 6
Distance **394 yds** / Par **4**
Stroke Index **5**

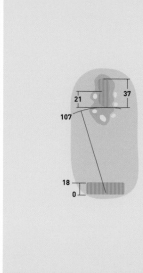

7 Hole 7
Distance **122 yds** / Par **3**
Stroke Index **17**

8 Hole 8
Distance **474 yds** / Par **5**
Stroke Index **9**

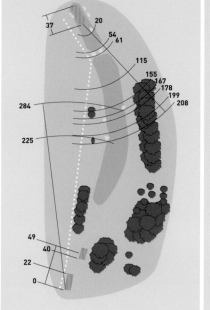

9 Hole 9
Distance **375 yds** / Par **4**
Stroke Index **1**

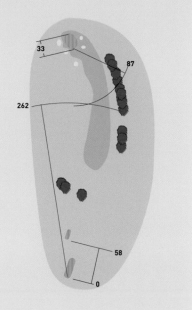

CONTACT DETAILS

Address
Rest Bay, Porthcawl
CF36 3UW

Telephone
01656 782251

Website
www.royalporthcawl.com

> **"** If there is one thing I have learned during my years as a professional, it is that the only thing constant about golf is its inconstancy **"**
>
> *JACK NICKLAUS*

15 Hole 15
Distance **466 yds** / Par **4**
Stroke Index **2**

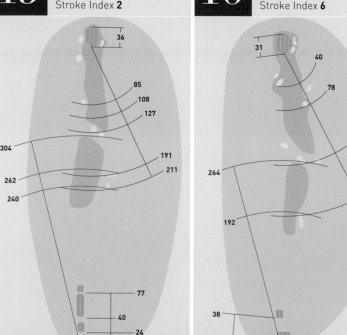

16 Hole 16
Distance **430 yds** / Par **4**
Stroke Index **6**

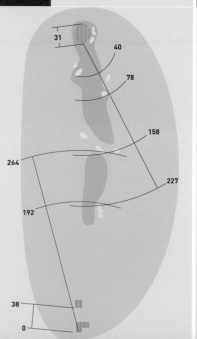

17 Hole 17
Distance **504 yds** / Par **5**
Stroke Index **14**

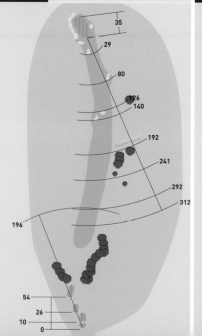

18 Hole 18
Distance **410 yds** / Par **4**
Stroke Index **10**

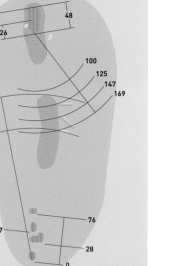

ROYAL PORTHCAWL COURSE

All distance measurements in yards from the blue tees.

All illustrations are based upon original Strokesaver artwork.

Out	
Distance	3408 yds
Par	36
In	
Distance	3421 yds
Par	36
Totals	
Distance	6829 yds
Par	72

IRELAND

(34) **Ballybunion**   150
Co. Kerry

(35) **Dromoland Castle**   154
Co. Clare

(36) **Druids Glen**   158
Co. Wicklow

(37) **Fota Island Resort**   162
Co. Cork

(38) **The K Club**   166
Co. Kildare

(39) **Mount Juliet**   170
Co. Kilkenny

(40) **Portmarnock**   174
Co. Dublin

(41) **Rathsallagh House**   178
Co. Wicklow

(42) **Royal County Down**   182
Co. Down

(43) **Royal Portrush**   186
Co. Antrim

Ballybunion
CO. KERRY

Ballybunion links has gained worldwide recognition for the fine development of the natural terrain, enabling the course to literally flow with the land. In 1892 the professional golfer James McKenna is believed to have laid out the original Old Course, although the Ballybunion Golf Club was not founded until 1906. With large sand dunes and a dramatic Atlantic backdrop, Ballybunion offers an exciting round of golf in a scenic location, but be warned, the Old Course is difficult to play in the wind.

Although overshadowed by the Old Course, the Cashen (see plan page152), designed by Robert Trent Jones and first opened for play in 1982, is also world class, characterized by narrow fairways, small greens and large dunes. The courses are virtually treeless, with tough grass and steep slopes open to the elements. Despite its remote location, top golfers from around the world are not deterred from coming to play a round on this exacting course.

Tour Notes

1980s America's Tom Watson forms a strong relationship with Ballybunion and brings many of the illustrious figures in the world of golf over to play, including Jack Nicklaus, Lee Trevino and Nick Faldo.

1995 Tom Watson updates the Old Course, tenderly nurturing and revitalizing the century-old course to meet the demands of a new millennium.

July 1998 The late Payne Stewart aces the testing 16th hole during his visit to Ballybunion. His playing partners are not as fortunate; Mark O'Meara gets his par but the great Tiger Woods takes two to get out of the bunker and records a bogey, demonstrating just how awkward this hole can be.

September 1998 President Clinton plays a round at Ballybunion with Irish golf legend Christy O'Connor on his historic visit to Ireland. A life-size statue of the president about to swing a golf club is unveiled outside the police station in the town.

Hole 1
Distance **522 yds** / Par **5**
Stroke Index **10**

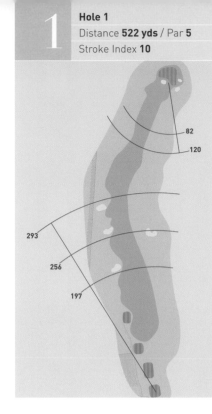

82
120
293
256
197

Hole 2
Distance **377 yds** / Par **4**
Stroke Index **4**

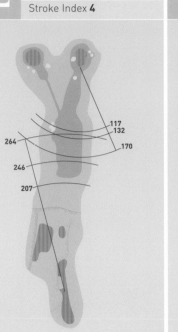

117
132
170
264
246
207

Hole 3
Distance **154 yds** / Par **3**
Stroke Index **18**

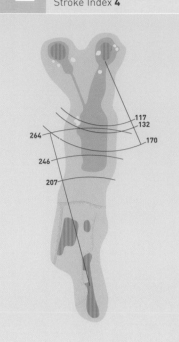

147

Hole 4
Distance **350 yds** / Par **4**
Stroke Index **8**

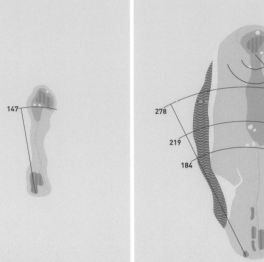

48
67
278
219
184

Hole 5
Distance **314 yds** / Par **4**
Stroke Index **16**

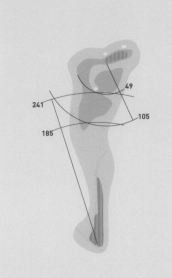

49
241
105
185

> " The game of golf would lose a great deal if croquet mallets and billiard cues were allowed on the putting green "
> *ERNEST HEMINGWAY*

Hole 10
Distance **324 yds** / Par **4**
Stroke Index **11**

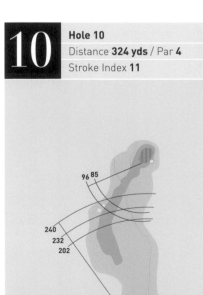

96 85
240
232
202

Hole 11
Distance **146 yds** / Par **3**
Stroke Index **17**

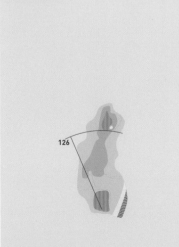

126

Hole 12
Distance **210 yds** / Par **3**
Stroke Index **13**

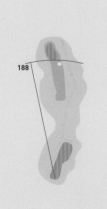

188

Hole 13
Distance **395 yds** / Par **4**
Stroke Index **1**

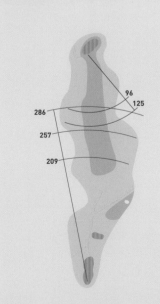

96
125
286
257
209

Hole 14
Distance **400 yds** / Par **4**
Stroke Index **7**

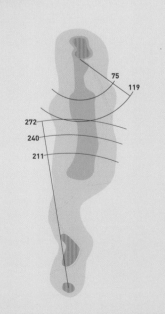

75
119
272
240
211

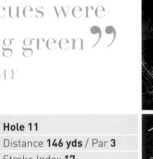

6
Hole 6
Distance **155 yds** / Par **3**
Stroke Index **12**

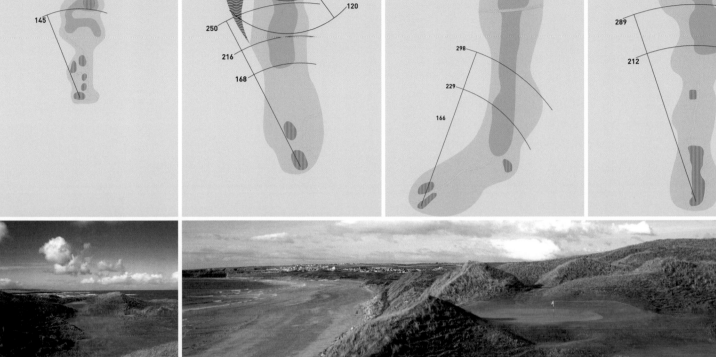

145

7
Hole 7
Distance **378 yds** / Par **4**
Stroke Index **6**

55
86
120
250
216
168

8
Hole 8
Distance **605 yds** / Par **5**
Stroke Index **2**

95
136
156
298
229
166

9
Hole 9
Distance **478 yds** / Par **5**
Stroke Index **14**

66
97
174
289
212

CONTACT DETAILS

Address
Sandhill Road, Ballybunion

Telephone
068 27146

Website
www.ballybuniongolfclub.ie

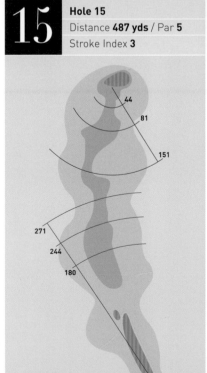

15
Hole 15
Distance **487 yds** / Par **5**
Stroke Index **3**

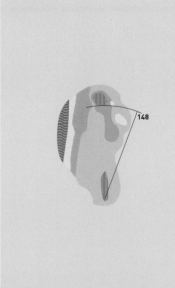

44
81
151
271
244
180

16
Hole 16
Distance **164 yds** / Par **3**
Stroke Index **15**

148

17
Hole 17
Distance **479 yds** / Par **5**
Stroke Index **13**

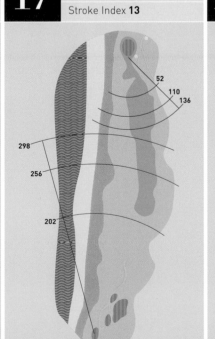

52
110
136
298
256
202

18
Hole 18
Distance **368 yds** / Par **4**
Stroke Index **5**

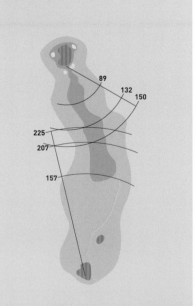

89
132
150
225
207
157

CASHEN COURSE

All distance measurements in yards from the blue tees.

Out	
Distance	**3333 yds**
Par	**37**
In	
Distance	**2973 yds**
Par	**35**

Totals	
Distance	**6306 yds**
Par	**72**

35 Dromoland Castle
CO. CLARE

You can't get a setting much better than this. Dromoland Castle lies in a secluded spot on the shores of Lough Dromoland, and the magnificent championship golf course is surrounded by parkland. Dromoland can trace its ancestry back to the Gaelic Royal families, even to the great Brian Boru, the High King of Ireland in the 10th century. The castle, with its delightful walled gardens, has been redesigned over the centuries, with the present building the result of an early 19th-century makeover. It is now been transformed into a luxury hotel.

Golf was first played at Dromoland in 1962. The opening hole eases you into the course with hazards incorporated from the second tee. The 7th hole is not only incredibly beautiful, with fine views across to the castle and lake, but testing, with its greenside bunker and water hazard. There is a challenge at the ninth that can be played two ways—with a two shot to the green or a daring one shot, but beware the pond. You can take a break at the clubhouse if you need to recharge your batteries before attempting the next nine holes. There are plenty of opportunities for practice with the first-class Golf Academy facility.

Tour Notes

2004 The course reopens for play following a 5 million euro restructuring. The new design is entrusted to golf course architect Ron Kirby and the late legendary Irish amateur J. B. Carr, who set out to create a course for the 21st century and produce spectacular results.

2004 Amid high security, US President George Bush and his wife Laura visit Dromoland in advance of the European Union-United States summit, but despite being a keen golfer the President has no time to try out the course.

1 Hole 1
Distance **378 yds** / Par **4**
Stroke Index **8**

2 Hole 2
Distance **457 yds** / Par **4**
Stroke Index **4**

3 Hole 3
Distance **197 yds** / Par **3**
Stroke Index **10**

4 Hole 4
Distance **469 yds** / Par **4**
Stroke Index **14**

5 Hole 5
Distance **412 yds** / Par **4**
Stroke Index **12**

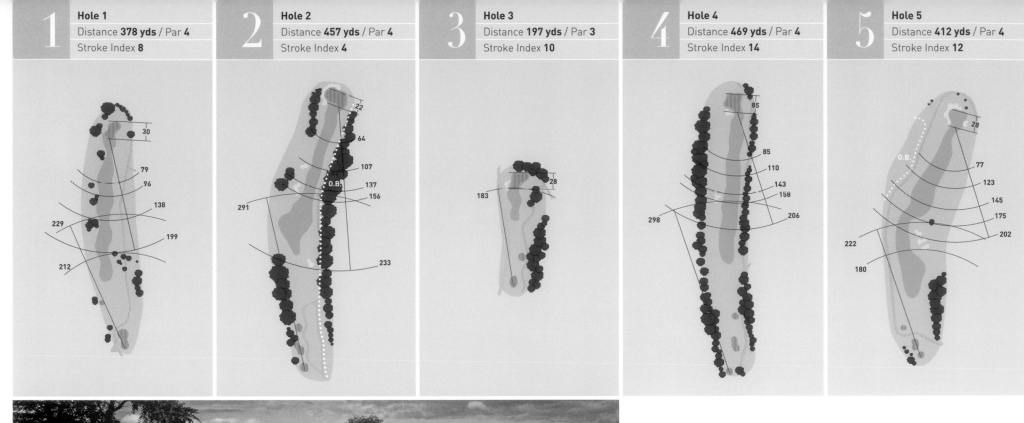

66 This is a game of misses.
The guy who misses the
best is going to win 99

BEN HOGAN

10 Hole 10
Distance **355 yds** / Par **4**
Stroke Index **13**

11 Hole 11
Distance **543 yds** / Par **5**
Stroke Index **5**

12 Hole 12
Distance **411 yds** / Par **4**
Stroke Index **11**

13 Hole 13
Distance **158 yds** / Par **3**
Stroke Index **15**

14 Hole 14
Distance **442 yds** / Par **4**
Stroke Index **3**

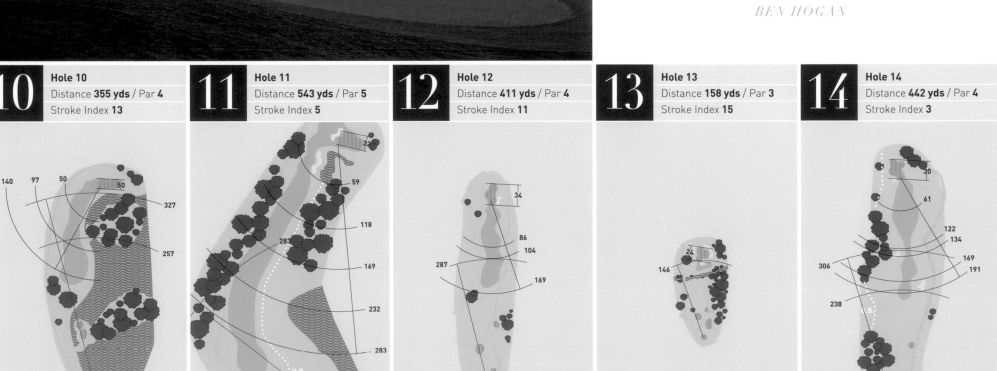

Hole 6
Distance **593 yds** / Par **5**
Stroke Index **2**

6

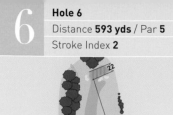
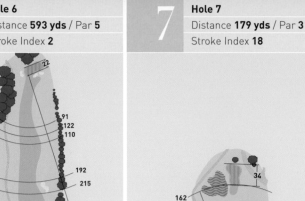

22
91
122
110
192
215
285
260
237

Hole 7
Distance **179 yds** / Par **3**
Stroke Index **18**

7

34
162

Hole 8
Distance **407 yds** / Par **4**
Stroke Index **6**

8

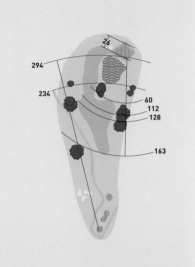

24
67
132
175
260
218
176

Hole 9
Distance **323 yds** / Par **4**
Stroke Index **16**

9

26
294
234
60
112
128
163

CONTACT DETAILS

Address
Newmarket-on-Fergus

Telephone
061 368444

Website
www.dromolandgolf.com

Hole 15
Distance **273 yds** / Par **4**
Stroke Index **17**

15

28
232
48
8
190
94
138

Hole 16
Distance **439 yds** / Par **4**
Stroke Index **1**

16

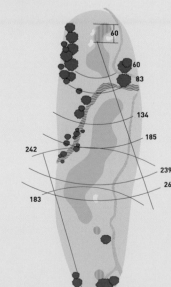

60
60
83
134
242
185
239
268
183

Hole 17
Distance **225 yds** / Par **3**
Stroke Index **9**

17

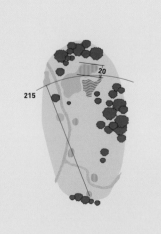

20
215

Hole 18
Distance **563 yds** / Par **5**
Stroke Index **7**

18

24
85
125
147
171
215
276
253
O.B.
192

DROMOLAND CASTLE COURSE

All distance measurements in yards from the blue tees.

Out	
Distance	**3415 yds**
Par	**36**
In	
Distance	**3409 yds**
Par	**36**

Totals	
Distance	**6824 yds**
Par	**72**

Druids Glen
CO. WICKLOW

From the very first tee to the 18th green, Druids Glen creates an exceptional golfing experience, with its distinguished surroundings and spectacular views. Inspirationally designed by Tom Craddock and Pat Ruddy and opened in 1995, it is the culmination of years of preparation, creating an inland course that challenges and satisfies in equal parts. Special features include an island green on the 17th hole and a striking Celtic Cross cleverly incorporated on the 12th.

Druids Glen hosted the Irish Open in 1996, 1997, 1998, and for an unprecedented fourth time in 1999. Known as the "Augusta of Europe", the world's top professionals and club golfers alike continue to take the challenge here. A variety of teeing positions are available and there is a practice area, including three full-length academy holes. The delightful 18th-century clubhouse is a welcoming sight after a strenuous round. Individual and corporate members enjoy generous reserved tee times; visitors are very welcome but it is recommended that you book well in advance.

Tour Notes

1999 Sergio Garcia wins his first professional tournament at Druids Glen with a dramatic victory at the Irish Open.

2000 Druids Glen is awarded the title of European Golf Course of the Year, presented by the International Association of Golf Tour Operators (IAGTO).

2002 The Seve Trophy, a biennial event between the leading Tour players of Great Britain and Ireland and mainland Europe, takes place at Druids Glen. Colin Montgomerie's home team outplay Seve Ballesteros's European players, a reversal of the 2000 match.

2002–2005 Ongoing development sees the formation of the Druids Glen Golf Resort with the opening of the Marriot Hotel and Country Club, and a new championship course at nearby Druids Heath. In 2005 the Druids Glen is named European Golf Resort of the Year by IAGTO.

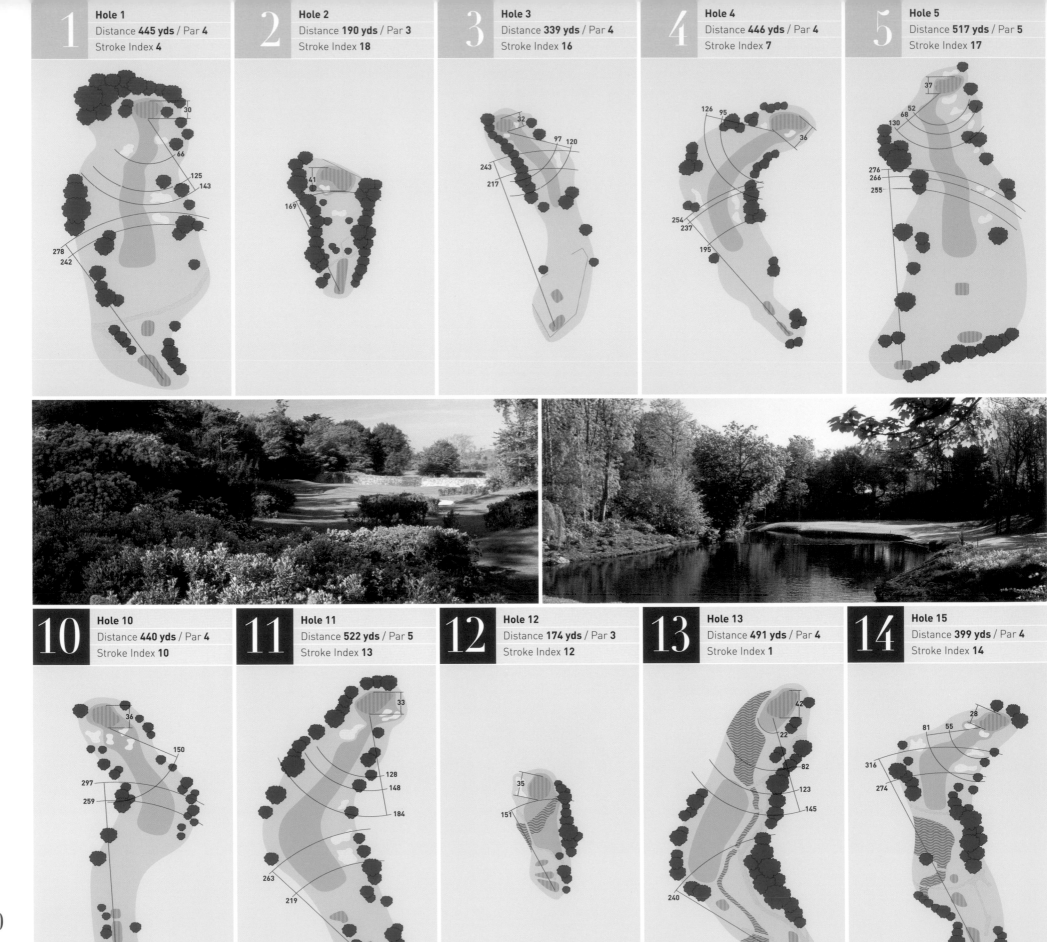

Hole 1
Distance **445 yds** / Par **4**
Stroke Index **4**

Hole 2
Distance **190 yds** / Par **3**
Stroke Index **18**

Hole 3
Distance **339 yds** / Par **4**
Stroke Index **16**

Hole 4
Distance **446 yds** / Par **4**
Stroke Index **7**

Hole 5
Distance **517 yds** / Par **5**
Stroke Index **17**

Hole 10
Distance **440 yds** / Par **4**
Stroke Index **10**

Hole 11
Distance **522 yds** / Par **5**
Stroke Index **13**

Hole 12
Distance **174 yds** / Par **3**
Stroke Index **12**

Hole 13
Distance **491 yds** / Par **4**
Stroke Index **1**

Hole 15
Distance **399 yds** / Par **4**
Stroke Index **14**

6	**Hole 6**
	Distance **476 yds** / Par **4**
	Stroke Index **2**

7	**Hole 7**
	Distance **405 yds** / Par **4**
	Stroke Index **6**

8	**Hole 8**
	Distance **166 yds** / Par **3**
	Stroke Index **11**

9	**Hole 9**
	Distance **389 yds** / Par **4**
	Stroke Index **15**

15	**Hole 15**
	Distance **456 yds** / Par **4**
	Stroke Index **9**

16	**Hole 16**
	Distance **538 yds** / Par **5**
	Stroke Index **18**

17	**Hole 17**
	Distance **203 yds** / Par **3**
	Stroke Index **5**

18	**Hole 18**
	Distance **450 yds** / Par **4**
	Stroke Index **3**

CONTACT DETAILS

Address
Newtownmountkennedy

Telephone
01 287 3600

Website
www.druidsglen.ie

DRUIDS GLEN COURSE

All distance measurements in yards from the blue tees.

Out	
Distance	**3373 yds**
Par	**35**
In	
Distance	**3673 yds**
Par	**36**
Totals	
Distance	**7046 yds**
Par	**71**

Fota Island Resort
CO. CORK

Magnificently set in the heart of a 780-acre island in Cork Harbour, Fota Island offers an amazing panorama, so much so it is included in the illustrious publication, the *Inventory of Outstanding Landscapes of Ireland*.

The Deerpark Course (see plan page 164), designed in 1993 by Ryder Cup hero Irishman Christy O'Connor and twice English Amateur Champion Peter McEvoy, is routed among mature woodlands with occasional views of the harbour. The course was upgraded to European Tour standard under the direction of Canadian designer Jeff Howes and reopened in 1999. During its short history, the Deerpark has been host to many professional and amateur championships. The traditional design features strategically placed bunkers and undulating putting surfaces. Welcome additions in 2006 were the Sheraton Fota Island Hotel and Spa exclusive lodges, plus a new Golf Academy. Fota Island now boasts two new courses, the Belvelly and the Barryscourt, and a marina is planned for the future to enhance the resort.

Tour Notes

2001 The Irish Open is held for the first time at Fota Island. Colin Montgomerie takes the accolades for the third time, while Ireland's Padraig Harrington and Darren Clarke, and Sweden's Niclas Fasth come in joint second.

2002 Denmark's Soren Hansen wins the Irish Open after a four-way play off with South African Darren Fichardt, Swede Niclas Fasth and Briton Richard Bland. Fota's 4th hole, which requires pin-point accuracy to navigate the narrow entrance to the green, was the final hole for the sudden death decider.

2006 Sam Torrance triumphs at the Irish Seniors Open, having won the Irish Open in both 1981 and 1995. In a four-man play off he secures his victory in style after hitting a glorious 150-yard wedge shot to within 14ft of the flag at the second hole, and securing the eagle putt to end all challenge.

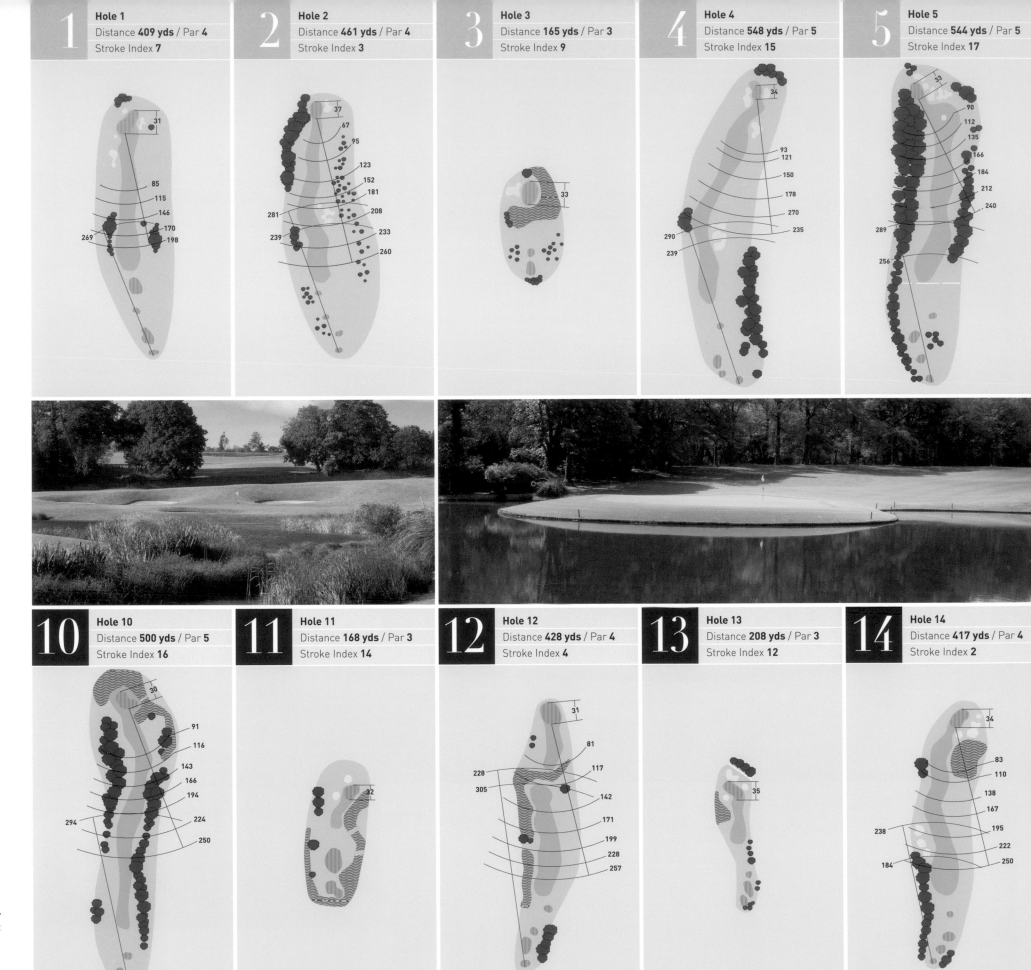

Hole 1
Distance **409 yds** / Par **4**
Stroke Index **7**

Hole 2
Distance **461 yds** / Par **4**
Stroke Index **3**

Hole 3
Distance **165 yds** / Par **3**
Stroke Index **9**

Hole 4
Distance **548 yds** / Par **5**
Stroke Index **15**

Hole 5
Distance **544 yds** / Par **5**
Stroke Index **17**

Hole 10
Distance **500 yds** / Par **5**
Stroke Index **16**

Hole 11
Distance **168 yds** / Par **3**
Stroke Index **14**

Hole 12
Distance **428 yds** / Par **4**
Stroke Index **4**

Hole 13
Distance **208 yds** / Par **3**
Stroke Index **12**

Hole 14
Distance **417 yds** / Par **4**
Stroke Index **2**

6 Hole 6
Distance **376 yds** / Par **4**
Stroke Index **13**

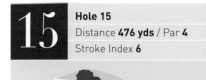

30
82
110
138
218
173
201
229

7 Hole 7
Distance **179 yds** / Par **3**
Stroke Index **11**

29

8 Hole 8
Distance **478 yds** / Par **4**
Stroke Index **1**

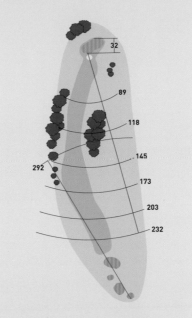

37
90
150
171
200
222
243
336
263

9 Hole 9
Distance **424 yds** / Par **4**
Stroke Index **5**

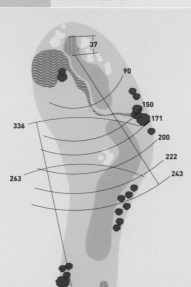

32
89
118
145
173
203
232
292

CONTACT DETAILS

Address
Fota Island

Telephone
021 488 3700

Website
www.fotaisland.ie

> 66 Golf is very much like a love
> affair. If you don't take it
> seriously, it's fun, if you do,
> it breaks your heart 99
>
> *LOUISE SUGGS*

15 Hole 15
Distance **476 yds** / Par **4**
Stroke Index **6**

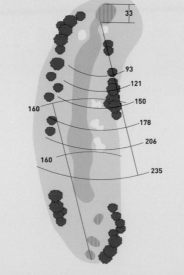

37
67
99
127
154
182
212
237
270
225
257

16 Hole 16
Distance **417 yds** / Par **4**
Stroke Index **8**

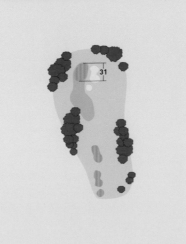

33
93
121
150
160
178
206
160
235

17 Hole 17
Distance **222 yds** / Par **3**
Stroke Index **10**

31

18 Hole 18
Distance **507 yds** / Par **5**
Stroke Index **18**

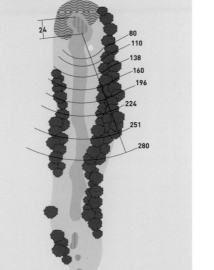

24
80
110
138
160
196
224
251
280

DEERPARK COURSE

All distance measurements in
yards from the blue tees.

Out	
Distance	**3584 yds**
Par	**36**
In	
Distance	**3343 yds**
Par	**35**

Totals	
Distance	**6927 yds**
Par	**71**

The K Club
CO. KILDARE

The K Club was the venue for the 2006 Ryder Cup, the first time that Ireland had hosted this esteemed event. A unique atmosphere prevails here; the courses are both cavalier and charismatic and reflect the personality of their architect, Arnold Palmer. Covering 550 acres of Kildare woodland, with 14 man-made lakes and the River Liffey providing the water hazards, it is one of life's great pleasures to play here.

The Palmer Course (see plan page 168) competes with any in Europe, spectacular, charming, enticing and invariably bringing out the very best in your game. The Smurfit European Course is designed to give you the experience of an inland links. Its many attributes include dramatic landscapes with dunes moulded throughout, while some 14 acres of water have been worked into the design—a watery grave awaits many on the home stretch. The Smurfit is entirely different from the Palmer Course, which is located just across the River Liffey.

Tour Notes

1995 The Smurfit European Open is held for the first time at The K Club with Bernard Langer of Germany clinching victory.

2006 In September the 36th Ryder Cup is hosted at The K Club and the Palmer Course is hailed as one of the world's best. European captain Ian Woosnam collects the trophy, his team beating the US by a massive 18 and a half points to 9 and a half points. This win equals the record made in the previous Ryder Cup in 2004, when the team from Europe was once again victorious.

2007 Having been held here annually since 1995, the newly named Smurfit Kappa European Open is won by Colin Montgomerie. It's his first victory for 19 months, and gives him his 31st European title.

Left: Tiger Woods chips onto the green during the 2006 Ryder Cup at The K Club

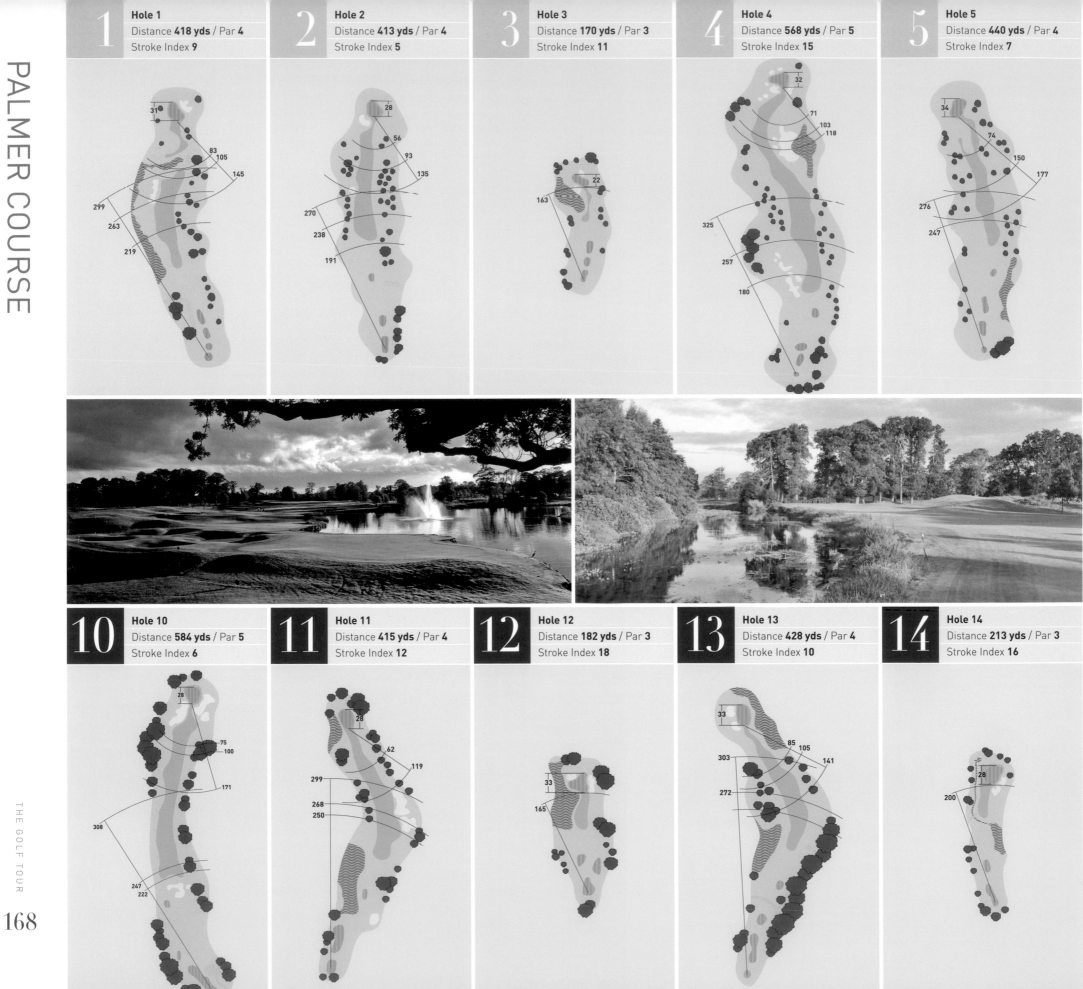

1
Hole 1
Distance **418 yds** / Par **4**
Stroke Index **9**

2
Hole 2
Distance **413 yds** / Par **4**
Stroke Index **5**

3
Hole 3
Distance **170 yds** / Par **3**
Stroke Index **11**

4
Hole 4
Distance **568 yds** / Par **5**
Stroke Index **15**

5
Hole 5
Distance **440 yds** / Par **4**
Stroke Index **7**

10
Hole 10
Distance **584 yds** / Par **5**
Stroke Index **6**

11
Hole 11
Distance **415 yds** / Par **4**
Stroke Index **12**

12
Hole 12
Distance **182 yds** / Par **3**
Stroke Index **18**

13
Hole 13
Distance **428 yds** / Par **4**
Stroke Index **10**

14
Hole 14
Distance **213 yds** / Par **3**
Stroke Index **16**

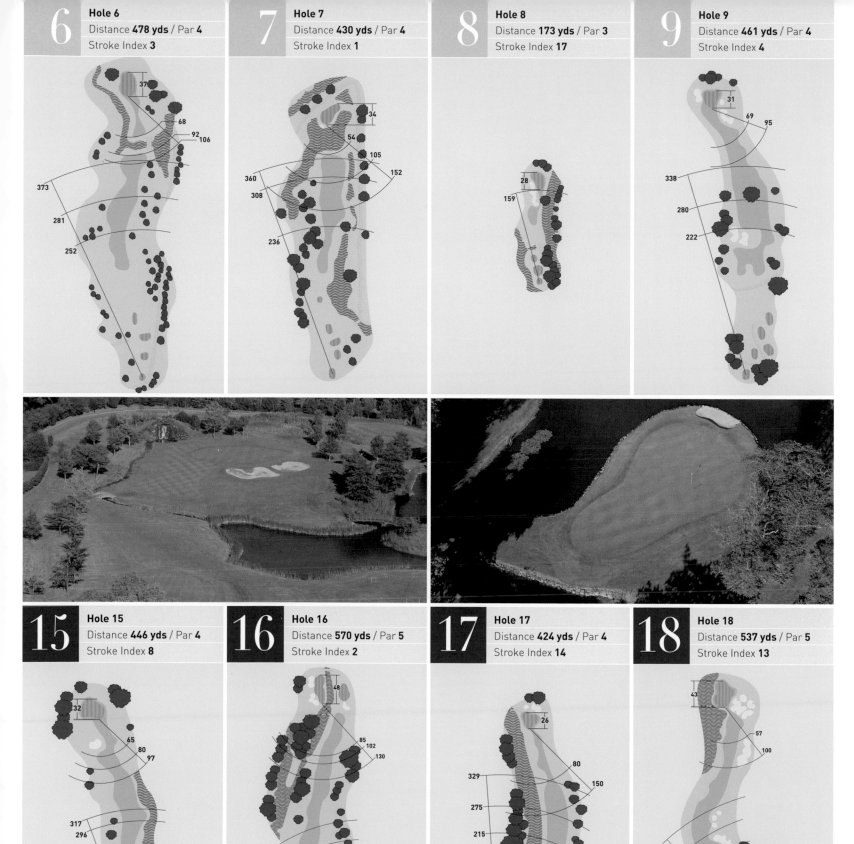

| **6** | **Hole 6**
Distance **478 yds** / Par **4**
Stroke Index **3** | **7** | **Hole 7**
Distance **430 yds** / Par **4**
Stroke Index **1** | **8** | **Hole 8**
Distance **173 yds** / Par **3**
Stroke Index **17** | **9** | **Hole 9**
Distance **461 yds** / Par **4**
Stroke Index **4** |

| **15** | **Hole 15**
Distance **446 yds** / Par **4**
Stroke Index **8** | **16** | **Hole 16**
Distance **570 yds** / Par **5**
Stroke Index **2** | **17** | **Hole 17**
Distance **424 yds** / Par **4**
Stroke Index **14** | **18** | **Hole 18**
Distance **537 yds** / Par **5**
Stroke Index **13** |

The K Club CO. KILDARE

CONTACT DETAILS

Address
Straffan

Telephone
01 601 7200

Website
www.kclub.com

PALMER COURSE

All distance measurements in
yards from the blue tees.

Out	
Distance	**3351 yds**
Par	**35**
In	
Distance	**3799 yds**
Par	**37**

Totals	
Distance	**7150 yds**
Par	**72**

Mount Juliet
CO. KILKENNY

Set within the beautiful Mount Juliet estate, this superb 18-hole course was designed by Jack Nicklaus and opened in 1991. It has hosted many respected events, including the Irish Open on three occasions. A cleverly concealed drainage and irrigation system makes the course perfect even when inclement weather would otherwise halt play. The course takes advantage of the estate's mature landscape to provide a world-class challenge for professionals and high-handicap golfers alike.

A particular feature is the 3rd hole, with an elevated tee to green guarded by a natural stream and lake. The final hole has water all down the left-hand side and a narrow approach that has sorted out many a tournament result. A three-hole golfing academy allows novice and experienced players ample opportunity to improve their game, while a new 18-hole putting course is the venue for the National Putting Championship.

1993–1995 England's Nick Faldo is triumphant in the Irish Open at Mount Juliet when he outplays Spaniard Jose Maria Ozabal in a play off. Bernhard Langer of Germany takes the honours in 1994 and in 1995 Scotland's Sam Torrance beats Englishmen Howard Clarke and Stuart Cage in a play off.

2002 The World Golf Championships-American Express Championship is held for the first time at Mount Juliet and won by Tiger Woods, who nets a massive $1 milliion prize.

With 49 of the top 50 players in the world at the event, Woods beats his nearest rival Retief Goosen by just one stroke.

2004 Tiger Woods returns to defend the title he won here in 2002 in front of a huge crowd, but fails on this occasion. The brilliance of South African Ernie Els, who finishes 18 under par, edges out his nearest rival Thomas Bjorn of Denmark on the final hole.

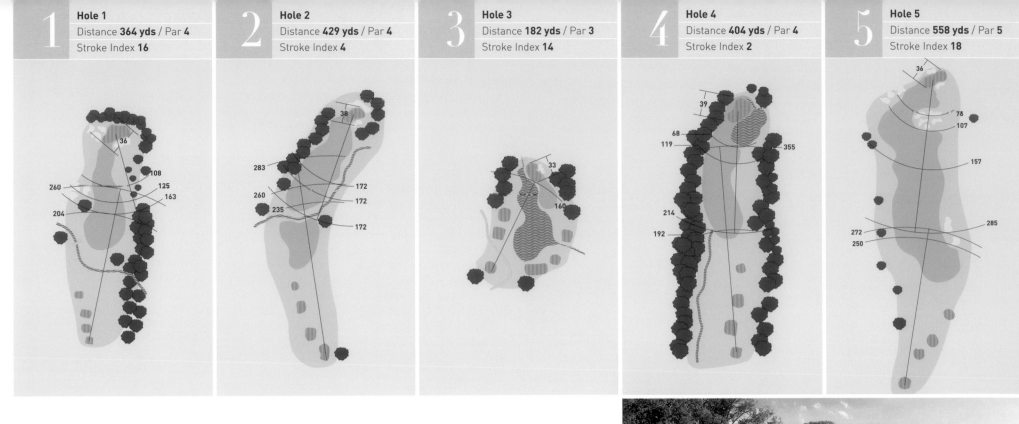

1
Hole 1
Distance **364 yds** / Par **4**
Stroke Index **16**

2
Hole 2
Distance **429 yds** / Par **4**
Stroke Index **4**

3
Hole 3
Distance **182 yds** / Par **3**
Stroke Index **14**

4
Hole 4
Distance **404 yds** / Par **4**
Stroke Index **2**

5
Hole 5
Distance **558 yds** / Par **5**
Stroke Index **18**

> " You get to know more of the character of a man in a round of golf than in six months of political experience "
>
> *DAVID LLOYD GEORGE*

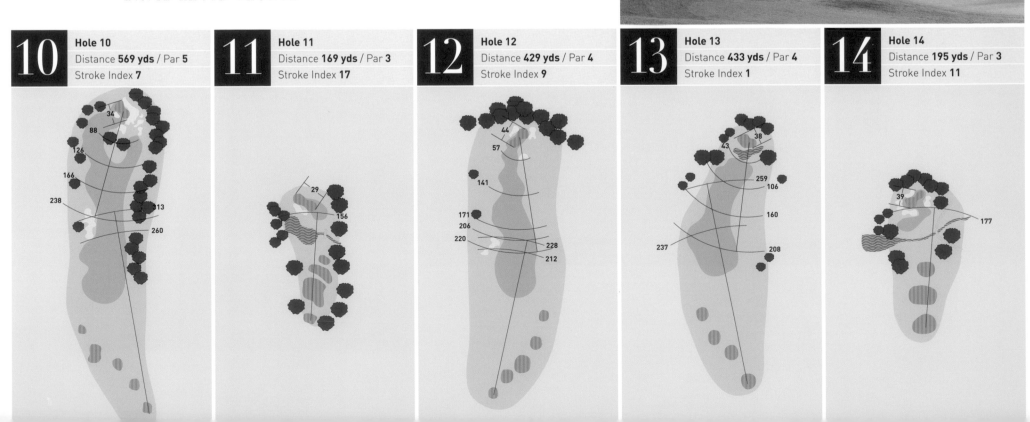

10
Hole 10
Distance **569 yds** / Par **5**
Stroke Index **7**

11
Hole 11
Distance **169 yds** / Par **3**
Stroke Index **17**

12
Hole 12
Distance **429 yds** / Par **4**
Stroke Index **9**

13
Hole 13
Distance **433 yds** / Par **4**
Stroke Index **1**

14
Hole 14
Distance **195 yds** / Par **3**
Stroke Index **11**

6
Hole 6
Distance **229 yds** / Par **3**
Stroke Index **6**

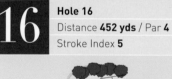

42
209

7
Hole 7
Distance **438 yds** / Par **4**
Stroke Index **12**

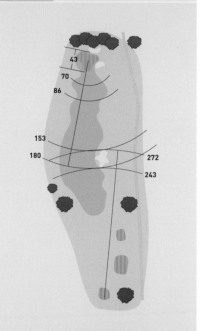

40
74
132
145
305
280

8
Hole 8
Distance **603 yds** / Par **5**
Stroke Index **10**

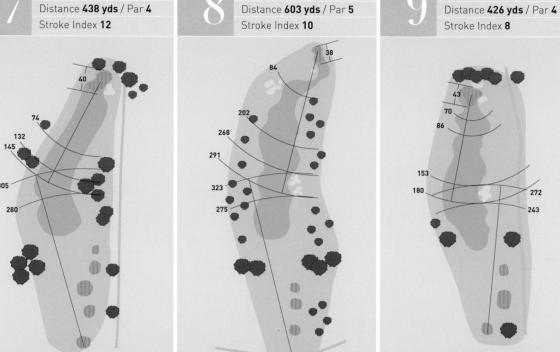

38
84
202
268
291
323
275

9
Hole 9
Distance **426 yds** / Par **4**
Stroke Index **8**

43
70
86
153
180
272
243

Mount Juliet CO. KILKENNY

CONTACT DETAILS

Address
Thomastown

Telephone
056 777 3000

Website
www.mountjuliet.ie

15
Hole 15
Distance **370 yds** / Par **4**
Stroke Index **15**

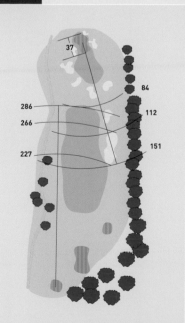

37
84
286
112
266
227
151

16
Hole 16
Distance **452 yds** / Par **4**
Stroke Index **5**

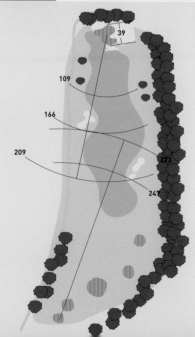

39
109
166
209
273
247

17
Hole 17
Distance **534 yds** / Par **5**
Stroke Index **13**

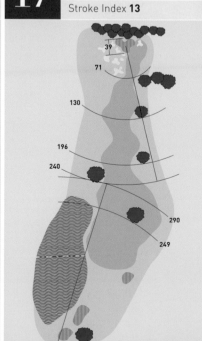

39
71
130
196
240
290
249

18
Hole 18
Distance **480 yds** / Par **4**
Stroke Index **3**

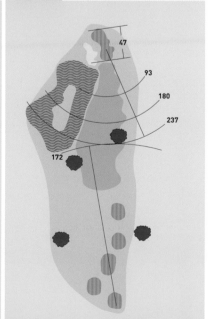

47
93
180
237
172

MOUNT JULIET COURSE

All distance measurements in
yards from the blue tees.

Out	
Distance	**3633 yds**
Par	**36**
In	
Distance	**3631 yds**
Par	**36**
Totals	
Distance	**7264 yds**
Par	**72**

Portmarnock
CO DUBLIN

Set within the curve of the coastline formed by Howth Peninsula, Portmarnock offers stunning views of Ireland's Eye and Lambay Island. Universally acknowledged as one of the truly great links courses, Portmarnock has staged many major events, from the British Amateur Championships of 1949 and the Canada Cup in 1960 to Irish Opens. Founded in 1894, the championship course offers a classic challenge: it is surrounded by water on three sides and no two successive holes play in the same direction. Unlike many courses that play nine out and nine home, Portmarnock demands a continual awareness of wind direction. This wind, combined with the wild surroundings and the sense of space and solitude makes for a truly memorable game of golf.

Extraordinary holes include the 14th, which Sir Henry Cotton regarded as the finest hole in golf; the 15th, which Arnold Palmer rates as the best par 3 in the world; and the 5th, considered by Harry Bradshaw as the top hole on the course. Bradshaw was Portmarnock's golf professional for 40 years and runner-up to A. D. Locke in the 1949 British Open, playing his ball from an empty bottle of stout.

Tour Notes

1960 The Canada cup is won at Portmarnock by the United States, a team comprising Arnold Palmer and Sam Snead. Surprisingly, it is Palmer's first experience of playing links golf.

1991 Portmarnock becomes the first Irish course to host the Walker Cup, held biennially since 1922. The Americans beat the combined team of Great Britain and Ireland by 14 points to 10.

2003 A nail-biting three-way play off, between Michael Campbell of New Zealand, Denmark's Thomas Bjorn and Sweden's Peter Hedblom, at the 18th Irish Open is delayed for 40 minutes due to a thunderstorm. Campbell's brilliant second shot on the first play-off hole pitches just 18 inches from the pin, securing him the lead and eventual victory.

1
Hole 1
Distance **320 metres** / Par **4**
Stroke Index **12**

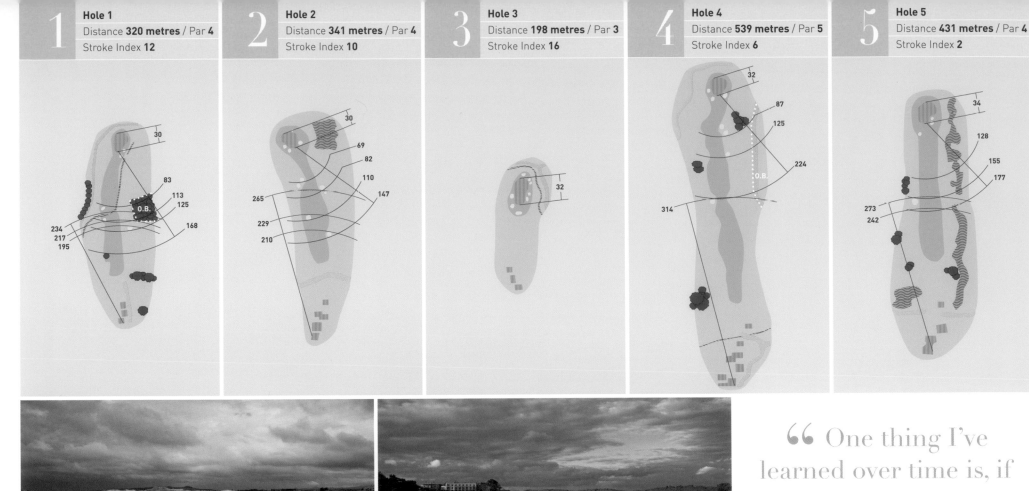

30
83
113
125
168
234
217
195
O.B.

2
Hole 2
Distance **341 metres** / Par **4**
Stroke Index **10**

30
69
82
110
147
265
229
210

3
Hole 3
Distance **198 metres** / Par **3**
Stroke Index **16**

32

4
Hole 4
Distance **539 metres** / Par **5**
Stroke Index **6**

32
87
125
224
314
O.B.

5
Hole 5
Distance **431 metres** / Par **4**
Stroke Index **2**

34
128
155
177
273
242

10
Hole 10
Distance **342 metres** / Par **4**
Stroke Index **7**

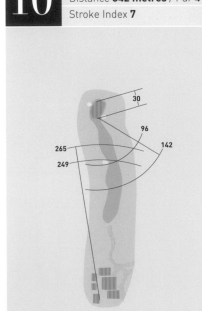

30
96
142
265
249

11
Hole 11
Distance **150 metres** / Par **3**
Stroke Index **17**

34

12
Hole 12
Distance **419 metres** / Par **4**
Stroke Index **1**

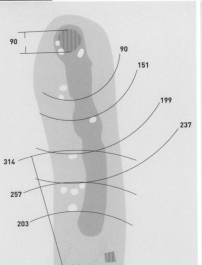

34
83
96
331
320
140
272
215

13
Hole 13
Distance **507 metres** / Par **5**
Stroke Index **11**

90
90
151
199
237
314
257
203

14
Hole 14
Distance **327 metres** / Par **4**
Stroke Index **15**

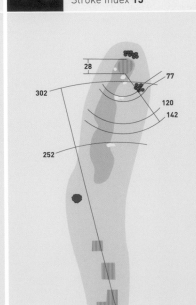

28
77
120
142
302
252

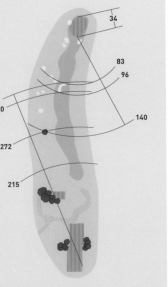
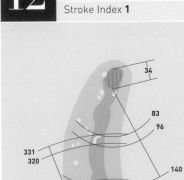

6	**Hole 6**
	Distance **520 metres** / Par **5**
	Stroke Index **14**

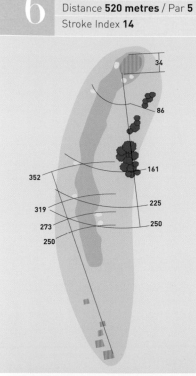

34
86
161
352
319 225
273 250
250

7	**Hole 7**
	Distance **412 metres** / Par **4**
	Stroke Index **4**

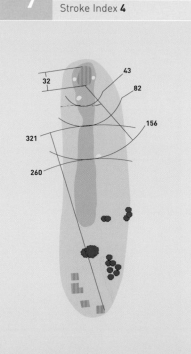

43
32 82
156
321
260

8	**Hole 8**
	Distance **374 metres** / Par **4**
	Stroke Index **8**

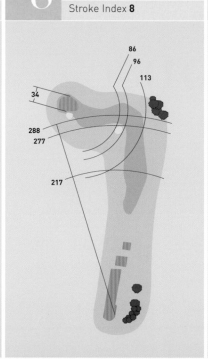

86
96
113
34
288
277
217

9	**Hole 9**
	Distance **156 metres** / Par **3**
	Stroke Index **18**

30
O.B.

CONTACT DETAILS

Address
Strand Road, Portmarnock

Telephone
01 846 2968

Website
wwwportmarnockgolfclub.ie

15	**Hole 15**
	Distance **402 metres** / Par **4**
	Stroke Index **5**

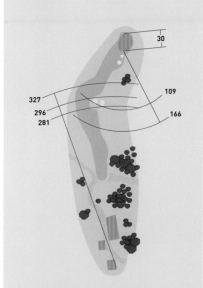

30
327 109
296 166
281

16	**Hole 16**
	Distance **383 metres** / Par **4**
	Stroke Index **9**

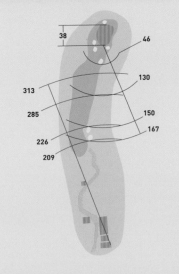

38 46
130
313
285 150
226 167
209

17	**Hole 17**
	Distance **193 metres** / Par **3**
	Stroke Index **13**

30

18	**Hole 18**
	Distance **408 metres** / Par **4**
	Stroke Index **3**

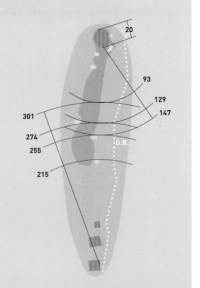

20
93
129
301 147
274
255 O.B.
215

OLD COURSE

All distance measurements in
metres from the blue tees.

Out	
Distance	**3291 metres**
Par	**36**
In	
Distance	**3131 metres**
Par	**36**

Totals	
Distance	**6422 metres**
Par	**72**

41 Rathsallagh House
CO. WICKLOW

Designed by Peter McEvoy and Christy O'Connor Jnr., this is a spectacular course, which will test professionals without intimidating the club golfer. Opened in 1994, it is set in 530 acres of lush parkland with thousands of mature trees, natural water hazards and a gently rolling landscape. Visit in the autumn and the course is magnificent, with the huge trees sporting leaves of crimson and gold. The greens are of a high quality in design, construction and condition.

Hole 3 catches many golfers out with its left-hand dogleg and fairway sloping sharply to the right. Considered one of the best and most challenging holes of any course in Ireland, the 8th is a blind shot from the tee, followed by hazards that include a lake, large bunker and stream. The 18th provides a spectacular finish, and you can then relax in the clubhouse with a birds-eye view of the 9th, 10th and 18th holes. Rathsallagh also boasts the Brendan McDaid Golf Academy, offering a wide range of practice and coaching facilities. Other sports you can take part in during a stay at Rathsallagh House are croquet and tennis. The hotel has won awards for its excellent Edwardian-style breakfast, just the thing to set you up for a day on the course.

Tour Notes

1992 Peter Thompson, a former Open champion, visits Rathsallagh. Over a drink he mentions to owner Joe O'Flynn that his land would be ideal for a golf course, and that if he were to give up farming and invest in this venture he would return to play the first round. Three years later, Thompson officially opens a superb new course.

2001–2006 Rathsallagh begins a run of hosting numerous tournaments and events, including the European Buzz Golf Pro Tour 2001, Irish Ladies Open 2003 and the Irish PGA Club Pro Tournament 2006.

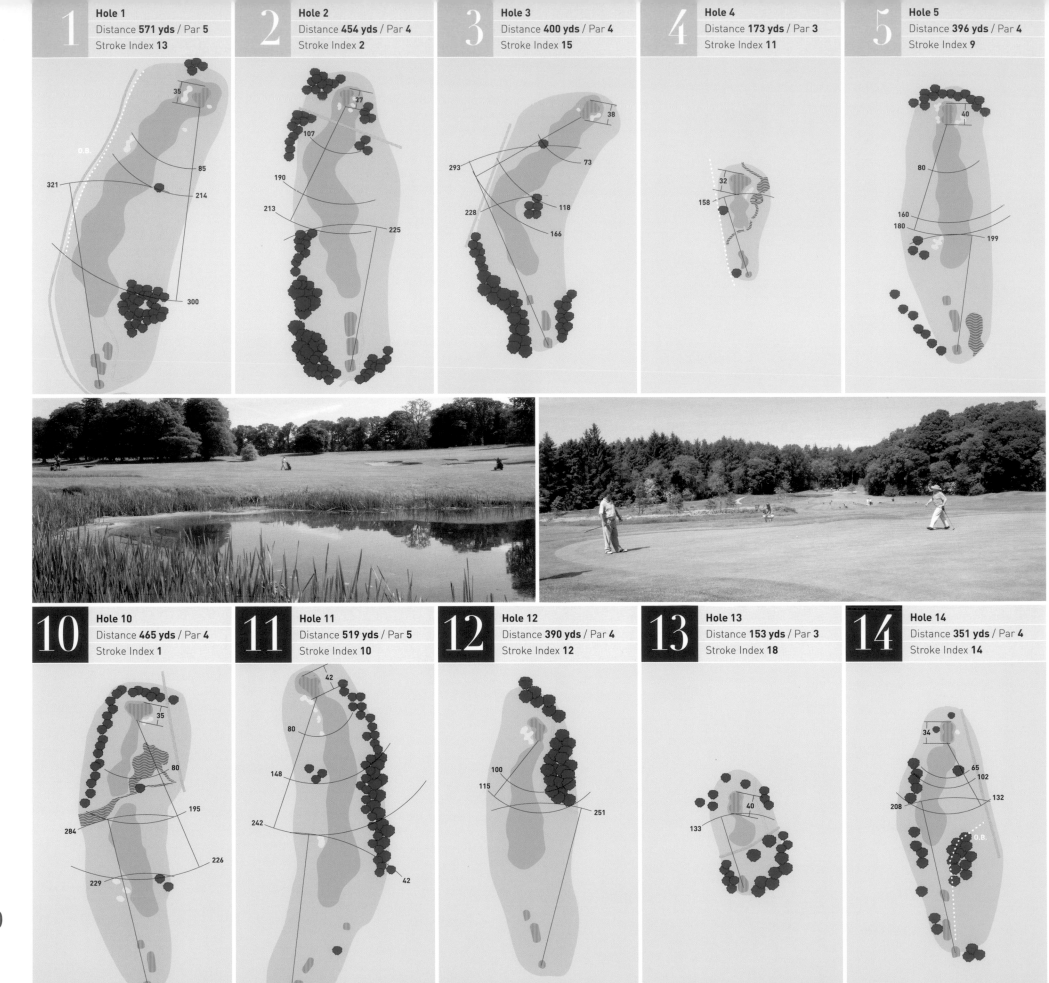

1 Hole 1
Distance **571 yds** / Par **5**
Stroke Index **13**

2 Hole 2
Distance **454 yds** / Par **4**
Stroke Index **2**

3 Hole 3
Distance **400 yds** / Par **4**
Stroke Index **15**

4 Hole 4
Distance **173 yds** / Par **3**
Stroke Index **11**

5 Hole 5
Distance **396 yds** / Par **4**
Stroke Index **9**

10 Hole 10
Distance **465 yds** / Par **4**
Stroke Index **1**

11 Hole 11
Distance **519 yds** / Par **5**
Stroke Index **10**

12 Hole 12
Distance **390 yds** / Par **4**
Stroke Index **12**

13 Hole 13
Distance **153 yds** / Par **3**
Stroke Index **18**

14 Hole 14
Distance **351 yds** / Par **4**
Stroke Index **14**

| **6** | **Hole 6**
Distance **502 yds** / Par **5**
Stroke Index **6** | **7** | **Hole 7**
Distance **176 yds** / Par **3**
Stroke Index **17** | **8** | **Hole 8**
Distance **382 yds** / Par **4**
Stroke Index **4** | **9** | **Hole 9**
Distance **416 yds** / Par **4**
Stroke Index **7** |

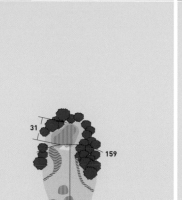
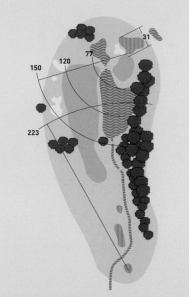
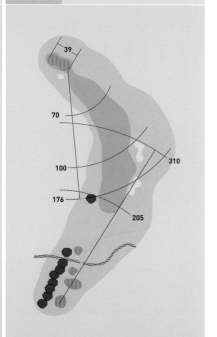

41

Rathsallagh House CO. WICKLOW

CONTACT DETAILS

Address
Dunlavin

Telephone
045 403316

Website
www.rathsallaghhousehotel.com

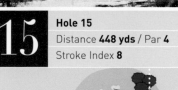

| **15** | **Hole 15**
Distance **448 yds** / Par **4**
Stroke Index **8** | **16** | **Hole 16**
Distance **536 yds** / Par **5**
Stroke Index **5** | **17** | **Hole 17**
Distance **169 yds** / Par **3**
Stroke Index **16** | **18** | **Hole 18**
Distance **450 yds** / Par **4**
Stroke Index **3** |

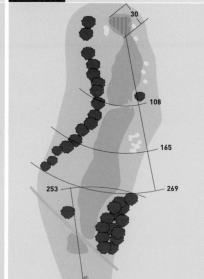
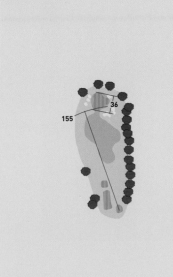
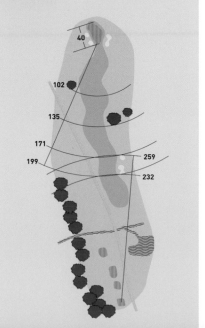

RATHSALLAGH COURSE

All distance measurements in yards from the blue tees.

Out	
Distance	**3470 yds**
Par	**36**
In	
Distance	**3481 yds**
Par	**36**

Totals	
Distance	**6951 yds**
Par	**72**

Royal County Down
CO. DOWN

Royal County Down is the signature course of Northern Ireland and was laid out in 1889 by the renowned links designer Old Tom Morris. The Championship Course (see plan page 184) is consistently rated among the world's top ten courses. Situated beneath the imperious Mourne Mountains, the course has the perfect setting as it stretches out along the shores of Dundrum Bay. As well as being one of the most beautiful courses, it is also one of the most demanding, with great swathes of heather and gorse lining fairways that tumble beneath vast sand hills, and wild tussock-faced bunkers defending small, subtly contoured greens; the 4th and 9th holes are particularly difficult.

The Annesley Links offers a less formidable yet extremely characterful game, played against the same incomparable backdrop. Substantially revised under the direction of Donald Steel, the course begins quite benignly before charging headlong into the dunes. Several charming and one or two teasing holes have been carved out amid the gorse, heather and bracken.

Tour Notes

1908 Harry Vardon modifies the Championship Course in the same year that King Edward VII bestows royal patronage on the club.

1968 The Curtis Cup comes to Royal County Down. In a very close competition, the United States ladies defeat the British Isles. This is the Americans, 11th win in 14 matches.

2000 Christy O'Connor Jnr. becomes only the second man in history to successfully defend the Senior British Open title, overcoming a one-shot overnight deficit to defeat South Africa's John Bland. Winning on his native soil is an extra special triumph for O'Connor.

2007 The amateur men's Walker Cup is played in September. Royal County Down is only the second club in Ireland to host the biennial event.

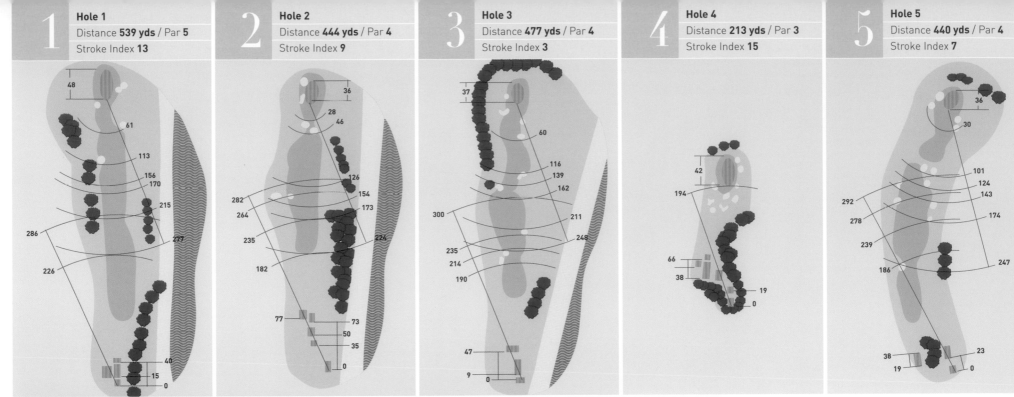

Hole 1
Distance **539 yds** / Par **5**
Stroke Index **13**

48
61
113
156
170
215
286
277
226
40
15
0

Hole 2
Distance **444 yds** / Par **4**
Stroke Index **9**

36
28
46
126
154
173
282
264
235
224
182
77
73
50
35
0

Hole 3
Distance **477 yds** / Par **4**
Stroke Index **3**

37
60
116
139
162
211
300
248
235
214
190
47
9
0

Hole 4
Distance **213 yds** / Par **3**
Stroke Index **15**

42
194
66
38
19
0

Hole 5
Distance **440 yds** / Par **4**
Stroke Index **7**

36
30
101
124
143
174
292
278
239
186
247
38
19
23
0

> 66 It is nothing new or original to say that golf is played one stroke at a time. But it took me many strokes to realize it 99
>
> *ROBERT TRENT JONES*

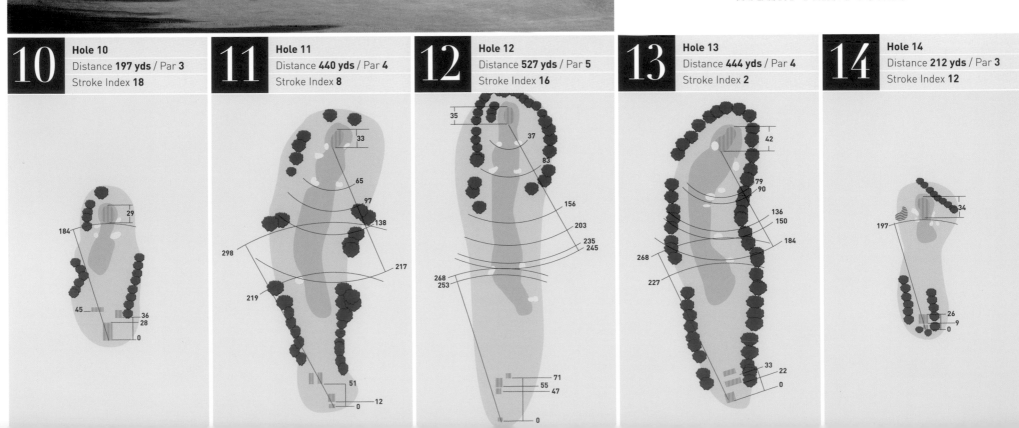

10 Hole 10
Distance **197 yds** / Par **3**
Stroke Index **18**

29
184
45
36
28
0

11 Hole 11
Distance **440 yds** / Par **4**
Stroke Index **8**

33
65
97
138
298
217
219
51
0   12

12 Hole 12
Distance **527 yds** / Par **5**
Stroke Index **16**

35
37
83
156
203
235
245
268
253
71
55
47
0

13 Hole 13
Distance **444 yds** / Par **4**
Stroke Index **2**

42
79
90
136
150
184
268
227
33
22
0

14 Hole 14
Distance **212 yds** / Par **3**
Stroke Index **12**

34
197
26
9

6 Hole 6
Distance **398 yds** / Par **4**
Stroke Index **11**

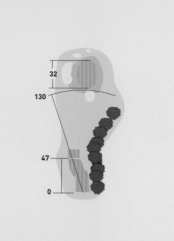

30
50
107
278
139
159
176
216
57
26
0

7 Hole 7
Distance **145 yds** / Par **3**
Stroke Index **17**

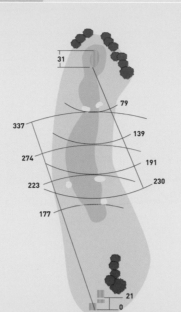

32
130
47
0

8 Hole 8
Distance **430 yds** / Par **4**
Stroke Index **1**

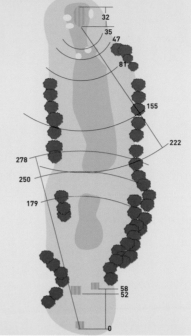

31
79
337
139
274
191
223
230
177
21
0

9 Hole 9
Distance **486 yds** / Par **4**
Stroke Index **5**

32
35
47
81
155
278
222
250
179
58
52

CONTACT DETAILS

Address
36 Golf Links Road,
Newcastle BT33 0AN

Telephone
028 4372 3314

Website
www.royalcountydown.org

Royal County Down CO. DOWN

15 Hole 15
Distance **467 yds** / Par **4**
Stroke Index **4**

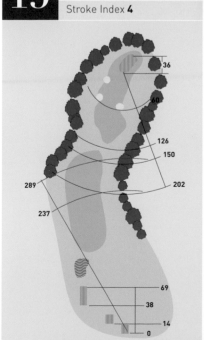

36
60
126
150
289
202
237
69
38
14
0

16 Hole 16
Distance **337 yds** / Par **4**
Stroke Index **14**

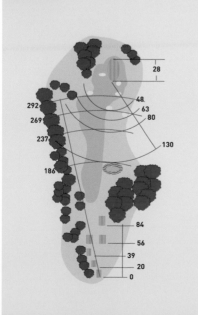

28
48
63
292
80
269
237
130
186
84
56
39
20
0

17 Hole 17
Distance **435 yds** / Par **4**
Stroke Index **10**

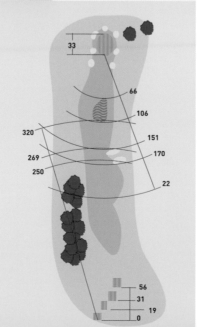

33
66
106
320
151
269
170
250
22
56
31
19
0

18 Hole 18
Distance **550 yds** / Par **5**
Stroke Index **6**

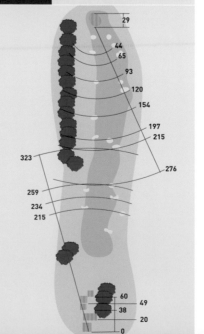

29
44
65
93
120
154
197
215
323
276
259
234
215
60
49
38
20
0

CHAMPIONSHIP COURSE

All distance measurements in
yards from the blue tees.

All illustrations are based upon
original Strokesaver artwork.

Out	
Distance	**3572 yds**
Par	**35**
In	
Distance	**3609 yds**
Par	**36**
Totals	
Distance	**7181 yds**
Par	**71**

43 Royal Portrush
CO. ANTRIM

This course, designed by Harry S. Colt, is deemed to be one of the best in the UK. Founded in 1888, it was the venue of the first professional golf event in Ireland, held in 1895, when Sandy Herd beat Harry Vardon in the final. Royal Portrush is spectacular and breathtaking, one of the tightest driving courses known to golfers. On a clear day there's a fine view of Islay and the Paps of Jura from the 3rd tee, and the Giant's Causeway from the 5th.

There are fairways up and down the valleys, and holes are aptly named Calamity Corner and Purgatory. The 2nd hole, Giant's Grave, is 509 yards long, but the 17th is even longer. This course is seriously tough and requires confident solid driving. There is much to intimidate, with enough natural hazards to cause problems without the necessity of man-made bunkers. And, of course, there is the ever-present, devilish wind to throw even the finest of golfers off course. A second course, the Valley, is one of the venues for the Causeway Coast Tournament, the largest amateur golf competition to be staged in the world.

Tour Notes

1951 The first Open to be held in Ireland is hosted by Royal Portrush. Max Faulkner triumphs and is the last British Open champion until Tony Jacklin wins in 1969.

1995–1999 Portrush hosts the Senior British Open. Winners include Brian Barnes of Scotland (1995, 1996), South African legend Gary Player (1997), Brian Huggett of Wales (after a sudden death play off, 1998) and Ireland's own Christy O'Connor Jnr. (1999).

2004 After a gap of four years, Portrush once again hosts the Senior British Open, when little-known American Peter Oakley produces the biggest upset victory in the history of the competition. Holding off an elite group of golfers, Oakley becomes the first qualifier to take the title in the 18-year history of the tournament.

Right: Catherine Lacoste wins the 1969 British Ladies Open at Portrush

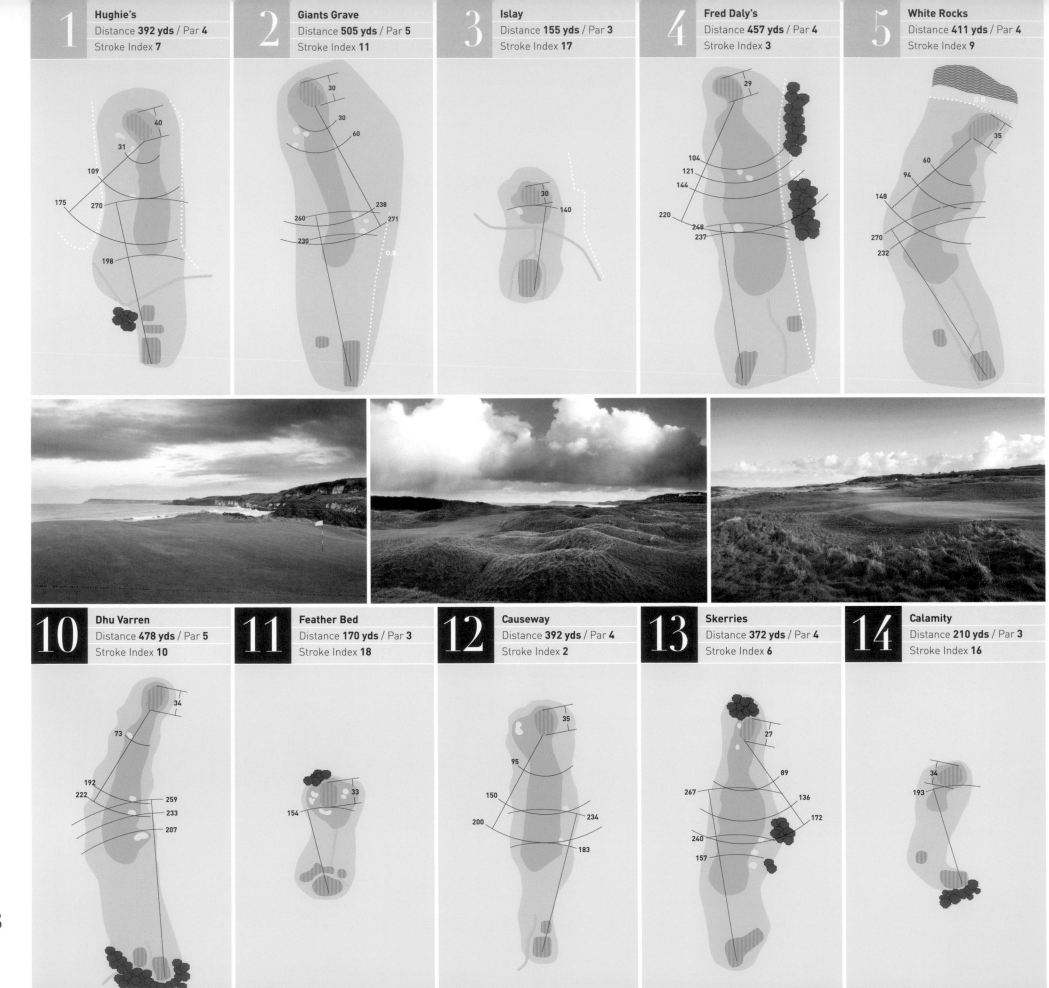

1 Hughie's
Distance **392 yds** / Par **4**
Stroke Index **7**

2 Giants Grave
Distance **505 yds** / Par **5**
Stroke Index **11**

3 Islay
Distance **155 yds** / Par **3**
Stroke Index **17**

4 Fred Daly's
Distance **457 yds** / Par **4**
Stroke Index **3**

5 White Rocks
Distance **411 yds** / Par **4**
Stroke Index **9**

10 Dhu Varren
Distance **478 yds** / Par **5**
Stroke Index **10**

11 Feather Bed
Distance **170 yds** / Par **3**
Stroke Index **18**

12 Causeway
Distance **392 yds** / Par **4**
Stroke Index **2**

13 Skerries
Distance **372 yds** / Par **4**
Stroke Index **6**

14 Calamity
Distance **210 yds** / Par **3**
Stroke Index **16**

6 Harry Colt's
Distance **189 yds** / Par **3**
Stroke Index **15**

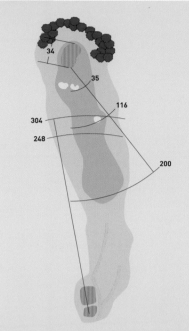

167
44

7 P. G. Stevenson's
Distance **431 yds** / Par **4**
Stroke Index **1**

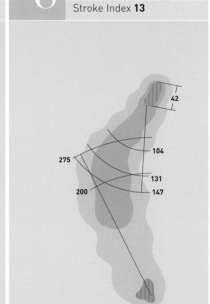

34
35
116
304
248
200

8 Himalayas
Distance **384 yds** / Par **4**
Stroke Index **13**

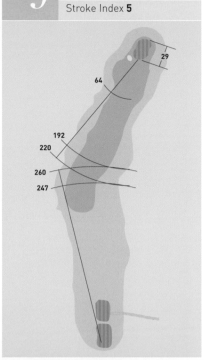

42
275
104
131
200
147

9 Tavern
Distance **475 yds** / Par **5**
Stroke Index **5**

29
64
192
220
260
247

CONTACT DETAILS

Address
Dunluce Road, Portrush
BT56 8JQ

Telephone
028 7082 2311

Website
www.royalportrushgolfclub.com

15 Purgatory
Distance **365 yds** / Par **4**
Stroke Index **12**

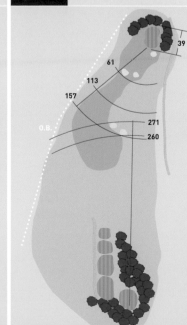

107
118
263
247
192
173

16 Babington's
Distance **442 yds** / Par **4**
Stroke Index **4**

39
61
113
157
271
260
O.B.

17 Glenarm
Distance **548 yds** / Par **5**
Stroke Index **14**

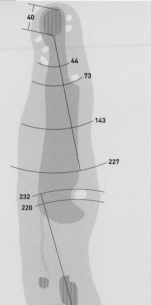

40
44
73
143
227
232
220

18 Greenaway
Distance **469 yds** / Par **4**
Stroke Index **8**

48
142
327
O.B.
213
233
256
236

ROYAL PORTRUSH COURSE

All distance measurements in yards from the blue tees.

Out	
Distance	3399 yds
Par	36
In	
Distance	3446 yds
Par	36

Totals	
Distance	6845 yds
Par	72

GLOSSARY OF GOLF TERMS

ace A hole made in one stroke.

address To position the body relative to the ball just before hitting it.

air shot When a player intends to play a shot but misses the ball completely.

approach shot Normally a short or medium shot played to the putting green or pin.

apron The grassy area surrounding the putting surface.

back door The rear of the hole.

back lip The edge of the bunker that is farthest from the green.

banana ball A slice that curves to the right in the shape of a banana.

beach A sand hazard on the course.

birdie One stroke under par for a hole. This expression possibly derived from the term

"It flew like a bird" to indicate a good shot.

bird's nest A lie in which the ball is cupped in deep grass.

blind hole If the putting green cannot be seen by the player as he approaches, the hole is called blind.

bogey A score of one over par for the hole. Double bogey is a score of two over par. Triple bogey is used when a golfer is 3 over par on a hole.

boundary The edge of the golf course that defines the area of play.

bowker This refers to a shot that appears to be horrible and then hits a tree, a rock, a spectator, etc. and bounces back into play.

bump and run A chip shot including the run of the ball after landing. Also known as "chip and run".

bunker A depression in bare ground that is covered with sand.

buzzard A score of two strokes over par for a hole.

caddie (caddy) Someone who carries a player's clubs during play and offers him assistance in accordance with the rules.

chili-dip To hit the ground before the ball, producing a weak lofted shot.

condor A four-under-par shot.

cross-bunker A lengthy bunker that is situated across the fairway.

cuppy A deep and enclosed lie.

dead ball A ball is said to be dead when there is no doubt that it will be sunk on the next shot.

divot A piece of turf removed with the club when making a shot.

dogleg A left or right bend in the fairway.

DQ'd Slang for a golfer being disqualified.

drain To sink a putt.

drive To hit the ball with maximum force and full stroke (usually with a driver from the tee).

drop To put the ball back in play after it has been declared unplayable or after the ball has been lost.

dub A missed or badly hit shot.

duff To mishit a shot by hitting the ground behind the ball and then hitting the top of the ball.

dunk To hit your ball into a water hazard.

eagle Two strokes under par for a single hole. Double eagle is a score of three under par for a single hole. Same as "albatross".

explosion shot A shot that takes large quantities of sand out of a sand trap.

fairway The area between the tee and the green that is well-maintained allowing a good lie for the ball.

fan To miss the ball completely.

flagstick A movable marker to show the location of the hole.

flash trap A shallow and small sand bunker.

flier A ball is hit without spin and goes for a greater distance than normal.

flier lie A good lie in the rough.

flub A poorly hit shot usually caused by hitting the ground before the ball.

fluffy A ball that is sitting up in grass.

fore This is shouted out to warn anyone who may be in danger from the flight of the ball.

free drop A drop where no penalty stroke is incurred.

fried egg A ball half-buried in the sand.

frog hair The short grass that borders the edge of the putting surface.

gimme A putt certain to be made on the next shot and is most likely to be conceded by an opponent.

gross score The actual number of strokes taken by a player for a hole or round before the player's handicap is deducted.

halved When a match is played without a decision. A hole is "halved" when both sides play it in the same number of strokes.

handicap The number of strokes a player may deduct from his actual score to adjust his scoring ability to the level of a scratch golfer.

hanging lie A ball resting on a downhill slope.

hazard A hazard is any sand trap, bunker or water on the course that may cause difficulty.

hog's back A ridge of ground or a hole having a ridge on a fairway.

hold To hit the ground and stay in place with little roll or bounce.

hole-in-one A hole made with one stroke. Same as "ace".

hook To hit the ball in a manner that causes it to curve from right to left in the case of a right-handed player or left to right for a left hander.

hustler A golfer with greater ability who purposely maintains a higher handicap in order to win more bets.

jail Help, I'm in jail! Stated

when you are faced with a very difficult shot.

jungle A slang term for heavy rough.

kick Another term for bounce.

kill the ball To hit a long shot.

lie The position in which the ball rests on the ground.

line The correct path of a putt to the hole when putting.

line up To study the green in order to determine how the putt should be played.

lip The top rim of the hole or cup.

loft The elevation of the ball in the air.

muff To mishit a shot.

net A player's final score after he subtracts his handicap.

nineteenth hole The bar at the clubhouse.

out-of-bounds The area outside of the course in which play is prohibited. A player is penalized stroke and distance. That is, he must replay the shot with a penalty of one stroke.

par The number of strokes a player should take to complete a round with good performance.

pawky Old Scottish term meaning cunning or tricky.

peg A tee.

penalty stroke An additional stroke added to a player's score for a rules violation.

pick up To take up one's ball before holing out.

pill Nickname for the ball.

pot bunker A small, deep sand trap with steep sides.

provisional ball A ball played if the previously played ball may be lost or out of bounds.

putt The shot made on the putting green. From a Scottish term meaning to push gently or nudge.

putting green The surface area around the hole that is specially prepared for putting.

rap To firmly hit a putt.

rifle To play a shot accurately and for a great distance.

rim out To run around the edge of the cup and fail to fall in.

rough Long grass areas adjacent to fairway, greens, tee-off areas or hazards.

round robin A tournament in which every player has the opportunity to play every other player.

sandbagger A golfer who lies about his ability in order to gain an edge in the game.

sandy Making par after being in a bunker.

scratch Par play. A zero handicap.

short game The part of the game that is made up of chip shots, pitching and putting.

shot hole A par-three hole.

sidehill lie A lie with the ball either above or below your feet.

sink a putt Make a putt.

skulling Hitting the ball at or above its centre causing the ball to be hit too hard and travel too great a distance.

sky To hit underneath the ball sending it much higher than intended.

slice A shot that curves strongly from left to right as a result of sidespin. The converse applies to a left-handed player.

smother To hit down on the ball so that it travels a short distance on the ground.

snake A very long putt that travels over several breaks in the green.

snipe A ball that is hooked and drops quickly.

spray To hit the ball erratically off line.

stableford A method of scoring that uses points instead of strokes.

stony To hit a ball close to the flagstick.

stymie When an opponent's ball is in the line of the other

player's putt. Since the ball may now be lifted, the term is used these days to refer to a tree or object in the way of a shot.

sudden death When in a match or stroke competition the score is tied after completing the round, play continues until one player wins a hole.

swale A moderately contoured depression or dip in terrain.

tee A disposable device, normally a wooden peg, on which the ball is placed for driving.

tee off To play a tee shot.

Texas wedge What the putter is called when it is used from off the green.

thread To direct the ball through a narrow opening.

tiger tee A slang expression for the back tee.

top To hit the ball above its centre causing it to roll or hop rather than rise.

trailing edge The backmost part of the sole of a golf club.

turn To start the back 9 holes.

up and down Getting out of trouble or out of a hazard and into the hole.

Vardon grip The overlapping grip.

waggle Movement of the club head prior to swinging.

whiff To swing and miss the ball completely.

whins A British term for heavy rough. Gorse bushes.

windcheater A shot played low against the wind.

wormburner A ball hit with adequate distance that hugs the ground.

yardage rating The rating of the difficulty in playing a hole based on yardage only.

yips Shakiness or nervousness in making a shot.

zoomie A drive that goes further than most drives ever hit by the golfer who smacked it.

ACKNOWLEDGEMENTS

The Automobile Association would like to thank the following photographers, companies and picture libraries for their assistance in the preparation of this book.

Abbreviations : l = left, r = right, t = top, b = below, c = centre.

Title page : Aberdovey Golf Club

2-3: Royal Cinque Ports Golf Club; 4-5: Corbis; 6t: The Art Archive/ British Library; 6c: Mary Evans Picture Library; 6b: Getty Images/ Hulton Archive/Don Price; 7t: Tony Roberts/Corbis; 7c: Tony Roberts/ Corbis; 7b: Gerry Penny/epa/Corbis; 8-9: Corbis; 10-11: The Belfry; 12l: Eddie Keogh/Reuters/Corbis; 12-13: The Belfry; 14-15t: Information supplied by 3DEagleview International; 14-15c: The Belfry; 14-15b: Information supplied by 3DEagleview International;16-17: East Sussex National Golf Resort and Spa; 18-19t: PremierPlan Golf Design; 18-19c: East Sussex National Golf Resort and Spa; 18-19b: PremierPlan Golf Design; 20-21: Manor House Hotel and Golf Club; 22-23t: Illustrations based on hole images supplied by The Golf Business Ltd; 22-23c: Manor House Hotel and Golf Club; 22-23b: Illustrations based on hole images supplied by The Golf Business Ltd; 24-25: Marriott Forest of Arden Hotel & Country Club; 26-27t: All Illustrations are based upon original Strokesaver artwork; 26-27c: Marriott Forest of Arden Hotel & Country Club; 26-27b: All Illustrations are based upon original Strokesaver artwork; 28-29: Marriott Hanbury Manor Hotel & Country Club; 30-31t: All Illustrations are based upon original Strokesaver artwork; 30-31c: Marriott Hanbury Manor Hotel & Country Club; 30-31b: All Illustrations are based upon original Strokesaver artwork; 32-33: The National Golf Centre, Woodhall Spa; 34-35t: All Illustrations are based upon original Strokesaver artwork; 34-35c: The National Golf Centre, Woodhall Spa; 34-35b: All Illustrations are based upon original Strokesaver artwork; 36-39: Courtesy of Old Thorns Golf and Country Estate; 40l: Alan C. Birch; 40c: popperfoto.com; 40-41: Alan C. Birch; 42-43t: All Illustrations are based upon original Strokesaver artwork; 42-43c: Alan C. Birch; 42-43b: All Illustrations are based upon original Strokesaver artwork; 44: Corbis; 44-45: Royal Cinque Ports Golf Club; 46-47t: All Illustrations are based upon original Strokesaver artwork; 46-47c: Royal Cinque Ports Golf Club; 46-47b: All Illustrations are based upon original Strokesaver artwork; 48l: David Alexander/Getty Images; 48r-49: Ross Kinnaird/Getty Images; 50-51t: All Illustrations are based upon original Strokesaver artwork; 50cl: Stephen Munday/Getty Images; 50cr: David Alexander/Getty Images; 50-51b: All Illustrations are based upon original Strokesaver artwork; 51c: Ross Kinnaird/Getty Images; 52l: popperfoto.com; 52-53c: Royal Lytham & St Annes Golf Club; 53t: Royal Lytham & St Annes Golf Club; 54-55t: All Illustrations are based upon original Strokesaver artwork; 54-55c: Royal Lytham & St Annes Golf Club; 54-55b: All Illustrations are based upon original Strokesaver artwork; 56-57: The Royal St. George's Golf Club; 58-59t: All Illustrations are based upon original Strokesaver artwork; 58-59c: The Royal St. George's Golf Club; 58-59b: All Illustrations are based upon original Strokesaver artwork; 60-61: St. Mellion International Hotel, Golf and Country Club; 62-63t: Original artwork courtesy of Eagle Promotions; 62-63c: St. Mellion International Hotel, Golf and Country Club; 62-63b: Original artwork courtesy of Eagle Promotions; 64-65: Sunningdale Golf Club; 66-67t: All Illustrations are based upon original Strokesaver artwork; 66-67c: Sunningdale Golf Club; 66-67b: All Illustrations are based upon original Strokesaver artwork; 68-69: Walton Heath Golf Club; 70-71t: All Illustrations are based upon original Strokesaver artwork; 70-71c: Walton Heath Golf Club; 70-71b: All Illustrations are based upon original Strokesaver artwork; 72-73: Wentworth Club; 74-75t: Illustrations based on hole images

supplied by PinPoint Golf; 74-75c: Wentworth Club; 74-75b: Illustrations based on hole images supplied by PinPoint Golf; 76-77: Woburn Golf Club; 78-79t: All Illustrations are based upon original Strokesaver artwork; 78-79c: Woburn Golf Club; 78-79b: All Illustrations are based upon original Strokesaver artwork; 80-81: Fairmont St. Andrews; 82b: Carnoustie Golf Links; 82c: Bettmann/ Corbis; 83: Carnoustie Golf Links; 84-85t: Original artwork graphics courtesy of Optimize Golf; 84-85c: Carnoustie Golf Links; 84-85b: Original artwork graphics courtesy of Optimize Golf; 86-87: The Duke's St Andrews; 88-89t: Information supplied by 3DEagleview International; 88-89c: The Duke's St Andrews; 88-89b: Information supplied by 3DEagleview International; 90-91: Fairmont St. Andrews; 92-93t: Original graphics courtesy of Pro-Guide Publishing, www.pro-guide.co.uk; 92-93c: Fairmont St. Andrews; 92-93b: Original graphics courtesy of Pro-Guide Publishing, www.pro-guide.co.uk; 94-95: Mike Caldwell; 96-97t: Original illustrations supplied by Golf Publishing Limited; 96-97c: Mike Caldwell; 96-97b: Original illustrations supplied by Golf Publishing Limited; 98-99: Marriott Dalmahoy Hotel & Country Club; 100-101t: All Illustrations are based upon original Strokesaver artwork; 100-101c: Marriott Dalmahoy Hotel & Country Club; 100-101b: All Illustrations are based upon original Strokesaver artwork; 102-103: Prestwick Golf Club; 104-105t: All Illustrations are based upon original Strokesaver artwork; 104-105c: Prestwick Golf Club; 104-105b: All Illustrations are based upon original Strokesaver artwork; 106-107: Royal Dornoch; 108-109t: Original artwork graphics courtesy of Optimize Golf; 108-109c: Royal Dornoch; 108-109b: Original artwork graphics courtesy of Optimize Golf; 110t: Hulton-Deutsch Collection/Corbis; 110b-111: Kenneth Ferguson; 112-113t: All Illustrations are based upon original Strokesaver artwork; 112-113c: Kenneth Ferguson; 112-113b: All Illustrations are based upon original Strokesaver artwork; 114t: St Andrews Links Trust; 114bl: St Andrews Links Trust; 114br: Bettmann/Corbis; 115t: St Andrews Links Trust; 115bl: St Andrews Links Trust; 115br Bettman/Corbis; 116-117t: Original artwork courtesy of St Andrews Links Trust; 116-117c St Andrews Links Trust; 118-119: The Westerwood Hotel; 120-121t: Original artwork courtesy of Eagle Promotions; 120-121c: The Westerwood Hotel; 120-121b: Original artwork courtesy of Eagle Promotions; 122-123: The Westin Turnberry Resort; 124-125t: Original illustrations supplied by Golf Publishing Limited; 124-125c: The Westin Turnberry Resort; 124-125b: Original illustrations supplied by Golf Publishing Limited; 126-127: The Celtic Manor Resort; 128-129: Aberdovey Golf Club; 130-131t: K & M PRINT; 130-131c: Aberdovey Golf Club; 130-131b: K & M PRINT; 132-133: The Celtic Manor Resort; 134-135t: All Illustrations are based upon original Strokesaver artwork; 134-135c: The Celtic Manor Resort; 134-135b: All Illustrations are based upon original Strokesaver artwork; 136-137: Marriott St. Pierre Hotel & Country Club; 138-139t: All Illustrations are based upon original Strokesaver artwork; 138-139c: Marriott St. Pierre Hotel & Country Club; 138-139b: All Illustrations are based upon original Strokesaver artwork; 140-141: Royal St David's Golf Club; 142-143t: All Illustrations are based upon original Strokesaver artwork; 142-143c: Royal St David's Golf Club; 142-143b: All Illustrations are based upon original Strokesaver artwork; 144-145: Royal Porthcawl Golf Club: 146-147t: All Illustrations are based upon original Strokesaver artwork; 146-147c: Royal Porthcawl Golf Club; 146-147b: All Illustrations are based upon original Strokesaver artwork; 148-149: David Cannon/Getty Images; 150-151: Ballybunion Golf Club; 152-153t: Illustrations based on hole images supplied by The Golf Business Ltd; 152-153c: Ballybunion Golf Club; 152-153b: Illustrations based on hole images supplied by The Golf Business Ltd; 154-155: Dromoland Castle Golf and Country Club; 156-157t: Illustrations based on hole images supplied by PinPoint Golf; 156-

157c: Dromoland Castle Golf and Country Club; 156-157b: Illustrations based on hole images supplied by PinPoint Golf; 158-159: Druids Glen Golf Resort; 160-161t: Original graphics courtesy of Coursemaster; 160-161c: Druids Glen Golf Resort; 160-161b: Original graphics courtesy of Coursemaster; 162-163: Fota Island Resort; 164-165c: Fota Island Resort; 166l: Gerry Penny/epa/Corbis; 166r-167: The K Club Golf and Spa Resort; 168-169t: Illustrations based on hole images supplied by The Golf Business Ltd; 168-169c: The K Club Golf and Spa Resort; 168-169b: Illustrations based on hole images supplied by The Golf Business Ltd; 170t: Mount Juliet; 170b: Laurence Griffiths/Getty Images; 171t: Andrew Redington/Getty Images; 171b: Mount Juliet; 172-173t: Information supplied by 3DEagleview International; 172-173c: Mount Juliet; 172-173b: Information supplied by 3DEagleview International; 174-175: Portmarnock Golf Club; 176-177t: Information supplied by 3DEagleview International; 176-177c: Portmarnock Golf Club; 176-177b: Information supplied by 3DEagleview International; 178-179: Rathsallagh House Hotel Golf and Country Club; 180-181t: Original graphics courtesy of Coursemaster; 180-181c: Rathsallagh House Hotel Golf and Country Club; 180-181b: Original graphics courtesy of Coursemaster; 182-183: David Cannon/Getty Images; 184-185t: All Illustrations are based upon original Strokesaver artwork; 184c: David Cannon/Getty Images; 185c: David Cannon/Getty Images; 184-185b: All Illustrations are based upon original Strokesaver artwork; 186l: popperfoto.com; 186-187: Royal Portrush Golf Club; 188-189t: Information supplied by 3DEagleview International; 188-189c: Royal Portrush Golf Club; 188-189b: Information supplied by 3DEagleview International; 188-189b: Royal Portrush Golf Club; 190-191: Corbis.

Golf Today: with thanks to Golf Today magazine for the quotes from their website.

Every effort has been made to trace the copyright holders, and we apologise in advance for any accidental errors. We would be happy to apply the corrections in the following edition of this publication.